THE POST-COMMUNION PRAYERS IN THE ORDINARY FORM OF THE ROMAN RITE

The Post-Communion Prayers in the Ordinary Form of the Roman Rite

Texts and Sources

Edited by Matthew P. Hazell

Lectionary Study Press

MMXX

First published 2020

ISBN: 979-8-696803-32-6 (pb)

DDC 264.'0203—dc23

CONTENTS

INTRODUCTION

The aim of this book is to provide easy access to the references and Latin source texts for every post-communion prayer in the Roman Missal of the Ordinary Form of the Roman Rite. This will, it is hoped, allow the reader to compare any given post-communion prayer with its source(s), in order to observe any differences between them, and how major or minor such differences might be in terms of tone, vocabulary, style, theology, etc. With regard to the arrangement and editing of sources before their inclusion in the post-conciliar Roman Missal, the substantial work of the *Consilium ad exsequendam* is, in my opinion, nowhere near as well known as it ought to be, particularly in the English-speaking world. Scholars such as Lauren Pristas have begun the process of examining the Consilium's work in this area with regard to the collects of the Missal,* and this is my own, modest attempt to provide some of the resources necessary for this work to continue for the post-communion orations.

Prayers in MR(2008) that are identical to their source in every way (except punctuation) are noted as such. For all other changes and edits made to the source prayers by the Consilium or the Congregation for Divine Worship and the Discipline of the Sacraments, attempts have been made to highlight these in order to assist the reader:

- Changes in vocabulary have been marked **in bold** in the MR(2008) text; more minor changes in, e.g., grammar have been *italicised*;

- Where prayers have been centonised—that is, newly-composed using parts from two or more existing prayers or other sources— solid underline and dashed underline are used to mark the relevant parts of the prayers (see, e.g., 1st Sunday of Advent, p. 3);

- Occasionally, only a single sentence or phrase in a much-longer text has been taken up by the Consilium; where this is the case, I have underlined it to make it easier to see (e.g., 1st Sunday of Lent, p. 25);

- Any textual omissions are marked with the symbol ° in the text of MR(2008) (e.g., 11th Sunday *per annum*, p. 63);

---

* In particular, see her work *The Collects of the Roman Missals: A Comparative Study of the Sundays in Proper Seasons before and after the Second Vatican Council* (London: Bloomsbury T&T Clark, 2013).

- No attempt has been made to mark any transpositions or changes in word order (e.g., Friday in Week 2 of Lent, p. 30); readers will have to observe these for themselves.

For those who would like to delve deeper into the history of the post-communion prayers, references to the *Corpus Orationum* (*CO*) and *Corpus Praefationum* (*Pref*) have been provided where possible. These two sets of volumes list, in alphabetical order, the orations and prefaces contained in over 200 extant manuscripts from before the liturgical reforms carried out after the Council of Trent, and make it possible for one to determine how widely a given prayer was used, when it was used, in what contexts, and whether there are any textual variants. These are vital resources for those who wish to examine the history of the orations of the Roman Missal, and readers are enthusiastically encouraged to make use of this book alongside *CO* and *Pref.*

It should be noted that the existing lists of sources sometimes designate a post-communion oration as a 'new composition'. Of course, not all of these have been composed completely from scratch, and I have made an attempt to reference the extra-liturgical sources (e.g. biblical, conciliar) where they seemed obvious to me. Still, there is much more investigation to be carried out on the sources and inspirations for many of these texts.

Some supplementary material is provided after this introduction, with the goal of facilitating further research in this area. A bibliography of works relating to the sources and composition of the post-Vatican II *Missale Romanum* is supplied, as well as some relevant extracts from various Church documents regarding the revision of the orations of the Roman Missal. This includes English translations of two sections from the unpublished schemata of the Consilium, from Group XIII (votive and *ad diversa* Masses) and Group XVIII *bis* (prayers and prefaces of the Missal). Finally, various indices, statistics and other data have placed at the end of the book.

It is my hope that readers find this book to be both beneficial for their own studies in the sacred liturgy, and a helpful resource for the ongoing critical assessment of the post-Vatican II liturgical reforms.

Matthew P. Hazell
12th October 2020
Feast of St Wilfrid of York

ABBREVIATIONS

A	P. Cagin (ed.), *Le sacramentaire gélasien D'Angoulême* (Paris, Bibl. Nat. ms. lat. 816) (Angoulême, 1919)
B	A. Paredi (ed.), *Sacramentarium Bergomense del secolo IX. Monumenta Bergomensia VI* (Ms. del sec. IX, Bibl. di S. Alessandro in Colonna in Bergamo) (Bergamo, 1962).
Bo	*E.A. Lowe, A. Wilmart & H.A. Wilson (eds.), The Bobbio Missal. A Gallican Mass-Book.* (Paris, Bibl. Nat. lat. 13264) (London: Henry Bradshaw Society, 1920)
C	Collect
CMBMV	*Collectio Missarum de Beata Maria Virgine, editio typica* (Libreria Editrice Vaticana, 1987)
CO	E. Moeller, J.M. Clément, B.C. 't Wallant & L.-M. Couillaud (eds.), *Corpus Orationum* (CCSL 160-160M; Brepols, 1992-2020, 15 vols.)
Cong. Pass.	*Congregatio Passionis Iesu Christi, Proprium Missarum* (Rome, 1974) [Passionists]
DOL	International Commission on English in the Liturgy, *Documents on the Liturgy 1963-1979: Conciliar, Papal, and Curial Texts* (Collegeville, MN: Liturgical Press, 1982)
EL	*Ephemerides Liturgicae*
Fulda	G. Richter & A. Schönfelder, *Sacramentarium Fuldense saeculi X* (Fulda, 1912). Reprinted by the Henry Bradshaw Society (vol. 101; Saint Michael's Abbey Press, 1977).
Gell	A. Dumas, *Liber Sacramentorum Gellonensis* (CCSL 159A-B; Turnhout, 1981)
GeV	L. C. Mohlberg, L. Eizenhöfer & P. Siffrin (eds.), *Liber Sacramentorum Romanae Aeclesiae Ordinis Anni Circuli. Rerum Ecclesiasticarum Documenta, Series Maior, Fontes III* (Cod. Vat. Reg. 316/Paris Bibl. Nat. 7193, 41/56) (Rome, 1968). [Gelasian Sacramentary]
Go	L.C. Mohlberg (ed.), *Missale Gothicum. Rerum Ecclesiasticarum Documenta, Series Maior, Fontes V* (Vat. Reg. lat. 317) (Rome, 1961)

IMC	*Istituto Missioni Consolata, Messe Proprie* (1975) [Consolata Missionaries]
LMS	M. Férotin (ed.), *Le Liber Mozarabicus Sacramentorum et les Manuscrits Mozarabes. Monumenta Ecclesiae Liturgica VI* (Paris, 1912)
MA(1981)	*Missale Ambrosianum. Iuxta rituum sanctae Ecclesiae Mediolanensis. Ex decreto Sacrosancti Oecumenici Concilii Vaticanii II instauratum* (Milan, 1981)
MP	C. Johnson & A. Ward, *Missale Parisiense anno 1738 publici iuris factum* (Instrumenta Liturgica Quarreriensia 1; Rome: C.L.V. Edizioni Liturgiche, 1993)
MP(1841)	*Missale Parisiense* (Societatis bib. ed. liturgiae Parisiensis: Paris, 1841)
MR	P. Bruylants (ed.), *Les Oraisons du Missel Romain: Texte et Historie. Etudes Liturgiques: Collection dirigée par le Centre du Pastorale Liturgique* (Louvain, 1952, 2 vols.)
	Reprinted in M. Sodi & A. Toniolo (eds.), *Liturgia tridentina. Fontes, indices, concordantia (1568-1962)* (Rome: Libreria Editrice Vaticana, 2010)
MR(1962)	*Missale Romanum ex decreto SS. Concilii Tridentini restitutum, Summorum Pontificum cura recognitum. Editio typica* (Typis Polyglottis Vaticanis, 1962)
MR(1970)	*Missale Romanum. Ex decreto Sacrosancti Œcumenici Concilii Vaticani II instauratum, auctoritate Pauli PP. VI promulgatum. Editio typica* (Typis Polyglottis Vaticanis, 1970)
MR(1975)	*Missale Romanum. Ex decreto Sacrosancti Œcumenici Concilii Vaticani II instauratum, auctoritate Pauli PP. VI promulgatum. Editio typica altera* (Typis Polyglottis Vaticanis, 1975)
MR(2008)	*Missale Romanum. Ex decreto Sacrosancti Œcumenici Concilii Vaticani II instauratum, auctoritate Pauli PP. VI promulgatum, Ioannis Pauli PP. II cura recognitum. Editio typica tertia* (Libreria Editrice Vaticana, 2008 reimpressio emendata)
O.Carm	*Missale Ordinis Fratrum B.M.V. de Monte Carmelo* (Rome, 1935) [Carmelites]
O.Cist	*Missale Cisterciense* (Westmallensis, 1890) [Cistercians]
OFM	*Missale Seraphicum cum Lectionario ad usum Fratrum Minorum S. Francisci conventualium* (Rome, 1974). [Franciscans]

OP	*Missale Iuxta Ritum Ordinis Praedicatorum* (Rome, 1965) [Dominicans]
OV	J. Vives & J. Claveras (eds.), *Oracional Visigotico. Monumenta Hispaniae Sacra, Serie Liturgica I* (Barcelona, 1946)
PAL	*Pro aliquibus locis* (Proper of Saints)
PC	Post-Communion
PL	J.-P. Migne (ed.), *Patrologiae cursus completus, Series Latina* (Paris-Montrouge, 1844-1864)
Pref	E. Moeller (ed.), *Corpus Praefationum* (CCSL 161-161D; Brepols, 1980-81)
QL	*Questions Liturgique*
RB	T. Fry (ed.), *Regula Sancti Benedicti* (Collegeville, MN: Liturgical Press, 1981)
RL	*Rivista Liturgica*
SAC	*Societas Apostolatus Catholici, Proprium Missarum* (Vatican City, 1972) [Pallottines]
SL	*Studia Liturgia*
SO	Secret / *Super oblata* (Prayer over the Offerings)
Soc.M	*Societas Mariae, Proprium missarum* (Rome, n.d.) [Marists].
SP	*Super populum* (Prayer over the People)
Triplex	O. Helming, *Das Sacramentarium Triplex* (Liturgiewissenschaftliche Quellen und Forschungen, 49; Münster, 1968)
Ve	L.C. Mohlberg, L. Eizenhöfer & P. Siffrin (eds.), *Sacramentarium Veronense. Rerum Ecclesiasticarum Documenta, Series Maior; Fontes I* (Cod. Bibl. Capit. Veron. LXXXV/80) (Rome, 1966)

BIBLIOGRAPHY OF STUDIES ON THE SOURCES OF THE POST-VATICAN II *MISSALE ROMANUM*

Henry Ashworth, "The Prayers for the Dead in the Missal of Pope Paul VI", *EL* 85.1 (1971), 3-15

Matthias Augé, "Le collette del Proprio del Tempo nel nuovo Messale", *EL* 84.4-5 (1970), 275-298

————, "Le collette di Avvento-Natale-Epifania del Messale Romano", *RL* 59 (1972), 614-627

————, "L'eucologia quaresimali del nuovo Messale", *RL* 60 (1973), 22-33

Maurizio Barba, "Il Comune della Beata Vergine Maria nel nuovo Messale Romano", *Notitiae* 436 (2002), 588-601

————, "Alcune varianti testuali nella Colletta della Domenica XVIII", *Notitiae* 439-440 (2003), 147-151

————, "L'Eucologia della Festa di Nostro Signore Gesù Cristo Sommo ed Eterno Sacerdote", *Notitiae* 551-552 (2012), 383-405

B. Baroffio, "Le orazioni dopo la comunione del Tempo di Avvento", *RL* 59 (1972), 649-662

Carlo Braga, "Il « *Proprium de Sanctis* »", *EL* 84.6 (1970), 401-431

F. Brovelli, "Le orazioni del Tempo pasquale", *RL* 62 (1975), 191-206

Vincenzo Calabrese, "Le orazioni collette « *in professione religiosa* ». Dalla *lex orandi* alla *lex vivendi*", *Notitiae* 587-592 (2015), 522-541

A. Catella, "La « *Collectio Missarum de Beata Maria Virgine* ». Analisi della eucologia", *RL* 75 (1988), 82-111

Antoine Dumas, "Pour mieux comprendre les textes liturgiques du Missel Romain", *Notitiae* 54 (1970), 194-213

————, "Les Préfaces du nouveau Missel", *EL* 85.1 (1971), 16-28

————, "Le sources du nouveau Missel Romain", *Notitiae* 60 (1971), 37-42

————, "Le sources du Missel Romain (II)", *Notitiae* 61 (1971), 74-77

————, "Le sources du Missel Romain (III)", *Notitiae* 62 (1971), 94-95

————, "Le sources du Missel Romain (IV)", *Notitiae* 63 (1971), 134-136

————, "Le sources du Missel Romain (V)", *Notitiae* 65 (1971), 276-280

————, "Le sources du Missel Romain (VI)", *Notitiae* 68 (1971), 409-410

————, "Les oraisons du nouveau Missel", *QL* 25 (1971), 262-270

Jean Evenou, "Les séries de collectes pour les dimanches au cours des siècles", *Notitiae* 406-407 (2000), 171-197

Walter Ferretti, "Le orazioni « post Communionem » de Tempore nel nuovo Messale Romano", *EL* 84.4-5 (1970), 323-341

Nicola Giampietro, "S. Lorenzo, diacono e martire: il Formulario della Messa", *Notitiae* 509-510 (2009), 54-64

Matthew P. Hazell, *The Proper of Time in the Post-Vatican II Liturgical Reforms* (Lectionary Study Press, 2018)

Cuthbert Johnson, "The Sources of the Roman Missal (1975), *Proprium de Tempore, Proprium de Sanctis*", *Notitiae* 354-356 (1996), 1-180

Cuthbert Johnson & Anthony Ward, "The Sources of the Roman Missal, I: Advent–Christmas", *Notitiae* 240-242 (1986), 445-747

————, "The Sources of the Roman Missal, II: Prefaces", *Notitiae* 252-254 (1987), 413-1009

————, *The Prefaces of the Roman Missal: A Source Compendium with Concordance and Indices* (Rome: Tipografia Poliglotta Vaticana, 1989)

Thomas A. Krosnicki, *Ancient Patterns in Modern Prayer* (Washington, DC: Catholic University of America Press, 1973)

Emil J. Lengeling, "*Pro unitate Christianorum* im neuen *Missale Romanum*" in B. Bobrinskoy (ed.), *Communio Sanctorum: mélanges offerts à Jean-Jacques von Allmen* (Geneva: Labor et fides, 1982), 204-223

Alessandro Pistoia, "Messe e orazioni rituali, « *ad diversa* » e votive", *EL* 84.6 (1970), 402-446

Lauren Pristas, "The Orations of the Vatican II Missal: Policies for Revision", *Communio* 30 (Winter 2003), 621-653

————, "The Pre- and Post-Vatican II Collects of the Dominican Doctors of the Church", *New Blackfriars* 86 (2005), 604-621

————, *The Collects of the Roman Missals: A Comparative Study of the Sundays in Proper Seasons before and after the Second Vatican Council* (London: Bloomsbury T&T Clark, 2013)

Vincenzo Raffa, "Le orazione sulle offerte del Proprio del Tempo nel nuovo Messale", *EL* 84.4-5 (1970), 299-322

Dylan Schrader, "The Revision of the Feast of Christ the King", *Antiphon* 18.3 (2014), pp. 227-253

Innocent Smith, "The Formularies *Pro unitate Christianorum* in the 2002 *Missale Romanum*", *SL* 45 (2015), 1-15

Dietmar Thönnes, *Die Euchologie der Collectio Missarum de Beata Maria Virgine* (Frankfurt am Main: Peter Lang, 1993)

Achille M. Triacca, "La strutturazione eucologia dei Prefazi. Contributo metodologico per una loro retta esegesi (In margine al nuovo « *Missale Romanum* »)", *EL* 86.3 (1972), 233-279

Anthony Ward, "A Magnificent Oration for the Easter Octave Day", *Notitiae* 559-560 (2013), 109-121

————, "The Origins of the Collect for the Eleventh Sunday *per annum*", *Notitiae* 453-454 (2004), 308-312

————, "The Origins of the Collect for the Twelfth Sunday *per annum*", *Notitiae* 455-456 (2004), 446-448

————, "The Solemn Blessings of the Postconciliar *Missale Romanum*", *EL* 118.4 (2004), 417-484

————, "The Collects of weeks I-XXVI *per annum* in the present Roman Missal", *EL* 120.4 (2006), 457-506

————, "The Collects of weeks XXVII-XXXIV *per annum* in the present Roman Missal", *EL* 121.1 (2007), 108-125

————, "The *Rotulus* of Ravenna as a source in the 2000 *Missale Romanum*", *EL* 121.1 (2007), 129-176

————, "The Orations of Lent before the First Sunday in the 2000 *Missale Romanum*", *EL* 121.3 (2007), 328-369

————, "The Orations of Lent for the First Week in the 2000 *Missale Romanum*", *EL* 121.4 (2007), 443-488

————, "The Orations for Ash Wednesday in the Present Roman Missal", *Notitiae* 485-486 (2007), 45-64

————, "Euchology for the Mass *in Cena Domini* of the 2000 *Missale Romanum*", *Notitiae* 507-508 (2008), 611-634

————, "The Orations after the readings at the Easter Vigil in the 2000 *Missale Romanum*", *EL* 123.4 (2009), 460-507

————, "The Palm Sunday Mass Formulary in the 2000 *Missale Romanum*", *Notitiae* 515-516 (2009), 396-428

————, "Sources of the Four Structural Orations of the Solemn Good Friday Liturgy in the 2000 *Missale Romanum*", *Notitiae* 525-526 (2010), 298-317

————, "The Easter Mass formularies for the Vigil and the Mass *in die* in the 2002 *Missale Romanum*", *EL* 124.1 (2010), 90-128

————, "The Orations for the Solemnities of the Ascension and Pentecost in the 2000 *Missale Romanum*", *EL* 124.2 (2010), 219-247

————, "The Orations after the Readings at the Pentecost Vigil in the 2008 reprint of the *Missale Romanum*", *EL* 124.3 (2010), 354-382

————, "The Missal Orations of the Easter Octave from Monday to Sunday", *EL* 125.1 (2011), 63-126

————, "The Council and the Collects of SS. Catherine of Alexandria and Jane Chantal", *EL* 125.4 (2011), 490-510

————, "Preface VIII of the Sundays *per annum* in the *Missale* of Pope Paul VI", *Notitiae* 547-548 (2012), 172-192

————, "Weekday Orations of the Second Week of Easter in the 2000 *Missale Romanum*", *EL* 126.1 (2012), 68-123

————, "The Orations for the Third Week of Easter in the 2000 *Missale Romanum*", *EL* 126.2 (2012), 195-235

————, "The Orations for the Fourth Sunday of Easter in the 2000 *Missale Romanum*", *EL* 126.4 (2012), 480-504

————, "The Weekday Orations for the Fourth Week of Easter in the 2000 *Missale Romanum*", *EL* 127.1 (2013), 85-115

————, "The Orations for the Fifth Week of Easter in the 2000 *Missale Romanum*", *EL* 127.2 (2013), 189-225

————, "The Orations for the Sixth Week of Easter in the 2000 *Missale Romanum*", *EL* 127.3 (2013), 328-364

————, "The Orations for the Seventh Week of Easter in the 2000 *Missale Romanum*", *EL* 127.4 (2013), 444-493

————, "The Mass formularies *per annum* I-VIII in the 2000 Missale Romanum. Sources of the *super oblata* and postcommunions", *EL* 128.3 (2014), 292-346

————, "The Mass formularies *per annum* IX-X in the 2000 Missale Romanum. Sources of the *super oblata* and postcommunions", *EL* 129.1 (2015), 101-122

————, "The Mass formularies *per annum* XIII-XIX in the 2000 *Missale Romanum*. Sources of the *super oblata* and postcommunions", *EL* 129.2 (2015), 206-251

————, "The Mass formularies *per annum* XX-XXVIII in the 2000 *Missale Romanum*. Sources of the *super oblata* and postcommunions", *EL* 129.3 (2015), 314-375

————, "The Mass formularies *per annum* XXIX-XXXII in the 2000 *Missale Romanum*. Sources of the *super oblata* and postcommunions", *EL* 129.4 (2015), 446-495

————, "The Mass formularies *per annum* XXXIII-XXXIV in the 2000 *Missale Romanum*. Sources of the *super oblata* and postcommunions", *EL* 130.1 (2016), 58-85

————, "Orations for St Polycarp in the 2000 *Missale Romanum*, and Some Antecedents till 1738", *EL* 131.2 (2017), 183-228

————, "The Orations of the Memorial of the Holy Name of Jesus in the 2000 *Missale Romanum*", *EL* 131.4 (2017), 443-471

————, "Orations for the Votive Mass of the Holy Name of Jesus in the Missal of Paul VI", *EL* 133.2 (2019), 129-160

Thomas R. Whelan, "Mass in Time of War or Civil Disturbance (*Missale Romanum* 2008): Elements of a Liturgical Theology in a Collect", *SL* 43 (2013), 155-168

NB: Issues of *Notitiae* are freely available online from the website of the Congregation for Divine Worship and the Discipline of the Sacraments (http://www.cultodivino.va/)

EXTRACTS FROM DOCUMENTS RELATING TO THE REVISION OF THE MISSAL AND ITS PRAYERS

Paul VI: Address to the members and *periti* of the Consilium, 29 October 1964 (DOL 622)

The portion of the work particularly entrusted to you involves taking up the revision of the liturgical books. That, it need hardly be said, is a work of immense importance and entails the most serious difficulties. Formulation of the prayers of the liturgy is the issue. To evaluate them, to revise them or compose new ones, you need not only the highest wisdom and perspicacity, but also an accurate sense of contemporary needs combined with a full understanding of the traditional liturgical heritage handed on to us.

You must have the conviction that the formularies of public prayer cannot be worthy of God unless they faithfully express Catholic teaching. They are to be so composed as to measure up to the norms of the highest art, as befits the majesty of divine worship. The prayers should breathe with the religious spirit of devotion; they should evince a splendour in their brevity and clear simplicity that will assure right understanding and the ready perception of their truth and beauty. Only then will the public prayer of the Church correspond to the nature and inner spirit of the liturgy and serve the Christian people's offering of the glory due to God.

Consilium ad exsequendam, Coetus XVIII *bis*: Schema 186 (*De Missali, 27*), 19th September 1966, "Concerning the revision of the orations and prefaces", pp. 1-4*

[1] About the work of revising the orations and prefaces of the Roman Missal, entrusted to Group 18 *bis* of the Consilium, the following principles are proposed:

1. That, in the Missal, there may be no repetition or iteration of the same texts.

It seems good to us for this to be avoided:

---

* English translation from Matthew P. Hazell, *The Proper of Time and the Post-Vatican II Liturgical Reforms* (Lectionary Study Press, 2018), pp. 220-227.

a) firstly, because it is, if I may be permitted to use the inelegant phrase, "formularistic" that the same texts are repeated up to 26 times per year, merely because they sound good, or as a result of an innate shortcoming;

b) secondly, that we may remedy the concerning defect in variety that means the same texts, e.g. the *super oblata* and postcommunion for the Sunday within the Octave of Christmas and for Palm Sunday, are used without any respect for their proper character or the nature of the celebration.

In a certain sense, albeit not its original one, it seems good to us that, even in these things, the desire of the Constitution on the Sacred Liturgy that "richer fare may be provided for the faithful at the table of God's word" (no. 51) be used to introduce into the Roman Missal the venerable riches of Latin euchology, not only because their form is beautiful, but also because of their true, important, theological strength.

Therefore, for every text that frequently occurs in the Missal, its ancient use is to be retained, with very few exceptions.

For Masses which lack orations after this, new texts are to be selected.

[2] QUESTION 1: Does it please the Fathers that, in revising the Roman Missal, the text of orations not be repeated?

2. Many texts, over the course of time, have become corrupted.

There is no question here of any archeologism, where older readings are considered better by that fact alone. However, certain alterations of ancient texts, carried out for theological or pastoral reasons, are in truth impairments or corruptions.

E.g. the insertion, in the 10th century, of the word "ad" in the following oration, which completely changed its theology:

> *Haec hostia, Domine, quaesumus, emundet nostra delicta:*
> *et, AD sacrificium celebrandum, subditorum tibi corpora*
> *mentesque sanctificet.*

Another change, about which we all unanimously feel pain, was made in the second part of the collect for Easter Sunday, and there is no doubt that this greatly diminished its theology. In the *Gelesianum Vetus* we read the following:

> *Deus, qui hodierna die per Unigenitum tuum aeternitatis nobis aditum,*
> *devicta morte reserasti, da nobis, quaesumus, ut qui resurrectionis*

dominicae sollemnia colimus, per innovationem tui Spiritus a morte animae resurgamus.

QUESTION 2: Does it please the Fathers that, in the way indicated, about which we have spoken, the text of orations is to be revised or, in certain cases, amended?

3. Just now, we have discussed erroneous readings, whether philological or theological.

In addition, there are some orations that have lost their historic value, or that no longer conform to the norms of Christian life today.

As an example of the first type, allow me to present the collect for Thursday in Week 3 of Lent, in which Saints Cosmas and Damian are mentioned.

For the second type, the majority of the Lenten orations will suffice as an example. For the remembrance of and preparation for Baptism, which according to the Constitution on the Sacred Liturgy is the primary nature of this season, are almost entirely absent. With respect to the second nature, namely the penitential character, *[3]* it is evident almost exclusively in the language of fasting, and neither the spirit of penance in general nor the preparation for the paschal mystery is sufficently treated.

QUESTION 3: Does it please the Fathers:

   a) that the commemoration of local or historical events that have lost their significance to the universal Church be removed from orations?
   b) does it please you that, in certain cases, orations be accommodated to the customs of Christian life today?

4. In many orations and prefaces, it is greatly disturbing that the so-called proper "literary genre" has been utterly lost. Indeed, from the beginning of their preparation in liturgical books, they are not always rightly used.

   a) a large portion of the prefaces are not a true "thanksgiving", but rather supplication, a merely dogmatic exposition, or even the life of a saint; but this is a matter we will discuss afterwards;
   b) there are some orations given as *super oblata* and postcommunions in which neither a gift (in the first) nor our participation in the sacrifice (in the second) are mentioned;

c) many of the orations *"super populum"* are actually collects, and do not appear clearly as these types of orations, which implore the blessing of God over the people gathered for the celebration of the Eucharist.

QUESTION 4: Does it please the Fathers that for each oration in the Missal that appears or is inserted, its proper literary genre be preserved or restored?

5. It is almost unanimously desired, and in our group all are of the same mind, that all orations be directed to the Father, so that our prayer, at least in the liturgy, is always made to the Father, through the Son, in the Holy Spirit.

Furthermore, many orations, especially of the Saints, should be revised. This is often the case among the orations in the Proper of Time, except for the collects of the Sundays of Advent. On account of their antiquity and more venerable character, we have not changed them. New orations, however, that have been selected for all [4] the ferial days of this season are all addressed to the Father.

QUESTION 5: Does it please the Fathers:

a) that all the orations of the Roman Missal be directed to the Father?
b) do you desire that even the collects of the Sundays of Advent be revised in this way?

6. A difficult and quite arduous part of our labours has been the selection of new orations:

a) in cases where, in the current Roman Missal, orations are repeated, and should be substituted for others;
b) in cases where certain days lack proper orations, especially those of Advent and Eastertide.

This gives rise to a very important question about unity, that is, the unity of the theological form of the orations of the Missal.

In addition, as we have seen, these new texts will be given over to be translated into the language proper to each region, as the "objective norms" will provide for, so that these extant orations might be known, that they be made suitable and easy, and be properly understood.

Therefore, insofar as a number of them need to be present, new orations have been, in the first place, selected from ancient sacramentaries, in conformity with the norms that have already been explained above.

Nevertheless, sometimes it is necessary that new texts are cultivated. For these, we might make use of the method called "centonisation", which is a very ancient tradition in Latin euchology. We have a notable example in the preface of the Ascension, which has been cultivated from two prefaces in the Verona Sacramentary.

These centonised elements are taken from sacramentaries, from sacred Scripture and from the works of the Fathers.

Besides the necessity of protecting the unity of which we spoke earlier, this has the possibility of saving the most beautiful elements from the sacramentaries, which are often placed in banal contexts.

QUESTION 6: Does it please the Fathers that new texts, composed chiefly by means of centonisation, be inserted into the Roman Missal?

Paul VI: Address to the members and *periti* of the Consilium, 13 October 1966 (DOL 631-632)

[631] Your first charge is an investigation into the sacred rites of long usage in the Church, which you are then to revise and to put into an improved form. The investigation presents no special problems, since the ceremonies are well known; it does, nevertheless, require certain qualilties of spirit. One is a reverence for the sacred that prompts us to honour the ceremonies used by the Church in worshipping God. Another is respect for tradition, which has passed on a priceless heritage worthy of veneration. Necessary as well is a sense of history, which has bearing on the way the rites under revision were formed, on ther genuine meaning, either as prayer or symbol, and on other similar points.

No predisposition to change everything without reason must govern this investigation, nor a hastiness, typical of the iconoclast, to emend and revise everything. The guides must be a devout prudence and a reverence combined with wisdom. The search must be for what is best rather than for what is new. With the new, whatever bears the treasures of the most inspired ages of faith should receive preference over present-day inventions. Nevertheless, the voice of the Church today must not be so constricted that it could not sing a new song, should the inspiration of the Holy Spirit move it to.

[632] Your second, extremely delicate duty is this: an examination of the modes of liturgical expression—whether words, including music and song, or gestures and ritual actions. The biblical sources of the particular rites must receive the most careful consideration. Intense effort must be brought to bear on the agreement of the lex orandi with the lex credendi, so that in its meaning prayer preserves the riches of dogma and religious language is suited to both the dogmatic realities it bears and to the balanced expression of the scale of values among the realities celebrated. All of this requires you to expend your learning as men dedicated to doctrine, your special skills as men of letters and the arts; but it also requires you to give your hearts, burning with love for God, for Christ and his kingdom—hearts, we believe, that in prayer have experienced the mystical. Your abilities will be put to the test by this endeavour, which derives its energies and inner force from prayer addressed to God then lived and which enlists the help of the arts. The effect on your work of revision will be, besides the mysterious stamp of beauty, the heavenly gift of being universal and lasting, the charism of being ever young. The liturgy deserves the adornment of such special gifts.

Consilium ad exsequendam, Coetus XIII: Schema 306 (*De Missali*, 52), 9th September 1968, "The Masses and Orations *ad Diversa*, and also Votive", p. 7*

[III. THE PRINCIPLES TO BE ADHERED TO IN THE REVISION OF MASSES *AD DIVERSA* EITHER EXTANT IN THE ROMAN MISSAL, OR FOR NEWLY-COMPOSED MASSES]

5. The orations

It is often impossible to preserve either orations that are found in the [current] Roman Missal or to borrow suitable orations from the treasury of ancient euchology. Indeed, prayer ought to express the mind of our current age, especially with regard to temporal necessities like the unity of Christians, peace and famine.

For example, the collect for the unity of Christians was composed to obtain the cessation of the 'great Western schism', which has not existed for four centuries now. This oration, which asks that Catholics divided

---

* English translation by Matthew P. Hazell.

between two or three Supreme Pontiffs may come together, is not able to give expression to post-conciliar, ecumenical prayer. The orations in the Mass for peace ask God to prevent tribulation in any nearby city and pour supernatural peace into our hearts: this is absurd if we wish to pray for peace in remote nations such as Vietnam and Biafra.[*]

In addition, it seems to us that it is not always possible for the Church on every occasion to make use of ancient orations, which do not correspond with the doctrinal progress visible in recent encyclicals such as *Pacem in terris* and *Populorum progressio,* and in conciliar documents such as *Gaudium et spes.* For the renewal of liturgical speech, accommodated to the mind of our age, is it not possible to begin with the Masses *ad diversa,* which may consider the concrete objects and necessities of today?

Finally, it is often agreed that more orations may be proposed and chosen *ad libitum* according to different conditions: for example, in Masses for those suffering hunger, two series of orations be present, as this Mass may be celebrated with the very people who are starving or with those who are ready to bring help to the hungry.

Paul VI: Address to the members and *periti* of the Consilium, 14 October 1968 (DOL 670-671)

[670] But we did not want to talk to you just to congratulate you for your work well done. Even more intense is the desire to exhort you and encourage you for the long road yet to be travelled. First, there is the revision of the Roman Missal, now on the verge of completion; then the revision of the Roman Breviary, Ritual, Pontifical, and Martyrology. You will still need a long time to revise all these liturgical books properly.

Clearly the Church today attaches supreme importance to the liturgy, which must be regarded, in the words of the Council, "as the summit towards which the activity of the Church is directed and at the same time as the fount from which all its power flows." [*SC* 10] It is also clear how necessary it is that as you go about your work you keep always in mind

---

[*] Translator's note: the Republic of Biafra declared its de facto independence from Nigeria on 30th May 1967, precipitating the Nigerian Civil War (July 1967–January 1970). The humanitarian crisis caused by the war came to particular prominence in Western media in mid-1968. At the end of the civil war, its leadership having surrendered to the (first) Supreme Military Council of Nigeria, Biafra was absorbed back into Nigeria.

the close relationship between the Church's lex orandi and the other sectors of religious life, especially faith, tradition, and canon law.

Since the lex orandi must be in harmony with the lex credendi and serve to manifest and corroborate the faith of the Christian people, the new prayer formularies you are preparing cannot be worthy of God unless they are the faithful reflections of Catholic teaching. It is easy to see that for these formularies to match the nature and character of liturgical worship, they must clearly bear the marks of majesty, simplicity, beauty, and have the power to stir the spirit and spark devotion.

[671] A further point is that reform of the liturgy must not be taken to be a repudiation of the sacred patrimony of past ages and a reckless welcoming of every conceivable novelty. You are well aware of the objective the conciliar Fathers set for themselves in this regard when they promulgated the Constitution on the Liturgy, namely, that the new should be in harmony with sound tradition so that "any new forms adopted should in some way grow organically from forms already existing." [SC 23] Hence a sound reform is to be seen as one having the power to combine the new and the old harmoniously.

These remarks clearly imply that to guarantee a true reform it is important that all accept the ecclesial and hierarchic character of the liturgy. That is to say, the rites and prayer formularies must not be regarded as a private matter, left up to individuals, a parish, a diocese, or a nation, but as the property of the whole Church, because they express the living voice of its prayer. No one, then, is permitted to change these formularies, to introduce new ones, or to substitute others in their place. The very dignity of the liturgy forbids this, for through the liturgy we are in contact with God. The good of souls and the effectiveness of pastoral activity, which would be imperilled, also forbid it. Remember that norm of the Constitution on the Liturgy: "Regulation of the liturgy depends solely on the authority of the Church." [SC 22.1; cf. 33]

Paul VI: Apostolic Constitution Missale Romanum, 3 April 1969 (DOL 1363)

This reform of the Roman Missal, in addition to the three changes already mentioned (the eucharistic prayer, the Order of Mass, and the readings), has also corrected and considerably modified other aspects of its components: the Proper of Seasons, the Proper of Saints, the Common of Saints, ritual Masses, and votive Masses. In all of these changes, particular care has been taken with the prayers. Their number has been increased, so that the new forms might better correspond to new needs, and the text of older prayers has been restored on the basis of the ancient sources. As a result, each weekday of the principal liturgical seasons, Advent, Christmas, Lent, and Easter, now has its own, distinct prayer.

Sacred Congregation of Divine Worship: Remarks of Benno Cardinal Gut, Prefect, at a papal audience for the Consilium, 10 April 1970 (DOL 688)

In these last six years we have lived through a remarkable period in the Church's history. It has been a period of hard and difficult work, not without problems; it has at times been marked by controversy; its passage has been measured by wise and often courageous experimentation. It is a period of history that has at once been serious and happy, bringing joy to the spirit.

Looking back over the course we have travelled, we gladly offer thanks to you, Holy Father, for having been so kind as to choose us to devote our energies to the work of renewing the inmost life of the Church. This work brings to realisation those things by which Vatican Council II has marked the Church and its structure with the spirit of genuine reform. That is a starting point from which the Church, entering on a new course pointed out by God, will advance toward more sublime and shining goals.

Like a ship that after a long voyage nears the harbour, the reform of the liturgy is fast approaching its successful outcome. The soon-to-be published Roman Missal as well as the divine office that we hope to be able to put in the hands of the people of God in a short time stand as the more notable achievements of the latest phase of the process.

Thirteen plenary and innumerable particular sessions, three hundred sixty-five schemata prepared for the plenary sessions, many other kinds of documents, including constitutions, decrees, instructions—this sums up the work done. By their silent but assiduous and dauntless work the fifty Fathers, cardinals and bishops, and the one hundred fifty periti, chosen from all parts of the world, have given a new form to the Church's lex orandi, in which the whole of God's family is raising a beautiful chorus of celebration.

Future historians will have the advantage of archives full of priceless records should they wish to reconstruct the development of the individual reformed rites or examine their texts, deriving from tradition or newly composed, or evaluate the particular reformed rubrical and pastoral norms. Then it will be utterly clear how conscious of their responsibility before God and the Church the members of that institution were in doing their work. It is the institution that you, Holy Father, with such foresight created on 3 January 1964 and that will be remembered in history as "the Consilium."

Paul VI: Address to the members and periti of the Consilium on the occasion of its final plenary meeting, 10 April 1970 (DOL 690)

In the light of such difficulties, it is amazing that so much is already finished; to mention only the highlights: the several instructions and other documents issued; the supporting writings of some of your members; the new Order of Mass; the changes for the liturgy of Holy Week; the rites for the baptism of infants, for diaconate, priesthood, episcopacy and marriage; the rite of funerals and of religious profession; the Roman Calendar. Soon to be published, after much hard work, is the Roman Missal, then (among other things) the Roman Breviary, the rites for confirmation and for the baptism of adults, the revised Roman Martyrology, the second book of the Roman Pontifical, and the Roman Ceremonial.

The principles approved by the Council's Constitution on the Liturgy has been the guiding light for all of your work. That "Magna Carta" of liturgical reform has initiated in the Church a new impetus in divine worship toward empowering people for a genuine, effective expression of their deepest sentiments in the liturgy and toward the preservation, as far as possible, of the heritage of the Latin Church.

Working along these two lines, not always easily coordinated, you have pursued the reform of the liturgy. Whether ancient or newly adapted and revised to suit the contemporary mind, texts have now been provided that are more numerous than those of former usage and richer in spiritual meaning; so too are new rites, simplified in accord with the intention of the Council and more clearly expressive of the realities they celebrate.

You have striven particularly to see to it that the word of God in Scripture receives greater prominence; that theology more strongly influences liturgical texts for a closer correspondence between the *lex orandi* and *lex credendi*; that as divine worship is ennobled by a genuine simplicity the people of God, especially with the sanctioning of a wider use of the vernacular, can understand the liturgical formularies more clearly and participate in the celebrations more actively.

The welcome outcome is that Vatican Council II, in no small measure because of your own efforts and care, is accomplishing a healthy renewal in the Church's life as to what concerns the encounter between God and his people that takes place in the liturgy.

Sacred Congregation of Divine Worship: Instruction *Calendaria particularia,* 24 June 1970 (DOL 4035)

Among the prayers, only the opening prayer has direct bearing on the saint being celebrated. It is well to give prominence to the saint's characteristics, some aspect of the saint's spiritual life or apostolate, without resorting to trite phrases, e.g., about miracles or establishing a religious institute. The prayer over the gifts and the prayer after communion, however, bear directly on the eucharistic mystery; any mention of the saint must only be incidental.

Secretariat of State: Letter of Cardinal J. Villot to Bishop C. Rossi (president of the *Centro di Azione Liturgica*), on the occasion of the 22nd National Liturgical Week of Italy at Oropa, on the new Roman Missal, 30 August 1971 (DOL 1779)

The Roman Missal is in fact the fundamental expression of the prayer of the Church: its purpose is to cast into formularies of doctrinal profundity, spiritual richness, and literary grace the praises and supplications that the Church in celebrating the eucharistic mystery addresses through Christ to the Father.

Further, the Missal takes up the whole mystery of Christ in the continuous march of each liturgical year toward the Easter of the eternal Jerusalem and casts the light of this mystery and its redemptive power on the Blessed Virgin, the saints, the Church, human existence, and world events. Thus it expresses concretely how in the Church the rule of prayer corresponds to the rule of faith.

What has always been true throughout the varied and progressive development of the Roman liturgy, from the ancient sacramentaries to the revered post-Tridentine Missal of St. Pius V, is true also of the new Roman Missal. While preserving the treasure of tradition, it has been rearranged and enhanced in consequence of the directives of Vatican Council II.

We might also say that in the new Missal there is further evidence and expression of the Church's perennial youth. That youth is the source of the Church's ever rediscovering itself, through continuous renewal against the toll of time, in order to present itself to humanity "without spot or wrinkle" (Eph. 5:27), as its divine Founder wished.

Accordingly this new Missal is marked by a greater cohesiveness in its texts. But it also recommends itself because of the remarkable richness and variety of these texts, embracing the new formularies added, especially for the more important seasons of the liturgical year, and the euchological collection, expanded to some two thousand prayers and many new prefaces. The result is that in contrast to the previous invariability of texts, explained in some providential way by special historical conditions, the new Missal offers flexible and well-advised options. While always respecting the norms for celebration, every celebrant has the opportunity and resources to meet the spiritual need of the participating assembly more effectively and to relate liturgical prayer in a vital way to the concrete situation of today's people. This was the reason for restoring certain ancient formularies, for a greater precision replacing the indefiniteness of certain prayers in the sanctoral cycle, for adding, along lines that follow the directions set by the Council, Mass texts and prayers "for special occasions."

Pope Paul therefore warmly urges priests to know the Missal, to study it, to meditate on it. An experiential knowledge and wise use of these texts will bring priests to see how it is possible and necessary to restore the style and spirit of liturgical prayer without recourse to an out-of-place, arbitrary improvisation.

Congregation for Divine Worship and Discipline of the Sacraments: *General Instruction of the Roman Missal*, 3rd edition, 2002 (nos. 6, 15)

[6] When it set out its instructions for the renewal of the Order of Mass, the Second Vatican Council, using, namely, the same words as did St. Pius V in the Apostolic Constitution Quo primum, by which the Missal of Trent was promulgated in 1570, also ordered, among other things, that a number of rites be restored "to the original norm of the holy Fathers." From the fact that the same words are used, it can be noted how the two Roman Missals, although four centuries have intervened, embrace one and the same tradition. Furthermore, if the inner elements of this tradition are reflected

upon, it is also understood how outstandingly and felicitously the older Roman Missal is brought to fulfillment in the later one.

[15] In this manner the Church, while remaining faithful to her office as teacher of truth, safeguarding "things old," that is, the deposit of tradition, fulfills at the same time the duty of examining and prudently adopting "things new" (cf. Mt. 13:52).

For part of the new Missal orders the prayers of the Church in a way more open to the needs of our times. Of this kind are above all the Ritual Masses and Masses for Various Needs, in which tradition and new elements are appropriately brought together. Thus, while a great number of expressions, drawn from the Church's most ancient tradition and familiar through the many editions of the Roman Missal, have remained unchanged, numerous others have been accommodated to the needs and conditions proper to our own age, and still others, such as the prayers for the Church, for the laity, for the sanctification of human labour, for the community of all nations, and certain needs proper to our era, have been newly composed, drawing on the thoughts and often the very phrasing of the recent documents of the Council.

On account, moreover, of the same attitude toward the new state of the world as it now is, it seemed to cause no harm at all to so revered a treasure if some phrases were changed so that the language would be in accord with that of modern theology and would truly reflect the current state of the Church's discipline. Hence, several expressions regarding the evaluation and use of earthly goods have been changed, as have several which alluded to a certain form of outward penance which was proper to other periods of the Church's past.

In this way, finally, the liturgical norms of the Council of Trent have certainly been completed and perfected in many particulars by those of the Second Vatican Council, which has carried into effect the efforts to bring the faithful closer to the Sacred Liturgy that have been taken up these last four centuries and especially those of recent times, and above all the attention to the Liturgy promoted by St. Pius X and his Successors.

PROPER OF TIME

I. ADVENT

1st Sunday of Advent

Source: Ve 173 + 1053 (*CO* 901 + 4718)

Ve 173   *Mense maii, preces in Ascensa Domini, C*

Da nobis, domine, non terrena sapere, sed amare caelestia, et inter praetereuntia constitutos iam nunc inhere mansuris.

Ve 1053   *Mense septembris, in natale episcoporum, XV alia missa, SO*

Prosint nobis, domine, frequentata mysteria, quae nos a cupiditatibus terrenis expediant, et instituant amare caelestia.

MR(2008)   *Dom. I Adv.*

Prosint nobis, quǽsumus, Dómine, frequentáta mystéria, quibus nos, inter prætereúntia **ambulántes**, iam nunc instítuis amáre cæléstia et inhærére mansúris.

2nd Sunday of Advent

Source: MR 970 (*CO* 5044 b)

MR 970   *Dom. II Adv, PC*

Repléti cibo spirituális alimóniæ, súpplices te, Dómine, deprecámur: ut, huius participatióne mystérii, dóceas nos terréna despícere et amáre cæléstia.

MR(2008)   *Dom. II Adv.*

Repléti cibo spiritális alimóniæ, súpplices te, Dómine, deprecámur, ut, huius participatióne mystérii, dóceas nos terréna **sapiénter perpéndere, et** cæléstibus **inhærére**.

3RD SUNDAY OF ADVENT

Source: MR 639 (*CO* 3076 b)

MR 639   *Dom. III Adv, PC*

Implorámus, Dómine, cleméntiam tuam: ut hæc divína subsídia, a vítiis expiátos, ad festa ventúra nos praeparent.

MR(2008)   *Dom. III Adv.*

Tuam, Dómine, cleméntiam implorámus, ut hæc divína subsídia, a vítiis expiátos, ad festa ventúra nos præparent.

4TH SUNDAY OF ADVENT

Source: Ve 741 + A 507 (*CO* 5579 + *Pref* 543)

Ve 741   *Mense augusti, natale sancti Laurenti, PC*

Sumpsimus, domine, pignus redemptionis aeternae. Sit nobis, quaesumus, interuenientibus sanctis tuis uitae praesentis auxilium pariter et futurae.

A 507   *Dom. V in Quadragesima, Pref*

VD: Maiestate tua propensius implorantes ut quanto magis dies salutifere festivitatis accedit tanto devotius ad eius digne celebrandum proficiamus paschale mysterium.

MR(2008)   *Dom. IV Adv.*

Sumpto pígnore redemptiónis ætérnæ, quǽsumus, omnípotens Deus, ut quanto magis dies salutíferæ festivitátis accédit, tanto devótius proficiámus ad Fílii tui digne **nativitátis** mystérium celebrándum.

Weekdays of Advent before 17th December

Mondays: See 1st Sunday of Advent (p. 3 above)

Tuesdays: See 2nd Sunday of Advent (p. 3 above)

Wednesdays: See 3rd Sunday of Advent (p. 4 above)

Thursdays: See 1st Sunday of Advent (p. 3 above)

Fridays: See 2nd Sunday of Advent (p. 3 above)

Saturdays: See 3rd Sunday of Advent (p. 4 above)

17th December

Source: GeV 1134 (*CO* 263)

GeV 1134   *De Adv. Domini, alia missa, PC*

Animae nostrae, quaesumus, omnipotens deus, hoc potiantur desiderio, ut a tuo spiritu inflammentur, et, sicut lampadas divino munere satiati, ante conspectum venientis Christi filii tui velut clara lumina fulgeamus.

MR(2008)   *Die 17 decembris*

° Divíno múnere satiáti, quǽsumus, omnípotens Deus, hoc desidério *potiámur*, ut, a tuo **accénsi** Spíritu, ° ante conspéctum veniéntis Christi ° tui, velut clara *luminária* fulgeámus.

18TH DECEMBER

Source: MR 1135 (*CO* 5845)

MR 1135   *Dom. I Adv., PC*

Suscipiámus, Dómine, misericórdiam tuam in médio templi tui: ut reparatiónis nostræ ventúra solémnia cóngruis honóribus præcedámus.

MR(2008)   *Die 18 decembris*

Suscipiámus, Dómine, misericórdiam tuam in médio templi tui, **et** redemptiónis nostræ ventúra sollémnia cóngruis honóribus præcedámus.

19TH DECEMBER

Source: A 1589 + Ve 1313 (*Pref* 1415 + 1390)

A 1589   *Dom. II ante natale Domini*

VD: <u>Referentes gratiarum de praeteritis muneribus actionem, promptius quae ventura sunt praestanda confidimus</u>. Nec est nobis seminum desperanda fecunditas, cum pro supplicationibus nostris annua devotione venerandus, etiam matris virginis fructus salutaris intervenit Christus dominus noster.

Ve 1313   *Mense decembri, XLIII. In ieiunio mensis decimi, III (item alia)*

VD: Quoniam salubri meditante ieiunio necessaria curatione tractamus, et per observantiae conpetentis obsequium de perceptis grati muneribus de percipiendis efficimur gratiores; ut non solum terrena fertilitate laetemur, sed <u>nativitatem panis aeterni purificatis suscipiamus mentibus honorandam</u>.

MR(2008)   *Die 19 decembris*

<u>Grátias</u> de **collátis** munéribus referéntes, **fac nos propítius**, omnípotens Deus, <u>quæ ventúra sunt</u> **desideráre** <u>præstánda</u>, ut <u>nativitátem</u> **Salvatóris nostri** <u>purificáti suscipiámus méntibus honorándam</u>.

20TH DECEMBER

Source: Gell 1887 (*CO* 4946 b)[*]

Gell 1887   *Missa in remissionem peccatorum, PC*

Quos munere caelesti reficis, domine, divino tuere praesidio, ut, tuis mysteriis perfruentes, nullis subdamur adversis et a cunctis iniquitatibus nostris exue nos, omnipotens deus, et in tua nos fac pace gaudere.

MR(2008)   *Die 20 decembris*

Quos múnere cælésti réficis, Dómine, divíno tuére præsídio, ut, tuis mystériis perfruéntes, ° in **vera** *fácias* pace gaudére.

21ST DECEMBER

Source: Ve 1305 (*CO* 5499)

Ve 1305   *Mensis decembris, in ieiunio mensis decimi, II alia missa, SP*

Sit plebi tuae, domine, continuata defensio divini participatio sacramenti, ut carnalibus vitiis non teneatur obnoxia, ut maiestati tuae plena sit devotione subiecta, ut salvationem mentis et corporis et incessabiliter expetet, et affluenter accipiat.

MR(2008)   *Die 21 decembris*

Sit plebi tuæ, Dómine, continuáta deténsio divíni participátio **mystérii**, ° ut, maiestáti tuæ plena ° devotióne subiécta, ° salvatiónem mentis et córporis ° affluénter accípiat.

---

[*] See also GeV 1352 (*CO* 4946 a): *Quos munere, domine, caelesti reficis, divino tuere praesidio, ut tuis mysteriis perfruentes nullis subdamur adversis.*

22ND DECEMBER

Source: Ve 1341 *(CO 6783)*

Ve 1341   *Item alia (Rotulus)*

Deus, qui via es veritatis et ineffabilis unitas trinitatis: concede propitius, tua in nobis gratia operante, ut venienti salvatori mereamur cum dignis operibus obviare et beatitudinis praemia promereri.

MR(2008)   *Die 22 decembris*

Róboret nos, Dómine, tui sacraménti percéptio, ut veniénti Salvatóri mereámur cum dignis opéribus obviáre, et beatitúdinis praemia promeréri.

23RD DECEMBER

Source: GeV 996 *(CO 528)*

GeV 996   *XVIII kalendas septembris, in Assumptione s. Mariae, PC*

Caelesti munere satiati, quaesumus, omnipotens deus, tua protectione custodi ut castimoniae pacem mentibus nostris atque corporibus, intercedente sancta Maria, propitiatus indulge, et veniente sponso filio tuo unigenito, accensis lampadibus eius digni praestolemur occursum.

MR(2008)   *Die 23 decembris*

Cælésti múnere satiátis, ° **Dómine,** ° pacem ° **tuam** propitiátus indúlge, ° **ut** Fílio tuo **dilectíssimo** *veniénti* accénsis lampádibus ° digni præstolémur occúrsum.

24TH DECEMBER (MORNING)

Source: MR 177 (CO 927)

MR 177   *Die 24 decembris, in vigilia nat. Domini, SO*

Da nobis, quǽsumus, omnípotens Deus: ut, sicut adoránda Fílii tui natalícia prævenímus, sic eius múnera capiámus sempitérna gaudéntes.

MR(2008)   *Dom. III Adv.*

Da nobis, **Dómine, hoc dono tuo mirábili recreátis**, ut, sicut adoránda Fílii tui natalícia prævenímus, sic eius múnera capiámus sempitérna gaudéntes.

PROPER OF TIME

II. CHRISTMASTIDE

CHRISTMAS DAY (VIGIL MASS)

Source: MR 169 (*CO* 904)

MR 177   *Die 24 decembris, in vigilia nat. Domini, PC*

Da nobis, quǽsumus, Dómine: unigéniti Fílii tui recensíta nativitáte respiráre; cuius cælésti mystério páscimur et potámur.

MR(2008)   *In Nat. Domini, ad Missam in Vigilia*

Text is the same as the source above.

CHRISTMAS DAY (MASS DURING THE NIGHT)

Source: MR 164 (*CO* 935 a)

MR 164   *In nat. Domini, ad primam Missam in nocte, PC*

Da nobis, quaesumus, Dómine Deus noster: ut, qui Nativitátem Dómini nostri Iesu Christi mystériis nos frequentáre gaudémus; dignis conversatiónibus ad eius mereámur perveníre consórtium.

MR(2008)   *In Nat. Domini, ad Missam in nocte*

Da nobis, quǽsumus, Dómine Deus noster, ut, qui nativitátem **Redemptóris** nostri ° frequentáre gaudémus, dignis conversatiónibus ad eius mereámur perveníre consórtium.

CHRISTMAS DAY (MASS AT DAWN)

Source: OV 216

OV 216   *Alia responsorium, Filia Syon consecrabis Domino*

Iesu, virtutum omnium Deus, qui per beatae genetricis tuae misterium consecras tibi multitudines populorum, dum novo miraculo virginem conceptione mirabili ditas, et matrem virginitatis honore non privas, ut incarnationis tuae misterium et singulare citra similitudinis exemplar manaret, et admirabile sine aliqua dissertione rationis existeret: dona nobis, huius arcana misterii et plena fide cognoscere et pleniori caritatis ardore diligere; ut per hoc, quod de te, quae vera sunt, eredimus, ad hoc, quod te diligentibus tribuis, ardentius veniamus.

MR(2008)   *In Nat. Domini, ad Missam in aurora*

Da nobis, Dómine, Fílii tui nativitátem læta devotióne coléntibus, huius arcána mystérii et plena fide cognóscere, et plenióre caritátis ardóre dilígere.

CHRISTMAS DAY (MASS DURING THE DAY)

Source: MR 858 (*CO 4365*)

MR 858   *In nat. Domini, ad tertiam Missam in die, PC*

Præsta, quaesumus, omnípotens Deus: ut natus hódie Salvátor mundi, sicut divínæ nobis generatiónis est auctor; ita et immortalitátis sit ipse largítor.

MR(2008)   *In Nat. Domini, ad Missam in die*

Præsta, ° **miséricors** Deus, ut natus hódie Salvátor mundi, sicut divínæ nobis generatiónis est auctor, ita et immortalitátis sit ipse largítor.

HOLY FAMILY (SUNDAY WITHIN THE OCTAVE OF CHRISTMAS)

Source: MR 956

MR 956   Dom. infra oct. Epiphaniae, S. familiae Iesu, Mariae, Ioseph, PC

Quos cæléstibus réficis sacraméntis, fac, Dómine Iesu, sanctæ Famíliæ tuæ exémpla iúgiter imitári: ut, in hora mortis nostræ, occurrénte gloriósa Vírgine Matre tua cum beáto Ioseph; per te in ætérna tabernácula récipi mereámur.

MR(2008)   S. Familiae Iesu, Mariae et Ioseph

Quos cæléstibus réficis sacraméntis, fac, **clementíssime Pater**, sanctæ Famíliæ ° exémpla iúgiter imitári, ut, **post ærúmnas sǽculi, eius consórtium consequámur ætérnum.**

5TH DAY IN THE OCTAVE OF CHRISTMAS (29TH DECEMBER)

Source: Ve 1067 (*CO* 1022 aA)

Ve 1067   Mense septembris, in nat. episcoporum, XVII alia missa, PC

Da, quaesumus, omnipotens deus, ut mysteriorum virtute sanctorum vita nostra firmetur.

MR(2008)   De V die infra oct. Nat. Domini

Da, quǽsumus, omnípotens Deus, ut mysteriórum virtúte sanctorum **iúgiter** vita nostra firmétur.

6TH DAY IN THE OCTAVE OF CHRISTMAS (30TH DECEMBER)

Source: Ve 1256 (*CO* 1919)

Ve 1256   *Mense decembris, in nat. Domini, V alia missa, PC*

Deus, qui nos sacramenti tui participatione contingis, virtutis eius effectus in nostris cordibus operare, ut suscipiendo muneri tuo per ipsum munus aptemur.

MR(2008)   *De VI die infra oct. Nat. Domini*

Text is the same as the source above.

7TH DAY IN THE OCTAVE OF CHRISTMAS (31ST DECEMBER)

Source: Ve 1299 (*CO* 2242)

Ve 1299   *Mense decembris, in ieiunio mensis decimi, prima missa, SP*

Diversis plebs tua, domine, gubernata subsidiis, et praesentia pietatis tuae remedia capiat et futura, ut, transeuntium rerum necessaria consolatione fovente, fiducialius ad aeterna contendat.

MR(2008)   *De VII die infra oct. Nat. Domini*

Text is the same as the source above.

MARY, THE HOLY MOTHER OF GOD (OCTAVE DAY OF CHRISTMAS)

Source: GeV 1252 (*CO* 3220 a)

GeV 1252   *Ordinarium Missae, alia oratio, PC*

Laeti, domine, sumpsimus sacramenta caelestia: intercedente pro nobis beata et gloriosa semperque virgine dei genetrice Maria ad vitam nobis proficiant sempiternam.

MR(2008)   *Sanctae Dei Genetricis Mariae*

Súmpsimus, Dómine, læti sacraménta cæléstia: **præsta, quæsumus, ut ad vitam** nobis profíciant sempitérnam, **qui** *beátam semper Vírginem Maríam* **Fílii tui** *Genetrícem* **et Ecclésiæ Matrem profitéri gloriámur.**

2ND SUNDAY AFTER CHRISTMAS

Source: MR 812 (*CO* 5708)

MR 812   *Dom. infra oct. Nativitatis, PC*

Per huius, Dómine, operatiónem mystérii, et vítia nostra purgéntur, et iusta desidéria compleántur.

MR(2008)   *Dom. II post Natvititatem*

Dómine **Deus noster, supplíciter te rogámus, ut,** huius operatióne mystérii, ° vítia nostra purgéntur, et iusta desidéria compleántur.

THE EPIPHANY OF THE LORD (VIGIL)*

Source: GeV 61 (*CO* 4061)

GeV 61   *VIII idus ianuarii, in Theophaniae, C*

Omnipotens sempiterne deus, qui verbi tui incarnationem praeclari testimonio sideris indicasti, quod videntes magi oblatis maiestatem tuam muneribus adorarunt, concede, ut semper in mentibus nostris tuae appareat stella iustitiae et noster in tua sit confessione thesaurus.

MR(2008)   *In Epiphania Domini, ad Missam in Vigilia*

Sacra alimónia renováti, tuam, Dómine, misericórdiam deprecámur, ut semper in méntibus nostris tuæ appáreat stella iustítiæ et noster in tua sit confessióne thesáurus.

THE EPIPHANY OF THE LORD (MASS DURING THE DAY)

Source: MR 92 (*CO* 524)

MR 92   *Die 13 ianuarii, In comm. Bapt. D.N.I.C., PC*

Cælésti lúmine, quaesumus, Dómine, semper et ubíque nos praeveni: ut mystérium, cuius nos partícipes esse voluísti, et puro cernámus intúitu, et digno percipiámus afféctu.

MR(2008)   *In Epiphania Domini, ad Missam in die*

Text is the same as the source above.

---

* This celebration was added to the *editio typica tertia*, so is not in MR(1970) or MR(1975).

The Baptism of the Lord (Sunday after Epiphany)

Source: New composition

MR(2008)   *Dom. post diem 6 ianuarii, In Baptismate Domini*

Sacro múnere satiáti, cleméntiam tuam, Dómine, supplíciter exorámus, ut, Unigénitum tuum fidéliter audiéntes, fílii tui vere nominémur et simu.

Weekdays of Christmastide

Mondays: See 5th Day in the Octave of Christmas (p. 15 above)

Tuesdays: See 6th Day in the Octave of Christmas (p. 16 above)

Wednesdays: See 7th Day in the Octave of Christmas (p. 16 above)

Thursdays: See 5th Day in the Octave of Christmas (p. 15 above)

Fridays: See 6th Day in the Octave of Christmas (p. 16 above)

Saturdays: See 7th Day in the Octave of Christmas (p. 16 above)

PROPER OF TIME

III. LENT, HOLY WEEK & TRIDUUM

Ash Wednesday

Source: MR 814 (*CO* 4194 B)

MR 814   *Feria IV Cinerum, PC*

Percépta nobis, Dómine, praebeant sacraménta subsídium: ut tibi grata sint nostra ieiúnia, et nobis profíciant ad medélam.

MR(2008)   *Feria IV Cinerum*

Text is the same as the source above.

Thursday after Ash Wednesday

Source: MR 104 (*CO* 554)

MR 104   *Feria V post Cineres, PC**

Cæléstis doni benedictióne percépta: súpplices te, Deus omnípotens, deprecámur; ut hoc idem nobis et sacraménti causa sit, et salútis.

MR(2008)   *Feria V post Cineres*

Cæléstis doni benedictióne percépta, súpplices te, Deus omnípotens, deprecámur, ut hoc idem nobis **semper** et **indulgéntiæ** causa sit et salútis.

---

* Also used on *Feria IV post Dominicam Passionis* (Wednesday after Passion Sunday).

Friday after Ash Wednesday

Source: Ve 868 + Ve 1255 (*CO* 3153 + *Pref* 1445)

Ve 868   *Mense septembris, ieiunii mensis septimi, II alia missa, SO*

Intende, quaesumus, domine, sacrificium singulare, ut huius participatione mysterii, quae speranda credimus, expectata sumamus.

Ve 1255   *Mense decembri, XL, VIII Nat. Domini, V item alia*

VD: Sollemnitas enim, domine, caelestis pacis ingreditur. Quaesumus, ut per eam gratiam, per quam tibi reconciliatus est mundus peccatorum remissione cunctorum, nos quoque delictis omnibus expiati, remediis tuae pietatis aptemur; et mysterium, quod extitit mundo salutare, principalis recordatione muneris adsequamur.

MR(2008)   *Feria VI post Cineres*

Quǽsumus, omnípotens Deus, ut, huius participatióne mystérii a delíctis ómnibus expiáti, remédiis tuæ pietátis aptémur.

Saturday after Ash Wednesday

Source: MR 107 (*CO* 562)

MR 107   *Sabbato post Cinerum, PC*

Cæléstis vitæ múnere vegetáti, quaesumus, Dómine: ut, quod est nobis in præsénti vita mystérium, fiat æternitátis auxílium.

MR(2008)   *Sabbato post Cineres*

Text is the same as the source above.

1ST SUNDAY OF LENT

Source: A 320 (*Pref* 501)

A 320   *Feria III hebd. I Quadrag.*

VD: In quo ieiunantium <u>fides additur, spes provehitur, caritas roboratur</u>. Ipse est enim <u>panis vivus et verus</u>, qui substantia aeternitatis et esca virtutis est. Verbum enim tuum, in quo facta sunt omnia, non solum humanarum mentium, sed ipse panis est angelorum. Hunc panem ministrare non desinas, et, ut eum indesinenter esuriamus, hortaris. Cuius carne, dum pascimur, roboramur, et sanguinem, dum potamur, abluimur.

MR(2008)   *Dom. I in Quadrag.*

Cælésti pane reféci, quo <u>fides **álitur**, spes provéhitur **et** cáritas roborátur</u>, quæsumus, Dómine, ut ipsum, qui <u>est panis vivus et verus</u>, esuríre discámus, et in omni verbo, quod procédit de ore tuo, vívere valeámus.

MONDAY IN WEEK 1 OF LENT

Source: MR 1063 (*CO* 5471)

MR 1063   *Dom. XI post Pent., PC*

Sentiámus, quaesumus, Dómine, tui perceptióne sacraménti, subsídium mentis et córporis: ut, in utróque salváti, cæléstis remédii plenitúdine gloriémur.

MR(2008)   *Feria II post Dom. I Quadrag.*

Text is the same as the source above.

TUESDAY IN WEEK 1 OF LENT

Source: MR 604 (*CO* 2912)

MR 604   *Dom. III post Pascha, SO*

His nobis, Dómine, mystériis conferátur, quo, terréna desidéria mitigántes, discámus amáre cæléstia.

MR(2008)   *Feria III post Dom. I Quadrag.*

Text is the same as the source above.

WEDNESDAY IN WEEK 1 OF LENT

Source: GeV 782 (*CO* 1921)

GeV 782   *In nat. episcopi, si infirmus aut absens fuerit, PC*

Deus, qui nos sacramentis tuis pascere non desistis, tribue, quaesumus, ut eorum nobis indulta refectio vitam conferat sempiternam.

MR(2008)   *Feria IV post Dom. I Quadrag.*

Deus, qui nos sacraméntis tuis páscere non desístis, tríbue, ut eórum nobis indúlta reféctio vitam, quǽsumus, cónferat sempitérnam.

Thursday in Week 1 of Lent

Source: MR 928 (*CO* 4831)

MR 928   *Sabbato Quat. Temp. Adv., PC*

Quaesumus, Dómine Deus noster: ut sacrosáncta mystéria, quæ pro reparatiónis nostræ munímine contulísti; et præsens nobis remédium esse fácias, et futúrum.

MR(2008)   *Feria V post Dom. I Quadrag.*

Text is the same as the source above.

Friday in Week 1 of Lent

Source: MR 1160 (*CO* 6001)

MR 1160   *Dom. I in Quadrag., PC**

Tui nos, Dómine, sacraménti libátio sancta restáuret: et a vetustáte purgátos, in mystérii salutáris fáciat transíre consórtium.

MR(2008)   *Feria VI post Dom. I Quadrag.*

Text is the same as the source above.

---

* Also used on *Feria VI Quat. Temp. Adv.* (Ember Friday in Advent).

SATURDAY IN WEEK 1 OF LENT

Source: GeV 132 (*CO* 4224)

GeV 132   *Feria VII hebd. I Quadrag., PC*

Perpetuo, domine, favore prosequere, quos reficis divino misterio, et, quos imbuisti caelestibus institutis, salutaribus comitare solatiis.

MR(2008)   *Sabbato post Dom. I Quadrag.*

Text is the same as the source above.

2ND SUNDAY OF LENT

Source: GeV 213 (*CO* 4209)

GeV 213   *Feria IV hebd. III Quadrag., PC*

Percipientes, domine, gloriosa mysteria referimus gratias, quod in terris positus iam caelestium praestas esse participes.

MR(2008)   *Dom. II in Quadrag.*

Percipiéntes, Dómine, gloriósa mystéria, grátias **tibi** *reférre* **satágimus**, quod, in terra pósitos, iam cæléstium præstas esse partícipes.

Monday in Week 2 of Lent

Source: MR 588 (*CO* 2841)

MR 588   *Feria II post Dom. II Quadrag., PC*

Hæc nos commúnio, Dómine, purget a crímine: et cæléstis remédii fáciat esse consórtes.

MR(2008)   *Feria II post Dom. II Quadrag.*

Hæc nos commúnio, Dómine, purget a crímine, et cæléstis **gáudii** fáciat esse consórtes.

Tuesday in Week 2 of Lent

Source: MR 989 (*CO* 5134 a)

MR 989   *Feria III post Dom. IV Quadrag., C*

Sacræ nobis, quaesumus, Dómine, observatiónis ieiúnia: et piæ conversatiónis augméntum, et tuæ propitiatiónis contínuum præstent auxílium.

MR(2008)   *Feria III post Dom. II Quadrag.*

Sacræ nobis, quǽsumus, Dómine, **mensæ reféctio**, et piæ conversatiónis augméntum, et tuæ propitiatiónis contínuum *præstet* auxílium.

Wednesday in Week 2 of Lent

Source: Ve 484 (*CO* 4827)

Ve 484   *Mensis iulii, orat. et preces diurnae, XII alia missa, PC*

Quaesumus, domine deus noster, ut quod nobis ad immortalitatis pignus esse voluisti, ad salutis aeternae tribuas provenire suffragium.

MR(2008)   *Feria IV post Dom. II Quadrag.*

Text is the same as the source above.

THURSDAY IN WEEK 2 OF LENT

Source: MR 583 (*CO* 2828)

MR 583   *Feria VI post Dom. II Quadrag., SO*

Hæc in nobis sacrifícia, Deus, et actióne permáneant, et operatióne firméntur.

MR(2008)   *Feria V post Dom. II Quadrag.*

Text is the same as the source above.

FRIDAY IN WEEK 2 OF LENT

Source: MR 551 (*CO* 2586)

MR 551   *Feria VI post Dom. II Quadrag., PC*

Fac nos, quaesumus, Dómine: accépto pígnore salútis ætérnæ, sic téndere congruénter; ut ad eam perveníre possímus.

MR(2008)   *Feria VI post Dom. II Quadrag.*

Accépto, Dómine, pígnore salútis ætérnæ, fac nos, quǽsumus, sic téndere congruénter, ut ad eam perveníre possímus.

SATURDAY IN WEEK 2 OF LENT

Source: MR 996 (*CO* 5152)

MR 996   *Sabbato post Dom. II Quadrag., PC*

Sacraménti tui, Dómine, divína libátio penetrália nostri cordis infúndat: et sui nos partícipes poténter effíciat.

MR(2008)   *Sabbato post Dom. II Quadrag.*

Sacraménti tui, Dómine, divína **percéptio** penetrália nostri cordis infúndat, et sui nos partícipes poténter effíciat.

3RD SUNDAY OF LENT

Source: Ve 23 (*CO* 5562)

Ve 23 *Sabbato post Dom. II Quadrag., PC*

Sumentes pignus caelestis arcani et, in terris positi, iam superno pane satiati, supplicamus, domine, deprecantibus sanctis tuis, ut, quod in nobis mystice geritur, veraciter impleatur.

MR(2008) *Dom. III in Quadrag.*

Suméntes pignus cæléstis arcáni, et in terra pósiti iam supérno pane satiáti, **te**, Dómine, *súpplices deprecámur*, ° ut, quod in nobis mystério géritur, **ópere** impleátur.

MONDAY IN WEEK 3 OF LENT

Source: MR 1159 (*CO* 6000)

MR 1159 *Dom. IX post Pent., PC*

Tui nobis, quaesumus, Dómine, commúnio sacraménti, et purificatiónem cónferat, et tríbuat unitátem.

MR(2008) *Feria II post Dom. III Quadrag.*

Text is the same as the source above.

TUESDAY IN WEEK 3 OF LENT

Source: MR 1178 (*CO* 6101 b)

MR 1178   *Dom. XII post Pent., PC*

Vivíficet nos, quaesumus, Dómine, huius participátio sancta mystérii: et páriter nobis expiatiónem tríbuat, et munímen.

MR(2008)   *Feria III post Dom. III Quadrag.*

Text is the same as the source above.

WEDNESDAY IN WEEK 3 OF LENT

Source: MR 1048 (*CO* 5394 A)

MR 1048   *Feria IV post Dom. III Quadrag., PC*

Sanctíficet nos, Dómine, qua pasti sumus, mensa cæléstis: et, a cunctis erróribus expiátos, supérnis promissiónibus reddat accéptos.

MR(2008)   *Feria IV post Dom. III Quadrag.*

Text is the same as the source above.

THURSDAY IN WEEK 3 OF LENT

Source: GeV 161 (*CO* 2938)

GeV 161   *Feria VI hebd. III Quadrag., PC*

Hos, quos reficis, domine, sacramentis attolle benignus auxiliis, ut tuae redemptionis effectum et mysteriis capiamus et moribus.

MR(2008)   *Feria V post Dom. III Quadrag.*

° Quos réficis, Dómine, saccraméntis, attólle benígnus auxíliis, ut tuæ **salvatiónis** efféctum et mystériis capiámus et móribus.

FRIDAY IN WEEK 3 OF LENT

Source: Ve 1121 (*CO* 3334)

Ve 1121 *Mense octobris, de siccitate temporis, II alia missa, PC*

Mentes nostras et corpora, domine, quaesumus, operatio tuae virtutis infundat, ut, quod participatione sumpsimus, plena redemptione capiamus.

MR(2008) *Feria VI post Dom. III Quadrag.*

Text is the same as the source above.

SATURDAY IN WEEK 3 OF LENT

Source: MR 172 (*CO* 919)

MR 172 *Dom. IV Quadrag., PC*

Da nobis, quaesumus, miséricors Deus: ut sancta tua, quibus incessánter explémur, sincéris tractémus obséquiis, et fidéli semper mente sumámus.

MR(2008) *Sabbato post Dom. III Quadrag.*

Text is the same as the source above.

4TH SUNDAY OF LENT

Source: MR 358 (*CO* 1721)

MR 358 *Orat. div. n. 25, Ad repellendas malas cogitationes, PC*

Deus, qui illúminas omnem hóminem veniéntem in hunc mundum: illúmina, quaesumus, corda nostra grátiæ tuæ splendóre; ut digna ac plácita maiestáti tuæ cogitáre semper et te sincére dilígere valeámus.

MR(2008) *Dom. IV Quadrag.*

Text is the same as the source above.

MONDAY IN WEEK 4 OF LENT

Source: Ve 1078 (*CO* 5298)

Ve 1078   *Mense septembris, in nat. episcoporum, XIX alia missa, PC*

Sancta tua nos, domine, quaesumus, et vivificando renovent, et renovando vivificent.

MR(2008)   *Feria II post Dom. IV Quadrag.*

Sancta tua nos, Dómine, quǽsumus, et renovándo vivíficent, **et sanctificándo ad ætérna perdúcant.**

TUESDAY IN WEEK 4 OF LENT

Source: MR 920 (*CO* 4775)

MR 920   *Dom. XVI post Pent., PC*

Purífica, quaesumus, Dómine, mentes nostras benígnus, et rénova cæléstibus sacraméntis: ut consequénter et córporum præsens páriter et futúrum capiámus auxílium.

MR(2008)   *Feria III post Dom. IV Quadrag.*

Text is the same as the source above.

WEDNESDAY IN WEEK 4 OF LENT

Source: MR 95 (*CO* 533)

MR 95   *Feria V post Dom. IV Quadrag., PC*

Cæléstia dona capiéntibus, quaesumus, Dómine: non ad iudícium proveníre patiáris, quæ fidélibus tuis ad remédium providísti.

MR(2008)   *Feria IV post Dom. IV Quadrag.*

Text is the same as the source above.

THURSDAY IN WEEK 4 OF LENT

Source: MR 922 (*CO 4784*)

MR 922   *Orat. div. n. 24, Pro tentatis et tribulatis, PC*

Puríficent nos, quaesumus, Dómine, sacraménta quæ súmpsimus: et fámulos tuos ab omni culpa líberos esse concéde; ut, qui consciéntiæ reátu constringúntur, cæléstis remédii plenitúdine gloriéntur.

MR(2008)   *Feria V post Dom. IV Quadrag.*

Text is the same as the source above.

FRIDAY IN WEEK 4 OF LENT

Source: MR(1962) (*CO 4455 b*)

MR(1962)   *Feria V in Cena Domini, de Missa Chrismatis, PC*

Præsta, quaesumus, Dómine: ut, sicut de prætéritis ad nova transímus; ita, vetustáte depósita, sanctificátis méntibus innovémur.

MR(2008)   *Feria VI post Dom. IV Quadrag.*

Text is the same as the source above.

SATURDAY IN WEEK 4 OF LENT

Source: MR 1151 (*CO 5962 c*)

MR 1151   *Sabbato post Dom. IV Quadrag., PC*

Tua nos, quaesumus, Dómine, sancta puríficent: et operatióne sua tibi plácitos esse perfíciant.

MR(2008)   *Sabbato post Dom. IV Quadrag.*

Text is the same as the source above.

5TH SUNDAY OF LENT

Source: MR 942 (*CO* 4889)

MR 942   *Sabbato post Dom. III Quadrag., PC*

Quaesumus, omnípotens Deus: ut inter eius membra numerémur, cuius córpori communicámus, et sánguini.

MR(2008)   *Dom. V in Quadrag.*

Text is the same as the source above.

MONDAY IN WEEK 5 OF LENT

Source: Ve 556 (*CO* 5165 a)

Ve 556   *Mense iulii, orat. et preces diurnae, XXV alia missa, PC*

Sacramentorum tuorum benedictione satiati, quaesumus, domine, ut per haec semper emundemur a vitiis et periculis exuamur.

MR(2008)   *Feria II post Dom. V Quadrag.*

Sacramentórum tuórum benedictióne **roboráti**, quǽsumus, Dómine, ut per hæc semper emundémur a vítiis, et **per sequélam Christi ad te festinánter gradiámur.**

TUESDAY IN WEEK 5 OF LENT

Source: MR 188 (*CO* 1023 a)

MR 188   *Feria III post Dom. de Passione, PC*

Da, quaesumus, omnípotens Deus: ut, quæ divína sunt, iúgiter exsequéntes, donis mereámur cæléstibus propinquáre.

MR(2008)   *Feria II post Dom. V Quadrag.*

Da, quǽsumus, omnípotens Deus, ut, quæ divína sunt iúgiter **ambiéntes**, donis **semper** mereámur cæléstibus propinquáre.

Wednesday in Week 5 of Lent

Source: GeV 1241 + MR 85 (*CO* 374 + 519)

GeV 1241   *Orat. et preces cum canone per dominicas dies, alia missa, PC*

Auxilientur nobis, domine, <u>sumpta mysteria, et sempiterna protectione</u> <u>confirment</u>.

MR 85   *Dom. XX post Pent., SO*

<u>Cæléstem nobis præbeant</u> hæc mystéria, quaesumus, <u>Dómine, medicínam:</u> <u>et vítia nostri cordis expúrgent</u>.

MR(2008)   *Feria IV post Dom. V Quadrag.*

<u>Cæléstem nobis, Dómine, præbeant</u> <u>sumpta mystéria</u> <u>medicínam</u>, **ut** <u>et</u> <u>vítia nostri cordis expúrgent</u>, <u>et sempitérna</u> **nos** <u>protectióne confírment</u>.

Thursday in Week 5 of Lent

Source: Ve 507 (*CO* 5456)

Ve 507   *Mense iulii, orat. et preces diurnae, XVI alia missa, PC*

Satiati munere salutari tuam, domine, misericordiam depracamur, ut hoc eodem sacramento, quo nos temporaliter vegetas, efficias perpetuae vitae participes.

MR(2008)   *Feria V post Dom. V Quadrag.*

Text is the same as the source above.

FRIDAY IN WEEK 5 OF LENT

Source: MR 1086 (*CO* 5614 D)

MR 1086   *Feria VI post Dom. Passionis, PC*

Sumpti sacrifícii, Dómine, perpétua nos tuítio non derelínquat: et nóxia semper a nobis cuncta depéllat.

MR(2008)   *Feria V post Dom. V Quadrag.*

Sumpti sacrifícii, Dómine, perpétua nos tuítio non *relínquat*, et nóxia semper a nobis cuncta depéllat.

SATURDAY IN WEEK 5 OF LENT

Source: Ve 525 (*CO* 3283)

Ve 525   *Mense iulii, orat. et preces diurnae, XIX alia missa, PC*

Maiestatem tuam, domine, supplices deprecamur, ut sicut nos corporis et sanguinis sacrosancti pascis alimento, ita divinae naturae facias esse consortes.

MR(2008)   *Sabbato post Dom. V Quadrag.*

Maiestátem tuam, Dómine, *supplíciter* deprecámur, ut, sicut nos Córporis et Sánguinis sacrosáncti pascis aliménto, ita divínæ natúræ fácias esse consórtes.

PALM SUNDAY

Source: MR 243 + MR 1022 (*CO* 1319 + 5251)

MR 243   *Dom. in Palmis, orat. 1a [pre-1955]*

Deus, quem diligere et amare iustitia est, ineffabilis gratiae tuae in nobis dona multiplica: et qui fecisti nos in morte Filii tui sperare quae credimus; fac nos eodem resurgente pervenire quo tendimus.

MR 1022   *Die 14 aprilis, Ss. Tiburtii et al, PC*

Sacro munere satiati, supplices te, Domine, deprecamur: ut, quod debitae servitutis celebramus officio, salvationis tuae sentiamus augmentum.

MR(2008)   *Dom. in Palmis de Passione Domini*

Sacro múnere satiáti, súpplices te, Dómine, deprecámur, ut, qui fecísti nos ° morte Fílii tui speráre *quod* crédimus, *fácias* nos, eódem resurgénte, perveníre quo téndimus.

MONDAY IN HOLY WEEK

Source: GeV 282 (*CO* 6086 b)

GeV 282   *Feria VII hebd. V Quadrag., SP*

Visita, quaesumus, domine, plebem tuam et corda, sacris dicata mysteriis, pietate tuere pervigili, ut remedia salutis aeternae, quae, te miserante, percipit, te protegente, custodiat.

MR(2008)   *Feria II hebd. Sanctae*

Text is the same as the source above.

TUESDAY IN HOLY WEEK

Source: *See Thursday in Week 5 of Lent, p. 37 above*

MR(2008)   *Feria III hebd. Sanctae*

Satiáti múnere salutári, tuam, Dómine, misericórdiam deprecámur, ut hoc eódem sacraménto, quo nos voluísti temporáliter vegetári, perpétuæ vitæ fácias esse partícipes.

WEDNESDAY IN HOLY WEEK

Source: MR 662 (CO 3243)

MR 662   *Feria IV maioris hebd., PC*

Largíre sénsibus nostris, omnípotens Deus: ut, per temporálem Fílii tui mortem, quam mystéria veneránda testántur, vitam te nobis dedísse perpétuam confídámus.

MR(2008)   *Feria IV hebd. Sanctae*

Text is the same as the source above.

MAUNDY THURSDAY (CHRISM MASS)

Source: MR 1103 + MR 83 (*CO* 5693 b + MR 83)

MR 1103   *Dom. infra octavam Epiphaniae, PC*

Supplices te rogamus, omnipotens Deus: ut quos tuis reficis sacramentis, tibi etiam placitus moribus dignanter deservire concedas.

MR 1022   *Die 30 augusti, S. Rosae, C*

Bonórum ómnium largítor, omnípotens Deus, qui beátam Rosam, cæléstis grátiæ rore prævéntam, virginitátis et patiéntiæ decóre Indis floréscere voluísti: da nobis fámulis tuis; ut, in odórem suavitátis eius curréntes, Christi bonus odor éffici mereámur.*

MR(2008)   *Feria V hebd. Sanctae, ad Missam chrismatis*

Súpplices te rogámus, omnípotens Deus, ut, quos tuis réficis sacraméntis, Christi bonus odor éffici mereántur.

MAUNDY THURSDAY (MASS OF THE LORD'S SUPPER)

Source: Go 214 (*CO* 698)

Ve 525   *Missa in Cena Domini, PC*

Concede nobis, omnipotens deus, ut, sicut temporali cena tuae passionis reficimur, ita satiari mereamur aeterna.

MR(2008)   *Sabbato post Dom. V Quadrag.*

Concéde nobis, omnípotens Deus, ut, sicut Cena **Fílii** *tui* ° refícimur temporáli, ita satiári mereámur ætérna.

---

* See also 2 Corinthians 2:15 (*quia Christi bonus odor sumus Deo in iis qui salvi fiunt*).

GOOD FRIDAY

Source: MR(1962)

MR(1962)   *Feria VI in Passione et Morte Domini, oratio 2a*

Omnípotens et miséricors Deus, qui Christi tui beáta passióne et morte nos reparásti: consérva in nobis óperam misericórdiæ tuæ; ut, huius mystérii participatióne, perpétua devotióne vivámus.

MR(2008)   *Feria VI in Passione Domini*

Omnípotens **sempitérne** Deus, qui nos Christi tui beáta morte et **resurrectióne** reparásti, consérva in nobis *opus* misericórdiæ tuæ, ut huius mystérii participatióne perpétua devotióne vivámus.

PROPER OF TIME

IV. EASTERTIDE

EASTER VIGIL

Source: MP 1313 (*CO* 5521 b)

MP 1313   *In die sancto paschae, PC*

Spiritum nobis, Domine, tuae caritatis infunde: ut quos sacramentis paschalibus satiasti, tua facias pietate concordes.

MR(2008)   *Dom. Paschae in Resurrectione Domini,*
Vig. Paschalis in Nocte Sancta

Text is the same as the source above.

EASTER SUNDAY

Source: B 564 (*CO* 4223)

B 564   *In die sancto paschae, PC*

Perpetuo, deus, ecclesiam tuam pio favore tuere, ut, paschalibus resuscitata mysteriis, ad resurrectionis perveniat claritatem.

MR(2008)   *Dom. Paschae in Resurrectione Domini, Ad missam in die*

Perpétuo, Deus, Ecclésiam tuam pio favóre tuére, ut, paschálibus **renováta** mystériis, ad resurrectiónis pervéniat claritátem.

EASTER MONDAY

Source: GeV 498 + 503 (*CO* 2580 + 3287)

GeV 498   *Feria VII in albis, PC*

Exuberet, quaesumus, Domine, mentibus nostris paschalis gratia
sacramenti, ut donis suis ipse nos dignos efficiat.

GeV 503   *Dom. in octava Paschae, PC*

Maiestatem tuam, domine, supplices exoramus, ut quos viam fecisti
perpetuae salutis intrare, nullis permittas errorum laquaeis inplicare.

MR(2008)   *Feria II infra octavam Paschae*

Exúberet, quǽsumus, Dómine, méntibus nostris paschális grátia
sacraménti, ut, quos viam fecísti perpétuæ salútis intráre, donis **tuis** dignos
effícias.

EASTER TUESDAY

Source: GeV 530 (*CO* 2527)

GeV 530   *Alia oratio paschalis, vespertinalis*

Exaudi nos, omnipotens deus, et familiae tuae corda, cui perfectam
baptismi gratiam contulisti, ad promerendam beatitudinem aptes
aeternam.

MR(2008)   *Feria III infra octavam Paschae*

Text is the same as the source above.

EASTER WEDNESDAY

Source: MR 4 (*CO* 10)

MR 4   *Feria IV infra octavam Paschae, PC*

Ab omni nos, quaesumus, Dómine, vetustáte purgátos: sacraménti tui veneránda percéptio in novam tránsferat creatúram.

MR(2008)   *Feria IV infra octavam Paschae*

Ab omni nos, quǽsumus, Dómine, vetustáte purgátos, sacraménti **Fílii** tui veneránda percéptio in novam tránsferat creatúram.

EASTER THURSDAY

Source: MR 531 (*CO* 2482)

MR 531   *Feria V infra octavam Paschae, PC*

Exáudi, Dómine, preces nostras: ut redemptiónis nostræ sacrosáncta commércia, et vitæ nobis cónferant præséntis auxílium, et gáudia sempitérna concílient.

MR(2008)   *Feria V infra octavam Paschae*

Text is the same as the source above.

EASTER FRIDAY

Source: GeV 532 (*CO* 5502)

GeV 532   *Alia oratio paschalis, vespertinalis*

Solita, quaesumus, domine, quos salvasti, pietate custodi, ut, quia tua sunt passione redempti, tua resurrectione laetentur.

MR(2008)   *Feria VI infra octavam Paschae*

Contínua, quǽsumus, Dómine, quos salvásti pietáte custódi, ut, *qui* **Fílii** *tui* passióne sunt redémpti, **eius** resurrectióne lætén tur.

EASTER SATURDAY

Source: MR 985 + St Leo the Great (*CO* 5125 + S. Leo, *Sermo* 71, 6)

MR 985   *Feria VI infra octavam Paschae, PC*

Réspice, quaesumus, Dómine, pópulum tuum: et, quem ætérnis dignátus es renováre mystériis, a temporálibus culpis dignánter absólve.

S. Leo   *Sermo 71, 6 (PL 54:389)*

Et quia antiquorum morborum difficilis et tarda curatio est, tanto velocius adhibeantur remedia, quanto recentiora sunt vulnera: ut semper ab omnibus offensionibus in integrum resurgentes ad illam incorruptibilem glorificandae carnis resurrectionem pervenire mereamur in Christo Jesu Domino nostro, qui vivit et regnat cum Patre et Spiritu sancto in saecula saeculorum. Amen.

MR(2008)   *Sabbato infra octavam Paschae*

Pópulum tuum, quǽsumus, Dómine, intuére benígnus, et, quem ætérnis dignátus es renováre mystériis, ad ° incorruptíbilem glorificándæ carnis resurrectiónem perveníre concéde.

2ND SUNDAY OF EASTER

Source: MR 133 (*CO* 754 a)

MR 133   *Feria III infra octavam Paschae, PC*

Concéde, quaesumus, omnípotens Deus: ut paschális percéptio sacraménti contínua in nostris méntibus persevéret.

MR(2008)   *Dom. II Paschae*

Text is the same as the source above.

Saturday in Week 2 of Easter[*]

Source: MR 1083 (*CO* 5583)

GeV 532   *Feria VI Quat. Temp. Pentecostes, PC*

Súmpsimus, Dómine, sacri dona mystérii: humíliter deprecántes; ut, quæ in tui commemoratiónem nos fácere præcepísti, in nostræ profíciant infirmitátis auxílium.

MR(2008)   *Sabbato post Dom. II Paschae*

Súmpsimus, Dómine, sacri dona mystérii, humíliter deprecántes, ut, quæ in **sui** commemoratiónem nos **Fílius tuus** fácere præcépit, in nostræ profíciant **caritátis augméntum**.

3rd Sunday of Easter

Text is the same as Easter Saturday, p. 48 above.

4th Sunday of Easter

Source: GeV 272 (*CO* 2774)

GeV 272   *Feria III hebd. V Quadrag., SP*

Gregem tuum, pastor bone, placatus intende et oves, quas pretioso sanguine filii tui redemisti, diabolica non sinas incursione lacerari.

MR(2008)   *Dom. IV Paschae*

Gregem tuum, Pastor bone, placátus inténde, et oves, quas pretióso Fílii tui sánguine redemísti, **in ætérnis páscuis collocáre dignéris**.

---

[*] For the other weekdays in Eastertide, up to Tuesday in Week 7, see p. 53 below.

5TH SUNDAY OF EASTER

Source: MR 36 + Ve 1297 (*CO* 126 a + *Pref 1320*)

MR 36   *Feria II infra octavam Paschae, PC*

Adésto, quaesumus, Dómine, pópulo tuo: et, quem mystériis cæléstibus imbuísti, ab hóstium furóre defénde.

Ve 1297   *Mense decembris, XLIII, in ieiunio mensis decimi*

VD: Quia, per ea quae conspiciuntur instruimur, quibus modis ad invisibilia tendere debeamus. Denique commonemur anni ducente successu, de praeteritis in futura, et ad novitatem vitae de vetustate transire. Ut terrenis sustentationibus expediti, caelestis doni capiamus desiderabilius ubertatem. Et per eum cibum, qui beneficiis praerogatur alternis, perveniamus ad victum sine fine mansurum.

MR(2008)   *Dom. V Paschae*

Pópulo tuo, quǽsumus, Dómine, adésto propítius, et, quem mystériis cæléstibus imbuísti, fac ad novitátem vitæ de vetustáte transíre.

6TH SUNDAY OF EASTER

Source: GeV 467 (*CO 3888*)

GeV 467   *Dom. Paschae., PC*

Omnipotens sempiterne deus, qui ad aeternam vitam in Christi resurrectione nos reparas, custodi opera misericordiae tuae et suavitatem corporis et sanguinis domini nostri Iesu Christi unigenti filii tui nostris infunde pectoribus.

MR(2008)   *Dom. VI Paschae*

Omnípotens sempitérne Deus, qui ad ætérnam vitam in Christi resurrectióne nos réparas, **fructus in nobis paschális multíplica sacraménti,** et **fortitúdinem cibi salutáris nostris** infúnde pectóribus.

THE ASCENSION OF THE LORD (VIGIL)*

Source: MP 1495

MP 1495   *Dom. in octava Ascensionis, PC*

Quae ex altari tuo, Domine, dona percepimus, accendant in cordibus nostris caelestis patriae desiderium, et quo praecursor pro nobis introivit Iesus, faciant nos, eius vestigia sectando, contendere.

MR(2008)   *In Ascensionis Domini, ad Missam in Vigilia*

Quæ ex altári tuo, Domine, dona percépimus, accéndant in córdibus nostris cæléstis pátriæ desidérium, et quo præcúrsor pro nobis introívit **Salvátor**, fáciant nos, eius vestígia *sectántes*, conténdere.

THE ASCENSION OF THE LORD (MASS DURING THE DAY)

Source: Ve 185 + 689 (*CO* 5924 a + 3972)

Ve 185   *Mense maii, in Ascensa Domini, VI alia missa, PC*

Tribue, quaesumus, domine, ut illuc tendat christianae nostrae devotionis affectus, quo tecum est nostra substantia.

Ve 689   *Mense augusti, nat. S. Stephani, VI alia missa, PC*

Omnipotens sempiterne deus, qui in terrena substantia constitutos divina tractare concedis: praesta depraecantibus sanctis tuis, ut eadem consequamur conversatione caelesti.

MR(2008)   *In Ascensionis Domini, ad Missam in die*

Omnípotens sempitérne Deus, qui in terra ° constitútos divína tractáre concédis, præsta, quæsumus, ut illuc tendat christiánæ ° devotiónis afféctus, quo tecum est nostra substántia.

---

* This celebration was added to the *editio typica tertia*, so is not in MR(1970) or MR(1975).

7TH SUNDAY OF EASTER

Source: Ve 174 (*CO* 2505)

Ve 174   *Preces in Ascensa Domini, SO*

Exaudi nos, deus salutaris noster, ut per haec sacrosancta mysteria in totius ecclesiae confidamus corpore faciendum, quod eius praecessit in capite.

MR(2008)   *Dom. VII Paschae*

Text is the same as the source above.

WEEKDAYS IN EASTERTIDE
(*up to Tuesday in Week 7*)

Mondays

> Weeks 2, 4, 6: See Saturday in Easter Octave, p. 48 above
>
> Weeks 3, 5: See 6th Sunday of Easter, p. 50 above
>
> Week 7: See 5th Sunday of Easter, p. 50 above

Tuesdays

> Weeks 2, 4, 6: See Thursday in Easter Octave, p. 47 above
>
> Weeks 3, 5: See Saturday in Easter Octave, p. 48 above
>
> Week 7: See Saturday in 2nd week of Easter p. 49 above

Wednesdays

> Weeks 2, 4, 6: See 5th Sunday of Easter, p. 50 above
>
> Weeks 3, 5: See Thursday in Easter Octave, p. 47 above

Thursdays

> Weeks 2, 4, (6[*]): See 6th Sunday of Easter, p. 50 above
>
> Weeks 3, 5: See 5th Sunday of Easter, p. 50 above

Fridays

> Weeks 2, 4, 6: See Friday in Easter Octave, p. 47 above
>
> Weeks 3, 5: See Saturday in 2nd week of Easter, p. 49 above

Saturdays

> Weeks 3, 5: See Friday in Easter Octave, p. 47 above
>
> Weeks 4, 6: See Saturday in 2nd week of Easter, p. 49 above

---

[*] Week 6 only in regions where Ascension is transferred to the 7th Sunday of Easter.

WEDNESDAY IN WEEK 7 OF EASTER

Source: Ve 924 (*CO* 2749)

Ve 924   *Mense septembris, XI alia missa, PC*

Gratiam tuam nobis, domine, semper accumulet divini participatio sacramenti, et, sua nos virtute mundando, tanti muneris capaces efficiat.

MR(2008)   *Feria IV post Dom. VII Paschae*

Grátiam tuam nobis, Dómine, semper accúmulet divíni participátio sacraménti, et, sua nos virtúte mundándo, tanti múneris capáces **indesinénter** effíciat.

THURSDAY IN WEEK 7 OF EASTER

Source: B 917 (*CO* 4193)

B 917   *VIII idus maii, nat. S. Victoris martyris, PC*

Percepta mysteria, quaesumus, domine, et eruditione nos instruant et participatione restaurent, ut ad spiritalia mereamur munera pervenire.

MR(2008)   *Feria V post Dom. VII Paschae*

Text is the same as the source above.

FRIDAY IN WEEK 7 OF EASTER

Source: Ve 208 + 969 (*CO* 1180 + 1921)

Ve 208   *Mense maii, in ieiunio mensis quarti, II alia missa, SO*

Deus, cuius mysteriis mundamur et pascimur: praesta, ut eadem sic temporaliter celebremus, ut nobis experiamur aeterna.

Ve 969   *Mense septembris, in nat. episcoporum, II alia missa, PC*

Deus, qui nos sacramentis tuis pascere non desistis, tribue, quaesumus, ut eorum nobis indulta refectio vitam conferat sempiternam.

MR(2008)   *Feria VI post Dom. VII Paschae*

Deus, cuius mystériis mundámur et páscimur, tríbue, quǽsumus, ut eórum nobis indúlta reféctio vitam cónferat sempitérnam.

SATURDAY IN WEEK 7 OF EASTER

Source: Ve 250 (*CO* 267)

Ve 250   *VIII idus maii, nat. S. Victoris martyris, PC*

Annue, domine, praecibus nostris, ut sicut de praeteritis ad nova sumus sacramenta translati, ita vetustate deposita sanctificatis mentibus innovemur.

MR(2008)   *Sabbato post Dom. VII Paschae*

Annue, Dómine, nostris précibus **miserátus**, ut, sicut de prætéritis ad nova sumus sacraménta transláti, ita, vetustáte depósita, sanctificátis méntibus innovémur.

PENTECOST VIGIL

Source: B 775 (*CO* 2837)

Ve 250   *Dom. Pentecostes, missa ambrosiana in eccl. maiore, PC*

Haec nobis, domine, munera sumpta proficiant, ut illo iugiter ferveamus spiritu, quem apostolis tuis ineffabiliter infudisti.

MR(2008)   *Dom. Pentecostes, ad Missam in Vigilia*

Text is the same as the source above.

PENTECOST SUNDAY

Source: Ve 419 + LMS 793 (*CO* 2398 a + 1480)

Ve 419   *Mense iulii, XIII alia missa, SP*

Ecclesia tua, domine, caelesti gratia repleatur et crescat atquem, ab omnibus vitiis expiata, percipiat <u>sempiternae redemptionis augmentum</u>; ut quod in membris suis copiosa temporum prorogatione veneratur, spiritalium capiat largitate donorum.

LMS 793   *Missa in die sancto Pentecostes, PC*

<u>Deus qui celestia famulis tuis dona largiris, custodi in nobis gratiam, quam dedisti. Vigeat</u> in sensibus nostris <u>munus infusum</u> mentesque nostras cum corporis sospitate <u>spiritalis esca proficiat</u>.

MR(2008)   *Dom. Pentecostes, ad Missam in die*

<u>Deus, qui **Ecclésiæ tuæ** cæléstia dona largíris, custódi ° grátiam quam dedísti,</u> ut Spíritus Sancti <u>vígeat **semper** munus infúsum,</u> et ad <u>*ætérnæ* redemptiónis augméntum spiritális esca profíciat</u>.

PROPER OF TIME

V. TEMPUS PER ANNUM

1ST WEEK *PER ANNUM*

Source: MR 1103 (*CO* 5693 b)

MR 1103   *Dom. infra octavam Epiphaniae, PC*

Súpplices te rogámus, omnípotens Deus: ut, quos tuis réficis sacraméntis, tibi étiam plácitis móribus dignánter deservíre concédas.

MR(2008)   *Hebdomada I per annum*

Text is the same as the source above.

2ND SUNDAY *PER ANNUM*

Source: MR 1069 (*CO* 5521 a)

MR 1069   *Feria VI post Cineres, PC*

Spíritum nobis, Dómine, tuæ caritátis infúnde: ut, quos uno pane cælésti satiásti, tua fácias pietáte concórdes.

MR(2008)   *Dom. II per annum*

Spíritum nobis, Dómine, tuæ caritátis infúnde, ut, quos uno cælésti pane satiásti, **una** fácias pietáte concórdes.

3RD SUNDAY *PER ANNUM*

Source: MR 840 (*CO* 4384)

MR 840   *Dom. II post Paschae, PC*

Præsta nobis, quaesumus, omnípotens Deus: ut, vivificatiónis tuæ grátiam consequéntes, in tuo semper múnere gloriémur.

MR(2008)   *Dom. III per annum*

Text is the same as the source above.

4TH SUNDAY *PER ANNUM*

Source: MR 959 (*CO* 4979 B)

MR 959   *Sabbato in albis, PC*

Redemptiónis nostræ múnere vegetáti, quaesumus, Dómine: ut hoc perpétuæ salútis auxílio fides semper vera profíciat.

MR(2008)   *Dom. IV per annum*

Text is the same as the source above.

5TH SUNDAY *PER ANNUM*

Source: OP 27/04 + John 15:16

OP 27/04   *27 aprilis, B. Hosannae a Catharo, PC*

Deus, qui de uno pane et de uno calice participantes unum in Christo corpus nos esse voluisti: per beatae Hosannae Virginis intercessionem fideles tuos in veritate confirma; et a recta fide aberrantes ad Ecclesiae tuae revoca unitatem.

John 15:16

Non vos me elegistis, sed ego elegi vos et posui vos, ut vos eatis et fructum afferatis, et fructus vester maneat, ut quodcumque petieritis Patrem in nomine meo, det vobis.

MR(2008)   *Dom. V per annum*

Deus, qui nos de uno pane et de uno cálice partícipes esse voluísti, da nobis, quǽsumus, ita vívere, ut, unum in Christo effécti, fructum afferámus pro mundi salúte gaudéntes.

6TH SUNDAY *PER ANNUM*

Source: MR 97 (*CO* 536)

MR 97   *Dom. VI post Epiphaniam, PC*

Cæléstibus, Dómine, pasti delíciis: quaesumus; ut semper éadem, per quæ veráciter vívimus, appetámus.

MR(2008)   *Dom. VI per annum*

Text is the same as the source above.

7TH SUNDAY *PER ANNUM*

Source: MR 940 (*CO* 4887)*

MR 940   *Dom. V post Epiphaniam, PC*

Quaesumus, omnípotens Deus: ut illíus salutáris capiámus efféctum, cuius per hæc mystéria pignus accépimus.

MR(2008)   *Dom. VII per annum*

Præsta, quǽsumus, omnípotens Deus, ut illíus *salútis* capiámus efféctum, cuius per hæc mystéria pignus accépimus.

8TH SUNDAY *PER ANNUM*

Source: *See Thursday in Week 5 of Lent, p. 37 above*

MR(2008)   *Dom. VIII per annum*

Satiáti múnere salutári, tuam, Dómine, misericórdiam deprecámur, ut, hoc eódem quo nos temporáliter végetas sacraménto, perpétuæ vitæ partícipes benígnus effícias.

---

* See also GeV 558 (*CO* 4347), a very similar oration: *Praesta, domine, quaesumus, ut illius salutis capiamus effectum, cuius per haec mysteria pignus accipimus.*

9TH SUNDAY *PER ANNUM*

Source: MP 1768

MP 1768   *Dom. VII post Pentecosten, PC*

Rege nos Spiritu tuo, quaesumus Domine, quos pascis corpore tuo; ut te non verbo, neque ligua, sed opere et veritate Dominum confitentes intrare mereamur in regnum caelorum.

MR(2008)   *Dom. IX per annum*

Rege nos Spíritu tuo, quǽsumus, Dómine, quos pascis **Fílii** *tui* Córpore **et Sánguine**, ut te, non **solum** verbo neque lingua, sed ópere et veritáte confiténtes, intráre mereámur in regnum cælórum.

10TH SUNDAY *PER ANNUM*

Source: MR 1146 (*CO* 5953 a)

MR 1146   *Dom. VII post Pentecostes, PC*

Tua nos, Dómine, medicinális operátio, et a nostris perversitátibus cleménter expédiat, et ad ea quæ sunt recta, perdúcat.

MR(2008)   *Dom. X per annum*

Text is the same as the source above.

11TH SUNDAY *PER ANNUM*

Source: MR 597 (*CO 2889*)

MR 597   *Missa Votivae, ad tollendem schisma, PC*

Hæc tua, Dómine, sumpta sacra commúnio: sicut fidélium in te uniónem præsígnat; sic in tua Ecclésia unitátis, quaesumus, operétur efféctum.

MR(2008)   *Dom. XI per annum*

Hæc tua, Dómine, sumpta sacra commúnio, sicut fidélium in te uniónem præsígnat, sic in Ecclésia tua unitátis ° operétur efféctum.

12TH SUNDAY *PER ANNUM*

Source: MR 150 (*CO 5182*)

MR 150   *Die 2 iulii, Ss. Processo et Martiniano, PC*

Córporis sacri et pretiósi Sánguinis repléti libámine, quaesumus, Dómine Deus noster: ut, quod pia devotióne gérimus, certa redemptióne capiámus.

MR(2008)   *Dom. XII per annum*

Sacri Córporis et Sánguinis pretiósi **alimónia renováti**, quǽsumus, Dómine, **cleméntiam tuam**, ut, quod gérimus devotióne **frequénti**, certa redemptióne capiámus.

13TH SUNDAY *PER ANNUM*

Source: MR 1177

MR 1177   *Missa Votivae, feria V, D.N.I.C. summi et aeterni Sacerdotis, PC*

Vivíficet nos, quaesumus, Dómine, divína quam obtúlimus et súmpsimus hóstia: ut, perpétua tibi caritáte coniúncti, fructum, qui semper máneat, afferámus.

MR(2008)   *Dom. XIII per annum*

Text is the same as the source above.

14TH SUNDAY *PER ANNUM*

Source: MR 1136 (*CO* 5854 b)

MR 1136   *Dom. I post Pentecosten, PC*

Tantis, Dómine, repléti munéribus: præsta, quaesumus; ut et salutária dona capiámus, et a tua numquam laude cessémus.

MR(2008)   *Dom. XIV per annum*

Text is the same as the source above.

15TH SUNDAY *PER ANNUM*

Source: MR 1090 (*CO* 5641)

MR 1090   *Dom. IV Adv., PC*

Sumptis munéribus, quaesumus, Dómine: ut, cum frequentatióne mystérii, crescat nostræ salútis efféctus.

MR(2008)   *Dom. XV per annum*

Text is the same as the source above.

16TH SUNDAY *PER ANNUM*

Text is the same as 5th Sunday of Easter, p. 50 above.

17TH SUNDAY *PER ANNUM*

Source: OP 28/04

OP 28/04   *28 aprilis, S. Ludovico Maria, PC*

Sumpsimus, Domine, divinum sacramentum, passionis tuae memoriale perpetuum: tribue, quaesumus, beato Ludovico Maria Confessore tuo interveniente, ut ad nostram salutem hoc munus proficiat; quod ineffabili nobis caritate donasti.

MR(2008)   *Dom. XVII per annum*

Súmpsimus, Dómine, divínum sacraméntum, passiónis **Fílii** *tui* memoriále perpétuum; tríbue, quǽsumus, ° ut ad nostram salútem hoc munus profíciat, quod ineffábili nobis caritáte **ipse** *donávit*.

18TH SUNDAY *PER ANNUM*

Source: MR 955 (*CO 4941*)

MR 955   *Orat. diversae, 17, Pro praelatis et congr. eis commissis, PC*

Quos cælésti récreas múnere, perpétuo, Dómine, comitáre præsídio: et, quos fovére non désinis, dignos fíeri sempitérna redemptióne concéde.

MR(2008)   *Dom. XVIII per annum*

Text is the same as the source above.

19TH SUNDAY *PER ANNUM*

Source: MR 1000 (*CO* 5166)

MR 1000   *Die 13 augusti, Ss Hippolyti et Cassiani, PC*

Sacramentórum tuórum, Dómine, commúnio sumpta nos salvet: et in tuæ
veritátis luce confírmet.

MR(2008)   *Dom. XIX per annum*

Text is the same as the source above.

20TH SUNDAY *PER ANNUM*

Source: MP 4470

MP 4470   *De uno vel pluribus Sanctis, PC*

Per haec sacramenta, Domine, Christi participes effecti, clementiam tuam
humiliter imploramus, ut quia imagini conformes in terris, et gloriae
consortes in caelis cum sancto/sancta N. fieri mereamur.

MR(2008)   *Dom. XX per annum*

Per hæc sacraménta, Dómine, Christi partícipes effécti, cleméntiam tuam
humíliter implorámus, ut, **eius** *imáginis* confórmes in terris, et **eius**
consórtes in cælis ° fíeri mereámur.

21st Sunday *per annum*

Source: MR 822 (*CO* 4279)

MR 822   *Missa Votivae, in consecratione Episcopi, PC*

Plenum, quaesumus, Dómine, in nobis remédium tuæ miseratiónis operáre: ac tales nos esse pérfice propítius, et sic fovéri; ut tibi in ómnibus placére valeámus.

MR(2008)   *Dom. XXI per annum*

Text is the same as the source above.

22nd Sunday *per annum*

Source: New composition

MR(2008)   *Dom. XXII per annum*

Pane mensæ cæléstis refécti, te, Dómine, deprecámur, ut hoc nutriméntum caritátis corda nostra confírmet, quátenus ad tibi ministrándum in frátribus excitémur.

23rd Sunday *per annum*

Source: MP 425

MP 425   *Dom. V post Epiphaniam, PC*

Da fidelibus tuis, Domine, quos et verbi tui, et caelestis Sacramenti pabulo nutris et vivificas, tantis muneribus sic proficere, ut in consummatione seculi, separati a reprobis, inter electos tuos numerari mereamur.

MR(2008)   *Dom. XXIII per annum*

Da fidélibus tuis, Dómine, quos et verbi tui et cæléstis sacraménti pábulo nutris et vivíficas, **ita dilécti Fílii tui** tantis munéribus ° profícere, ut **eius vitæ semper consórtes éffici** mereámur.

24TH SUNDAY *PER ANNUM*

Source: MR 677 (*CO* 3335)

MR 677   *Dom. XV post Pentecosten, PC*

Mentes nostras et córpora possídeat, quaesumus, Dómine, doni cæléstis operátio: ut non noster sensus in nobis, sed iúgiter eius prævéniat efféctus.

MR(2008)   *Dom. XXIV per annum*

Mentes nostras et córpora possídeat, quǽsumus, Dómine, doni cæléstis operátio, ut non noster sensus in nobis, sed eius prævéniat **semper** efféctus.

25TH SUNDAY *PER ANNUM*

Source: MR 958 (*CO* 2938)

MR 958   *Missa Votivae, in collatione sacrorum ordine, PC*

Quos tuis, Dómine, réficis sacraméntis, contínuis attólle benígnus auxíliis: ut tuæ redemptiónis efféctum et mystériis capiámus, et móribus.

MR(2008)   *Dom. XXV per annum*

Quos tuis, Dómine, réficis sacraméntis, contínuis attólle benígnus auxíliis, ut ° redemptiónis efféctum et mystériis capiámus et móribus.

26TH SUNDAY *PER ANNUM*

Source: MP 1782

MP 1782   *Dom. VIII post Pentecosten, PC*

Sit nobis, Domine, reparatio mentis et corporis caeleste mysterium; ut simus eius in gloria cohaeredes, cui, mortem ipsius annuntiando, compatimur.

MR(2008)   *Dom. XXVI per annum*

Text is the same as the source above.

27TH SUNDAY *PER ANNUM*

Source: St Leo the Great

S. Leo   *Sermo 63, 7 (PL 54:357)*

Dum fermento veteris malitiae abiecto, nova creatura de ipso Domino inebriatur et pascitur. Non enim aliud agit participatio corporis et sanguinis Christi, quam ut in id quod sumimus transeamus: et in quo commortui, et consepulti, et conresusciati sumus, ipsum per omnia et spiritu et carne gestemus dicente Apostolo...

MR(2008)   *Dom. XXVII per annum*

Concéde nobis, omnípotens Deus, ut de percéptis sacraméntis *inebriémur atque pascámur*, quátenus in id quod súmimus transeámus.

28TH SUNDAY *PER ANNUM*

Text is the same as Saturday in Week 5 of Lent, p. 38 above.

29TH SUNDAY *PER ANNUM*

Source: Ve 982 (*CO* 2703)

Ve 982   *Mense septembris, in nat. episcoporum, III alia missa, SP*

Gaudeat, domine, quaesumus, populus, tua semper benedictione confisus, et caelestium rerum frequentatione proficiat, ut et temporalibus beneficiis adiuvetur et erudiatur aeternis.

MR(2008)   *Dom. XXIX per annum*

Fac nos, quǽsumus, Dómine, ° cæléstium rerum frequentatióne *profícere*, ut et temporálibus benefíciis adiuvémur, et *erudiámur* ætérnis.

30TH SUNDAY *PER ANNUM*

Source: MR 817 (*CO* 4219)

MR 817   *Sabbato Quat. Temp. septembris, PC*

Perfíciant in nobis, Dómine, quaesumus, tua sacraménta quod cóntinent: ut, quæ nunc spécie gérimus, rerum veritáte capiámus.

MR(2008)   *Dom. XXX per annum*

Text is the same as the source above.

31ST SUNDAY *PER ANNUM*

Source: MR 63 (*CO* 5521 a)

MR 63   *Dom. II post Epiphaniam, PC*

Augeátur in nobis, quaesumus, Dómine, tuæ virtútis operátio: ut divínis vegetáti sacraméntis, ad eórum promíssa capiénda, tuo múnere præparémur.

MR(2008)   *Dom. XXXI per annum*

Augeátur in nobis, quǽsumus, Dómine, tuæ virtútis operátio, ut, **refécti cæléstibus** sacraméntis, ad eórum promíssa capiénda tuo múnere præparémur.

32ND SUNDAY *PER ANNUM*

Source: MR 576 + Go 541 (*CO* 2770 + 240)*

MR 576   *Dom. XVIII post Pentecosten, PC*

Grátias tibi reférimus, Dómine, sacro múnere vegetáti: tuam misericórdiam deprecántes; ut dignos nos eius participatióne perfícias.

Go 541   *Missa dom. VI, PC*

Agamus omnipotenti deo gratias, quia refecit nos pane caelesti et poculo spiritali, sperantes ab eius benigna clementia, ut per effusionem spiritus sancti sui, in quibus cibi caelestis virtus introivit, sinceritatis gratia perseveret.

MR(2008)   *Dom. XXXII per annum*

Grátias tibi, Dómine, reférimus sacro múnere vegetáti, tuam **cleméntiam implorántes**, ut, per **infusiónem** Spíritus ° **tui,** in quibus ° cæléstis virtus introívit, sinceritátis grátia persevéret.

---

* See also MP 1894: *Gratias tibi agimus, omnipotens Deus, qui refecisti nos pane coelesti et poculo spirituali; clementiam tuam implorantes, ut per infusionem Spiritus Sancti tui, in quibus coelestis cibi virtus introivit, sinceritatis gratia perseveret.*

33RD SUNDAY *PER ANNUM*

Text is the same as Saturday in Week 2 of Easter, p. 49 above.

34TH WEEK *PER ANNUM*

Source: MR 947 (*CO* 4828 b)

MR 947   *Dom. XXIII post Pentecosten, PC*

Quaesumus, omnípotens Deus: ut, quos divína tríbuis participatióne gaudére, humánis non sinas subiacére perículis.

MR(2008)   *Hebd. XXXIV per annum*

Quǽsumus, omnípotens Deus, ut, quos divína tríbuis participatióne gaudére, **a te numquam separári permíttas**.

PROPER OF TIME

VI. SOLEMNITIES OF THE LORD IN *TEMPUS PER ANNUM*

THE MOST HOLY TRINITY

Source: MR 897 (*CO 4657*)

MR 897   *In festo SS.mi Trinitatis, PC*

Proficiat nobis ad salútem córporis et ánimæ, Dómine Deus noster, huius sacraménti suscéptio: et sempitérnæ sanctæ Trinitátis eiusdémque indivíduæ Unitátis conféssio.

MR(2008)   *SS.mi Trinitatis*

Text is the same as the source above.

THE MOST HOLY BODY AND BLOOD OF CHRIST

Source: MR 552 (*CO 2597*)

MR 552   *In festo SS.mi Corporis Christi, PC*

Fac nos, quaesumus, Dómine, divinitátis tuæ sempitérna fruitióne repléri: quam pretiósi Córporis et Sánguinis tui temporális percéptio præfigúrat.

MR(2008)   *SS.mi Corporis et Sanguinis Christi*

Text is the same as the source above.

THE MOST SACRED HEART OF JESUS

Source: New composition

MR(2008)   *SS.mi Cordis Iesu*

Sacraméntum caritátis, Dómine, sancta nos fáciat dilectióne fervére, qua, ad Fílium tuum semper attrácti, ipsum in frátribus agnóscere discámus.

Our Lord Jesus Christ, King of the Universe

Source: MR 637

MR 1069   *Dom. ultima octobris, D.N.I.C. Regis, PC*

Immortalitátis alimóniam consecúti, quaesumus, Dómine: ut, qui sub Christi Regis vexíllis militáre gloriámur, cum ipso, in cælésti sede, iúgiter regnáre possímus.

MR(2008)   *Domini nostri Iesu Christi, Universorum Regis*

Immortalitátis alimóniam consecúti, quǽsumus, Dómine, ut, qui ° Christi Regis **universórum** gloriámur **obœdíre mandátis**, cum ipso in cælésti **regno sine fine vívere valeámus**.

PROPER OF SAINTS

2 January: Ss Basil the Great & Gregory Nazianzen[*]

Source: *See Common of Pastors, III.B.1, p. 136 below*

MR(2008)   *Die 2 ianuarii, Ss. Basilii Magni et Gregorii Nazianzeni*

Mensa cæléstis, omnípotens Deus, in ómnibus festivitátem beatórum Basilíi et Gregórii celebrántibus supérnas vires firmet et áugeat, ut et fídei donum íntegrum custodiámus, et per osténsum salútis trámitem ambulémus.

3 January: Holy Name of Jesus[†]

Source: MR 741

MR 741   *Ss.mi nominis Iesu, PC*

Omnipotens aeterne Deus, qui creasti et redemisti nos, respice propitius vota nostra: et sacrificium salutaris hostiae, quod in honorem nominis Filii tui, Domini nostri Iesu Christi, maiestati tuae obtulimus, placido et benigno vultu suscipere digneris; ut gratia tua nobis infusa, sub glorioso nomine Iesu, aeternae praedestinationis titulo gaudeamus nomina nostra scripta esse in caelis.

MR(2008)   *Ss.mi nominis Iesu*

° Hóstia **sumpta,** ° Dómine, ° **quam** Christi *nomen honorántes* tuæ obtúlimus maiestáti, *grátiam tuam,* **quæsumus, nobis infúndat ubérrime,** ut et nostra in cælis esse scripta nómina gaudeámus.

---

[*] Note that in MR(1970) and MR(1975), only a proper Collect is assigned to this celebration.

[†] This celebration was added to the *editio typica tertia*, so is not in MR(1970) or MR(1975); the direct source is the Votive Mass of the Most Holy Name of Jesus in MA(1981), 617/9.

17 January: St Anthony

Source: New composition*

MR(2008)   *Die 17 ianuarii, S. Antonii*

Sacraméntis tuis, Dómine, salúbriter enutrítos, cunctas fac nos semper insídias inimíci superáre, qui beáto António dedísti contra potestátes tenebrárum claras reférre victórias.

24 January: St Francis de Sales

Source: MR(1962)

MR(1962)   *PAL, die 29 ianuarii, S. Francisci Salesii, PC*

Concede, quaesumus, omnipotens Deus: ut, per sacramenta quae sumpsimus, beati Francisci caritatem et mansuetudinem imitantes in terris, gloriam quoque consequamur in caelis.

MR(2008)   *Die 24 ianuarii, S. Francisci de Sales*

Text is the same as the source above.

25 January: Conversion of St Paul

Source: *See Common of Pastors, I.1, p. 134 below*

MR(2008)   *Die 25 ianuarii, In conversione S. Pauli*

Sacraménta quæ súmpsimus, Dómine Deus noster, in nobis fóveant caritátis ardórem, quo beátus apóstolus Paulus veheménter accénsus, ómnium pértulit sollicitúdinem Ecclesiárum.

---

* Though this PC uses different vocabulary, it may have been inspired by Psalm 90 (e.g., v. 3: *quóniam ipse liberávit me de láqueo venántium, et a verbo áspero*), prayed at Sunday Compline in both the *Breviarium Romanum* and *Liturgia Horarum*.

26 January: Ss Timothy & Titus[*]

Source: *See Common of Pastors, V.2, p. 139 below*

MR(2008)   *Die 26 ianuarii, Ss. Timothei et Titi*

Sacraménta quæ súmpsimus, Dómine Deus noster, illam nobis fidem innútriant, quam et apostólica dócuit prædicátio, et beatórum Timóthei et Titi sollicitúdo custodívit.

2 February: The Presentation of the Lord (Candlemas)

Source: MP 2384

MP 2384   *Die 2 februarii, in praes. Domini et purif. B.M.V., PC*

Perfice in nobis, quaesumus Domine, gratiam tuam, qui justi Simeonis expectationem implesti, ut sicut ille mortem non vidit, priusquam Christum Dominum videre mereretur; ita et nos in amplexu Domini morientes, vitam obtineamus aeternam.

MR(2008)   *Die 2 februarii, In praesentatione Domini*

Per hæc sancta quæ súmpsimus, ° Dómine, pérfice in nobis grátiam tuam, qui exspectatiónem ° Simeónis implésti, ut, sicut ille mortem non vidit **nisi** *prius* Christum ° **suscípere** mererétur, ita et nos, in **occúrsum** Dómini **procedéntes**, vitam obtineámus ætérnam.

---

[*] Note that in MR(1970) and MR(1975), only a proper Collect is assigned to this celebration.

14 February: Ss Cyril & Methodius*

Source: New composition

MR(2008) *Die 14 februarii, Ss. Cyrilli et Methodii*

Deus, cunctárum Pater géntium, qui nos de uno pane et uno Spíritu partícipes éfficis ac ætérni herédes convívii, in hac festivitáte beatórum Cyrílli et Methódii benígnus concéde, ut tuórum multitúdo filiórum, in eádem fide persevérans, unánimis regnum iustítiæ et pacis ædíficet.

22 February: The Chair of St Peter

Source: Ve 552 + St Augustine (*CO* 2763 a + S. Aug, *Tr. Io.* 26, 17)

Ve 552 *Mense iulii, orat. et preces diurnae, XXIV alia missa, PC*

Gratias tibi, domine, laudesque persolvimus, qui nos <u>corporis et sanguinis dilectissimi filii tui domini nostri communione vegetasti</u>, misericordiam tuam suppliciter exorantes, ut hoc tuum, domine, sacramentum non sit nobis reatus ad poenam, sed fiat intercessio salutaris ad veniam.

S. Aug *Tractatus in Iohannis 26, 17*

Caro enim mea, inquit, vere est cibus, et sanguis meus vere est potus. Cum enim cibo et potu id appetant homines, ut non esuriant, neque sitiant, noc veraciter non praestat nisi iste cibus et potus, qui eos a quibus sumitur, immortales et incorruptibiles facit, id est societas ipsa sanctorum, ubi <u>pax erit et unitas</u> plena atque perfecta.

MR(2008) *Die 22 februarii, Cathedrae S. Petri*

Deus, qui nos, beáti Petri apóstoli festivitátem celebrántes, **Christi** Córporis et Sánguinis ° communióne vegetásti, præsta, quæsumus, ut hoc redemptiónis commércium sit sacraméntum nobis <u>unitátis et pacis</u>.

---

* Note that in MR(1970) and MR(1975), only a proper Collect is assigned to this celebration.

7 March: Ss Perpetua & Felicity*

Source: *See Common of Martyrs, V, p. 133 below*

MR(2008)   *Die 7 martii, Ss. Perpetuae et Felicitatis*

Suméntes, Dómine, gáudia sempitérna de participatióne sacraménti, et de memória beatárum Perpétuæ et Felicitátis supplíciter deprecámur, ut, quæ sédula servitúte, donánte te, gérimus, dignis sénsibus tuo múnere capiámus.

19 March: St Joseph, Spouse of the B.V.M.

Source: MR 35 (*CO* 160)

MR 35   *Die 19 martii, S. Ioseph sponsi B.V.M., PC*

Adésto nobis, quaesumus, miséricors Deus: et, intercedénte pro nobis beáto Ioseph Confessóre, tua circa nos propitiátus dona custódi.

MR(2008)   *Die 19 martii, S. Ioseph sponsi B.V.M.*

Famíliam tuam, quǽsumus, **Dómine, quam de** beáti Ioseph **sollemnitáte lætántem ex huius altáris alimónia satiásti, perpétua protectióne defénde,** et tua **in ea** propitiátus dona custódi.

---

* Note that in MR(1970) and MR(1975), only a proper Collect is assigned to this celebration.

25 MARCH: THE ANNUNCIATION OF THE LORD[*]

Source: MR 641 (*CO* 3094)

MR 641   *Die 25 martii, In annuntiatione B.M.V., SO*

In méntibus nostris, quaesumus, Dómine, veræ fídei sacraménta confirma: ut, qui concéptum de Vírgine Deum verum et hóminem confitémur; per eius salutíferæ resurrectiónis poténtiam, ad ætérnam mereámur perveníre lætítiam.

MR(2008)   *Die 25 martii, In annuntiatione Domini*

Text is the same as the source above.

25 APRIL: ST MARK

Source: MR 871 + MP 3692 (*CO* 4460 + MP 3692)

MR 871   *Die 18 octobris, S. Lucae, PC*

<u>Præsta, quaesumus, omnípotens Deus: ut, quod de sancto altári tuo accépimus</u>, précibus <u>beáti Evangelístæ tui Lucæ, sanctíficet</u> ánimas nostras, per quod tuti esse possímus.

MP 3692   *Die 18 octobris, S. Lucae, PC*

Praesta, quaesumus omnipotens Deus, ut quod de sancto altari accepimus, precibus beati Evangelistae tui Lucae, <u>in fide Evangelii</u> nos <u>immobiles efficiat</u>.

MR(2008)   *Die 25 aprilis, S. Marci*

<u>Præsta, quǽsumus, omnípotens Deus, ut, quod de sancto altári tuo accépimus</u>, ° **nos** <u>sanctíficet</u>, et <u>in fide Evangélii</u>, quod *beátus* ° **Marcus** prædicávit, **fortes** <u>effíciat</u>.

---

[*] In MR(1970) and MR(1975), this prayer is also used as the PC in the Mass formulary for Eastertide in the Common of the Blessed Virgin Mary.

29 April: St Catherine of Siena

Source: MR 45

MR 45   *Die 30 aprilis, S. Catherinae Senensis, PC*

Æternitátem nobis, Dómine, cónferat, qua pasti sumus, mensa cæléstis: quæ beátæ Catharínæ Vírginis vitam étiam áluit temporálem.

MR(2008)   *Die 30 aprilis, S. Catherinae Senensis*

Æternitátem nobis, Dómine, cónferat, qua pasti sumus, mensa cæléstis, quæ beátæ Catharínæ ° vitam étiam áluit temporálem.

1 May: St Joseph the Worker

Source: MR 98

MR 98   *PAL, die 22 maii, S. Ritae a Cassia, PC*

Cæléstibus, Dómine, pasti delíciis, súpplices te rogámus: ut, intercedénte sancta Rita, caritátis et passiónis tuæ in méntibus nostris signa ferámus, et perpétuæ pacis fructu iúgiter perfruámur.

MR(2008)   *1 maii, S. Ioseph opificis*

Cæléstibus, Dómine, pasti delíciis, súpplices te rogámus, ut, **exémplo beáti Ioseph**, caritátis ° tuæ in **córdibus** nostris **testimónia geréntes**, ° perpétuæ pacis fructu iúgiter perfruámur.

2 MAY: ST ATHANASIUS

Source: MP 2573

MP 2573   *Die 2 maii, S. Athanasii, PC*

Da nobis, quaesumus, omnipotens Deus, ut consubstantialis tibi Filii tui divinitas, quam cum beato Athanasio firmiter confitemur, per hoc sacramentum vivificet nos semper et muniat.

MR(2008)   *Die 2 maii, S. Athanasii*

Da nobis, quǽsumus, omnípotens Deus, ut ° **Unigéniti** tui **vera** divínitas, quam cum beáto Athanásio fírmiter confitémur, per hoc sacraméntum vivíficet nos semper et múniat.

3 MAY: SS PHILIP & JAMES

Source: MP 2563

MP 2563   *Die 1 maii, Ss. apostolorum Philippi et Iacobi, PC*

Purifica, quaesumus Domine, mentes nostras per haec sancta quae sumpsimus; ut, cum Apostolis tuis Philippo et Iacobo, te in Patre, et Patrem in te contemplantes, vitam aeternam habeamus.

MR(2008)   *Die 3 maii, Ss. Philippi et Iacobi*

Purífica, quǽsumus, Dómine, mentes nostras per hæc sancta quæ súmpsimus, ut, cum apóstolis ° Philíppo et Iacóbo te in **Fílio** ° contemplántes, vitam *habére* **mereámur** ætérnam.

14 MAY: ST MATTHIAS

Source: MP 2432

MP 2432   *Die 24 februarii, S. Matthiae, PC*

Placeant, quaesumus, omnipotens Deus, maiestati tuae sacrificia quae sumpsimus; et sicut beatum Matthiam Apostolorum tuorum numero sorte aggregasti; ita et nos, per misericordiam tuam, in partem sortis sanctorum ascribere digneris.

MR(2008)   *Die 14 maii, S. Matthiae*

Famíliam tuam, Dómine, divínis ne cesses replére munéribus, ut, beáto *Matthía* **pro nobis intercedénte**, in partem sortis sanctórum **in lúmine** nos dignéris **accípere**.

26 MAY: ST PHILIP NERI

Source: *See 6th Sunday* per annum, *p. 61 above.*

MR(2008)   *Die 26 maii, S. Philippi Neri*

Cæléstibus, Dómine, pasti delíciis, quǽsumus, ut, beáti Philíppi imitatióne, semper éadem, per quæ veráciter vívimus, appetámus.

31 MAY: VISITATION OF THE BLESSED VIRGIN MARY

Source: MP 2883

MP 2883   *Die 2 iulii, In visitatione B.M.V., PC*

Largire, quaesumus Domine, fidelibus tuis, ut quem in utero latentem beatus Ioannes cum exultatione praesensit, eiusdem in hoc sacramento absconditi praesentiam cum sancta laetitia sentiamus.

MR(2008)   *Die 31 maii, In visitatione B.M.V.*

Magníficet te, Deus, Ecclésia tua qui tuis **fecísti magna** fidélibus, **et,** quem ° laténtem beátus Ioánnes cum exsultatióne præsénsit, *eúndem* **semper vivéntem** cum lætítia in hoc **percípiat** sacraménto.

SATURDAY AFTER THE 2ND SUNDAY AFTER PENTECOST: IMMACULATE HEART OF THE BLESSED VIRGIN MARY

Source: New composition

MR(2008)   *Sabbato post dom. secundam post Pent., Immac. Cordis B.M.V.*

Redemptiónis ætérnæ partícipes effécti, quǽsumus, Dómine, ut, qui Genetrícis Fílii tui memóriam ágimus, et de grátiæ tuæ plenitúdine gloriémur, et salvatiónis contínuum sentiámus augméntum.

1 JUNE: ST JUSTIN

Source: *See Common of Doctors, 2, p. 140 below.*

MR(2008)   *Sabbato post dom. secundam post Pent., Immac. Cordis B.M.V.*

Cælésti alimónia refécti, súpplices te, Dómine, deprecámur, ut, beáti Iustíni mártyris mónitis obsequéntes, de accéptis donis semper in gratiárum actióne maneámus.

3 June: Ss Charles Lwanga & Companions

Source: MP 2913

MP 2913   *Die 10 iulii, Ss. mart. Septem Frat. et S. Felicitatis, PC*

Sumpsimus, Domine, divina sacramenta, sanctorum Martyrum tuorum triumphum recolentes: praesta quaesumus, ut quae ipsis ad tormenta perferenda robur contulerunt, nobis praebeant inter adversa constantiam.

MR(2008)   *Die 3 iunii, Ss Caroli Lwanga et sociorum*

Súmpsimus, Dómine, divína sacraménta, sanctórum mártyrum tuórum **victóriam** recoléntes: ° quǽsumus, ut, quæ ipsis ad perferénda **supplícia** ° contulérunt, **ea** nobis inter advérsa prǽbeant **fídei caritatísque** constántiam.

11 June: St Barnabas

Source: Ve 335 (*CO 228*)

Ve 335   *Mense iunii, in nat. apost. Petri et Pauli, XVII alia missa, PC*

Aeternae pignus vitae capientes, humiliter imploramus, ut, apostolicis fulti patrociniis, quod in imagine gerimus sacramenti, manifesta perceptione sumamus.

MR(2008)   *Die 11 junii, S. Barnabae*

Ætérnæ pignus vitæ capiéntes, **te, Dómine**, humíliter implorámus, ut, ° quod **pro beáti Bárnabæ** *apóstoli* **memória** in imágine gérimus sacraménti, manifésta perceptióne sumámus.

21 June: St Aloysius Gonzaga

Source: MR 48

MR 48   *Die 21 iunii, S. Aloisii Gonzagae, PC*

Angelórum esca nutrítos, angélicos étiam, Dómine, da móribus vívere: et eius, quem hódie cólimus, exémplo in gratiárum semper actióne manére.

MR(2008)   *Die 21 iunii, S. Aloisii Gonzagae*

Angelórum esca nutrítos, **fac nos,** Dómine, **pura tibi conversatióne servíre,** et, eius quem hódie cólimus exémplo, in gratiárum semper actióne manére.

24 June: Nativity of St John the Baptist (Vigil Mass)

Source: MR 73 (*CO* 423 b)*

MR 73   *Die 23 iunii, in vig. nat. S. Ioannis Baptistae, PC*

Beáti Ioánnis Baptístæ nos, Dómine, præclára comitétur orátio: et, quem ventúrum esse prædíxit, poscat nobis fore placátum, Dóminum nostrum Iesum Christum, Fílium tuum.

MR(2008)   *Die 24 iunii, in nat. S. Ioannis Baptistae, ad missam in vigilia*

Sacris dápibus satiátos, beáti Ioánnis Baptístæ nos, Dómine, præclára comitétur orátio, et, quem **Agnum nostra ablatúrum crímina nuntiávit, ipsum** Fílium tuum poscat nobis fore placátum.

---

* Some of the additions to this oration in the OF would seem to be inspired by John 1:29 (*Altera die vidit Ioannes Iesum venientem ad se, et ait: Ecce agnus Dei, ecce qui tollit peccatum mundi*).

24 June: Nativity of St John the Baptist (Day)

Source: MR 1074 (*CO* 5540)

MR 1074   *Die 24 iunii, in nat. S. Ioannis Baptistae, PC*

Sumat Ecclésia tua, Deus, beáti Ioánnis Baptístæ generatióne lætítiam: per quem suæ regeneratiónis cognóvit auctórem, Dóminum nostrum Iesum Christum, Fílium tuum.

MR(2008)   *Die 24 iunii, in nat. S. Ioannis Baptistae, ad missam in die*

Cæléstis Agni convívio refécti, quæsumus, Dómine, ut Ecclésia tua, *sumens* **de** beáti Ioánnis Baptístæ generatióne lætítiam, quem **ille prænuntiávit ventúrum,** suæ regeneratiónis cognóscat auctórem °.

28 June: St Irenaeus

Source: MP 2831*

MP 2831   *Die 28 iunii, Ss. Irenaei Lugdunensis ac sociorum, PC*

Per haec sacra mysteria, quaesumus Domine, da nobis fidei miseratus augmentum; ut quae sanctos Martyres tuos Irenaeum et socios usque ad sanguinem retenta glorificat, nos etiam iustificet veraciter hanc sequentes.

MR(2008)   *Die 28 iunii, S. Irenaei*

Per hæc sacra mystéria, quæsumus, Dómine, da nobis fídei miserátus augméntum, ut, quæ **beátum** ° Irenǽum **epíscopum** ° usque ad **mortem** reténta gloríficat, nos étiam iustíficet veráciter hanc sequéntes.

---

* See also Ve 713 (*CO* 900): *Da nobis, domine, fidei tuae miseratus augmentum, ut, quae sanctos martyres tuos, usque ad sanguinem retenta, glorificat, nos etiam iustificet, veraciter hanc sequentes.*

29 JUNE: SS PETER & PAUL (VIGIL MASS)

Source: MP 2840

MP 2840   *Die 28 iunii, Missa de vigilia Ss. Petri et Pauli, PC*

Caelestibus sacramentis, quaesumus Domine, mentes nostras corrobora: nec ullis non permittas perturbationibus concuti, quos in Apostolicae confessionis petra solidasti.

MR(2008)   *Ss. Petri et Pauli, ad missam in vigilia*

Cæléstibus sacraméntis, quǽsumus, Dómine, **fidéles tuos** corróbora, ° quos ° *Apostolórum* **doctrína illuminásti.**

29 JUNE: SS PETER & PAUL (MASS DURING THE DAY)

Source: MP 2711

MP 2711   *Die 11 iunii, S. Barnabae, PC*

Da nobis, Domine, videre Ecclesiam tuam, sicut erat in diebus antiquis; quando perseverantes in doctrina Apostolorum et in fractione panis Barnabus et alii discipuli, cor unum erant et anima una.

MR(2008)   *Die 29 iunii, Ss. Petri et Pauli, ad missam in die*

Da nobis, Dómine, **hoc sacraménto reféctis, ita in** *Ecclésia* **conversári, ut,** perseverántes in fractióne panis *Apostolorúmque* doctrína, ° cor unum **simus** et ánima una, **tua caritáte firmáti.**

3 July: St Thomas

Source: MP 2161

MP 2161   *Die 21 decembris, S. Thomae, PC*

Deus, cuius carnem in tuo sacramento non palpamus modo, sed intimo pectore suscipimus; praesta quaesumus, ut cum Apostolo tuo Thoma te Dominum Deum nostrum, fide per dilectionem operante, fateamur.

MR(2008)   *Die 3 iulii, S. Thomae*

Deus, cuius **Unigéniti Corpus** in **hoc veráciter** ° suscípimus saccraménto, præsta, quǽsumus, ut, **quem** Dóminum *Deúmque* nostrum cum apóstolo ° Thoma fide **cognóscimus, ipsum ópere quoque profiteámur et vita.**

11 July: St Benedict

Source: New composition

MR(2008)   *Die 11 iulii, S. Benedicti*

Accépto pígnore vitæ ætérnæ, te, Dómine, supplíciter deprecámur, ut, beáti Benedícti mónitis obsequéntes, óperi tuo fidéliter serviámus, et fratres fervénti diligámus caritáte.

22 July: St Mary Magdalene

Source: MP 2987

MP 2987   *Die 22 iulii, S. Mariae Magdalenae, PC*

Mysteriorum tuorum, Domine, sancta perceptio perseverantem illum nobis amorem infundat, quo beata Maria Magdalene tibi immobiliter adhaesit.

MR(2008)   *Die 22 iulii, S. Mariae Magdalenae*

Mysteriórum tuórum, Dómine, sancta percéptio perseverántem illum nobis amórem infúndat, quo beáta María Magdaléna **Christo magístro suo indesinénter** adhǽsit.

25 JULY: ST JAMES

Source: MR 71 (*CO 459*)

MR 71   *Die 25 iulii, S. Iacobi, PC*

Beáti Apóstoli tui Iacóbi, quaesumus, Dómine, intercessióne nos ádiuva: pro cuius festivitáte percépimus tua sancta lætántes.

MR(2008)   *Die 25 iulii, S. Iacobi*

Text is the same as the source above.

26 JULY: SS JOACHIM & ANNE

Source: MP 3048

MP 3048   *Die 28 iulii, Ss. Ioachim et Annae, PC*

Deus, qui ex hominibus nasci dignatus es, ut homines feceres filios Dei: quaesumus, ut quos pane filiorum satiasti, adoptionis Spiritu jugiter sanctifices.

MR(2008)   *Die 26 iulii, Ss Ioachim et Annae*

Deus, qui **Unigénitum tuum** ex homínibus nasci **voluísti**, ut hómines **ex te mirábili mystério renasceréntur**, quǽsumus, ut, quos filiórum pane satiásti, adoptiónis spíritu **benignitáte tua** sanctífices.

29 JULY: ST MARTHA

Source: *See Common of Virgins, II.2, p. 141 below*

MR(2008)   *Die 29 iulii, S. Marthae*

Córporis et Sánguinis Unigéniti tui sacra percéptio, Dómine, ab ómnibus nos cadúcis rebus avértat, ut, exémplo beátæ Marthæ, valeámus et sincéra in terris caritáte profícere, et tui perpétua in cælis visióne gaudére.

31 July: St Ignatius of Loyola

Source: MR 663

MR 663   *Die 31 iulii, S. Ignatii, PC*

Laudis hostia, Domine, quam pro sancto Ignatio gratias agentes obtulimus: ad perpetuam nos maiestatis tuae laudationem, ejus intercessione, perducat.

MR(2008)   *Die 31 iulii, S. Ignatii de Loyola*

Laudis hóstia, Dómine, quam pro **beáto** Ignátio grátias agéntes obtúlimus, ad perpétuam nos maiestátis tuæ laudatiónem ° perdúcat.

1 August: St Alphonsus Liguori

Source: MR 282

MR 282   *Die 2 augusti, S. Alfonsi Mariae de Ligorio, PC*

Deus, qui beátum Alfónsum Maríam Confessórem tuum atque Pontíficem fidélem divíni mystérii dispensatórem et præcónem effecísti: eius méritis precibúsque concéde; ut fidéles tui et frequénter percípiant, et percipiéndo sine fine colláudent.

MR(2008)   *Die 1 augusti, S. Alfonsi Mariae de' Liguori*

Deus, qui beátum Alfónsum Maríam ° fidélem dispensatórem et præcónem **tanti** mystérii **providísti**, ° concéde, ut fidéles tui **illud** frequénter percípiant, et, percipiéndo, **te** sine fine colláudent.

6 August: The Transfiguration of the Lord

Source: MP 3144

MP 3144   *Die 6 augusti, in Transfiguratione Domini, PC*

Caelestia, quaesumus Domine, alimenta quae sumpsimus, in eius nos transforment imaginem, cuius claritatem gloriosa Transfiguratione manifestare voluisti.

MR(2008)   *Die 6 augusti, in Transfiguratione Domini*

Text is the same as the source above.

8 August: St Dominic

Source: MP 3128

MP 3128   *Die 4 augusti, S. Dominici, PC*

Percipiat Ecclesia tua, Deus, beati Dominici festivitate, plenae devotionis effectum; ut cuius praedicatione floruit, eius intercessione iuvetur.

MR(2008)   *Die 8 augusti, S. Dominici*

Cæléstis, Dómine, virtútem sacraménti, quo in beáti **commemoratióne** Domínici **pasti sumus**, percípiat Ecclésia tua plenæ devotiónis **afféctu, et** cuius prædicatióne flóruit, eius intercessióne iuvétur.

10 August: St Lawrence

Source: *See Common of Holy Men & Women, I.B.2, p. 144 below*

MR(2008)   *Die 10 augusti, S. Laurentii*

Sacro múnere satiáti, súpplices te, Dómine, deprecámur, ut, quod in festivitáte beáti Lauréntii débitæ servitútis præstámus obséquium, salvatiónis tuæ sentiámus augméntum.

14 AUGUST: ST MAXIMILIAN KOLBE[*]

Source: OFM 14/08

OFM 14/08   *Die 14 augusti, B. Maximilian Mariae Kolbe, PC*

Quǽsumus, Dómine, ut refécti Córpore et Sánguine tuo, eo caritátis igne accendámur, quem ex hoc convívio beátus Maximiliánus María accépit.

MR(2008)   *Die 14 augusti, S. Maximilian Mariae Kolbe*

Quǽsumus, Dómine, ut, refécti Córpore et Sánguine Fílii tui, eo caritátis igne accendámur, quem ex hoc convívio **sanctus** Maximiliánus María accépit.[†]

15 AUGUST: THE ASSUMPTION OF THE B.V.M. (VIGIL)

Source: MR 676 (*CO* 3328)

MR 676   *Die 15 augusti, in Assumptione B.M.V., PC[‡]*

Mensae caelestis participes effecti, imploramus clementiam tuam, Domine Deus noster: ut qui Assumptionem Dei Genetricis colimus, a cunctis malis imminentibus ejus intercessione liberemur.

MR(2008)   *Die 15 augusti, in Assumptione B.M.V., ad missam in vigilia*

Mensæ cæléstis partícipes effécti, implorámus cleméntiam tuam, Dómine Deus noster, ut, qui Assumptiónem Dei Genetrícis cólimus, a cunctis malis imminéntibus ° liberémur.

---

[*] This celebration was added to the *editio typica tertia*, so is not in MR(1970) or MR(1975).

[†] Note that the Latin text of this prayer as originally promulgated (prot. no. CD 570/83) is identical to OFM 14/08: see *Notitiae* 202 (1983), p. 240.

[‡] This is the PC as it was before Pius XII's dogmatic definition of the Assumption, after which new propers were issued by the Sacred Congregation of Rites on 31 October 1950: see *AAS* (1950), pp. 793-795.

15 August: The Assumption of the B.V.M. (Day)

Source: MR 1087 *bis*

MR 1087 bis   *Die 15 augusti, in Assumptione B.M.V., PC*

Sumptis, Dómine, salutáribus sacraméntis: da, quaesumus; ut, méritis et intercessióne beátæ Vírginis Maríæ in cælum assúmptæ, ad resurrectiónis glóriam perducámur.

MR(2008)   *Die 15 augusti, in Assumptione B.M.V., ad missam in die*

Sumptis, Dómine, salutáribus sacraméntis, da, quǽsumus, ut, °
intercessióne beátæ Maríæ Vírginis in cælum assúmptæ, ad resurrectiónis glóriam perducámur.

20 August: St Bernard

Source: O.Cist 20/08

O.Cist 20/08   *Die 20 augusti, in festo S.P.N. Bernardi, PC*

Suum in nobis, omnipotens Deus, intercedente te beato Bernado, cibus, quem sumpsimus, operetur effectum: ut incorporet nos sibi esus edentes.

MR(2008)   *Die 20 augusti, S. Bernardi*

Cibus, quem súmpsimus, Dómine, **in celebratióne** *beáti Bernárdi*, suum in nobis operétur efféctum, ut, **eius exémplis roboráti et mónitis erudíti, Verbi tui incarnáti rapiámur amóre**.

21 AUGUST: ST PIUS X

Source: MR(1962)

MR(1962)   *Die 3 septembris, S. Pii X, PC*

Mensæ cæléstis virtúte refécti, quaesumus, Dómine Deus noster: ut, interveniénte sancto Pio Summo Pontífice; fortes efficiámur in fide, et in tua simus caritáte concórdes.

MR(2008)   *Die 21 augusti, S. Pii X*

Memóriam beáti *Pii* **papæ celebrántes**, quǽsumus, Dómine Deus noster, ut, virtúte ° mensæ cæléstis, **constántes** efficiámur in fide, et in tua simus caritáte concórdes.

22 AUGUST: QUEENSHIP OF THE B.V.M.

Source: MR 67

MR 67   *PAL, die 27 novembris, B.M.V. Immac. a sacro numismate, SO*

Beáta Vírgine María intercedénte, cuius précibus exorátus Iesus Christus, Fílius tuus, fecit inítium signórum: da nobis, Dómine Deus, sacraméntum Córporis et Sánguinis eiúsdem Fílii tui pura mente confícere; ut ætérni convívii mereámur esse partícipes.

MR(2008)   *Die 22 augusti, B.M.V. Reginae*

Sumptis, Dómine, **sacraméntis cæléstibus, te súpplices deprecámur**, ut, **qui** *beátæ Vírginis Maríæ* **memóriam venerándo recólimus**, ætérni convívii mereámur esse partícipes.

24 August: St Bartholomew

Source: *See Common of Pastors, IV.A, p. 137 below*

MR(2008)   *Die 24 augusti, S. Bartholomaei*

Súmpsimus, Dómine, pignus salútis ætérnæ, festivitátem beáti Bartholomǽi apóstoli celebrántes, quod sit nobis, quǽsumus, vitæ præséntis auxílium páriter et futúræ.

28 August: St Augustine

Source: St Augustine, *Sermon* 57, 7

S. Augustini   *Sermo 57, 7*

Virtus enim ipsa quae ibi intelligitur, unitas est, <u>ut</u> redacti in corpus eius, <u>effecti membra eius, simus quod accipimus</u>.

MR(2008)   *Die 28 augusti, S. Augustini*

Sanctíficet nos, quǽsumus, Dómine, mensæ Christi participátio, <u>ut, eius membra effécti, simus quod accépimus</u>.

29 August: Passion of St John the Baptist

Source: MR 142 (*CO* 792)

MR 142   *Die 29 augusti, in decollatione S. Ioannis Baptistae, PC*

Cónferat nobis, Dómine, sancti Ioánnis Baptístæ solémnitas: ut et magnífica sacraménta, quæ súmpsimus, significáta venerémur, et in nobis pótius édita gaudeámus.

MR(2008)   *Die 29 augusti, in passione S. Ioannis Baptistae*

Concéde nobis, Dómine, **beáti** Ioánnis Baptístæ **natále recenséntibus**, ut et **salutária** sacraménta quæ súmpsimus significáta venerémur, et in nobis pótius édita gaudeámus.

3 SEPTEMBER: ST GREGORY THE GREAT

Source: *See Common of Doctors, 1, p. 139 below*

MR(2008)   *Die 3 septembris, S. Gregorii Magni*

Quos Christo réficis pane vivo, eósdem édoce, Dómine, Christo magístro, ut in festivitáte beáti Gregórii tuam discant veritátem, et eam in caritáte operéntur.

8 SEPTEMBER: NATIVITY OF THE BLESSED VIRGIN MARY

Source: New composition

MR(2008)   *Die 8 septembris, In nativitate B.M.V.*

Exsúltet Ecclésia tua, Dómine, quam sacris mystériis refecísti, de beátæ Maríæ Vírginis Nativitáte congáudens, quæ univérso mundo spes fuit et auróra salútis.

12 SEPTEMBER: MOST HOLY NAME OF MARY[*]

Source: Triplex 271 (*CO* 506 b)

Triplex 271   *Kalendas maii, nat. sanctae Waltpurgae virginis, PC*

Benedictionis tuae, domine, gratiam, intercedente beata Waltpurgae virgine tua, consequamur, ut, cuius venerando gloriam praedicamus, eius in omnibus nostris necessitatibus auxilium sentiamus.

MR(2008)   *Die 12 septembris, Ss.mi nominis Mariae*

Benedictiónis tuæ, Dómine, intercedénte **Dei Genetríce María**, grátiam consequámur, ut, cuius *veneréndum* **nomen celebrámus**, eius in ómnibus ° necessitátibus auxílium **percipiámus**.

---

[*] This celebration was added to the *editio typica tertia*, so is not in MR(1970) or MR(1975).

13 SEPTEMBER: ST JOHN CHRYSOSTOM

Source: MP 3478

MP 3478   *Die 18 septembris, S. Ioannis Chrysostomi, PC*

Da nobis, misericors Deus, interveniente beato Joanne Chrysostomo Pontifice, ut tremenda mysteria quae sumpsimus, nos in tua caritate confirment, et constantes veritatis defensores efficiant.

MR(2008)   *Die 13 septembris, S. Ioannis Chrysostomi*

Concéde, miséricors Deus, ut ° mystéria, quæ **pro** *beáti Ioánnis Chrysóstomi* **commemoratióne** súmpsimus, nos in tua caritáte confírment, et **tuæ fidéles confessóres** veritátis ° effíciant.

14 SEPTEMBER: THE EXALTATION OF THE HOLY CROSS

Source: MR 967 + 438 (*CO* 5040 + 2032)

MR 967   *Die 3 maii, in inventiones S. Crucis, PC*

Repleti alimonia caelesti, et spiritali poculo recreati, quaesumus, omnipotens Deus: ut ab hoste maligno defendas, <u>quos per lignum sanctae Crucis</u> Filii tui, arma iustitiae pro salute mundi, triumphare iussisti.

MR 438   *Feria IV maioris hebd., oratio 2a*

Deus, qui pro nobis Filium tuum crucis patibulum subire voluisti, ut inimici a nobis expelleres potestatem: concede nobis famulis tuis; ut <u>resurrectionis gratiam consequamur</u>.

MR(2008)   *Die 14 septembris, in Exaltatione S. Crucis*

Refectióne tua sancta enutríti, Dómine Iesu Christe, súpplices deprecámur, ut, <u>quos per lignum</u> ° crucis vivíficæ redemísti, ad <u>resurrectiónis</u> **glóriam perdúcas**.

15 September: Our Lady of Sorrows

Source: New composition (cf. Colossians 1:24)

Col. 1:24

Nunc gaudeo in passionibus <u>pro vobis et adimpleo ea quae desunt passionum Christi</u> in carne mea pro corpore eius, <u>quod est ecclesia.</u>

MR(2008)   *Die 15 septembris, B.M.V. Perdolentis*

Sumptis, Dómine, sacraméntis redemptiónis ætérnæ, súpplices deprecámur, ut, compassiónem beátæ Maríæ Vírginis recoléntes, <u>ea in nobis pro Ecclésia adimpleámus, quæ desunt Christi passiónum.</u>

16 September: Ss Cornelius & Cyprian

Source: MP 3457

MP 3457   *Die 16 septembris, S. Cypriani Carthaginensis, PC*

Deus, cujus Sacerdos et Martyr Cyprianis Evangelium tenens, Christi praecepta custodiens, occidi potuit, vinci non potuit: indue nos, per haec divina mysteria, fortitudine Spiritus tui: ut Evangeli veritati et voce et opere valeamus testimonium perhibere.

MR(2008)   *Die 16 septembris, Ss. Cornelii et Cypriani*

Per hæc mystéria quæ súmpsimus, Dómine, súpplices exorámus, ut, beatórum *mártyrum* **Cornélii et** *Cypriáni* **exémplo,** spíritus tui fortitúdine **confirmáti,** *evangélicæ* veritáti **possímus** testimónium perhibére.

20 September: Ss Andrew Kim Tae-Gŏn, Paul Chŏng Ha-Sang & Companions*

Source: New composition†

MR(2008)   *Die 20 septembris, Ss. Andreae Kim Tae-Gŏn,*
                                    et Pauli Chŏng Ha-Sang, et sociorum

Fórtium esca enutríti in celebratióne beatórum mártyrum, te, Dómine, supplíciter exorámus, ut, Christo fidéliter inhæréntes, in Ecclésia ad salútem ómnium operémur.

21 September: St Matthew

Source: MP 3497

MP 3497   *Die 21 septembris, S. Matthaei, PC*

Salutaris illius gaudii participes, quos Dominum Iesum in domo sua convivam beatus Matthaeus excepit, suppliciter te, Domine, deprecamur, ut eius sanet nos gratia medicinalis, qui venit vocare peccatores, Dominus noster Iesus Christus Filius tuus.

MR(2008)   *Die 21 septembris, S. Matthaei*

Salutáris ° gáudii partícipes, Dómine, quo **lætus Salvatórem** in domo sua convívam beátus Matthǽus excépit, **da,** ut **cibo semper reficiámur illíus,** qui **non iustos sed** peccatóres vocáre venit **ad salútem** °.

---

* This celebration was added to the *editio typica tertia*, so is not in MR(1970) or MR(1975).

† Note, however, that the second half of this PC is taken from Common of Martyrs, I.A.1; see p. 127 below.

26 September: Ss Cosmas & Damian

Source: *See Common of Martyrs, I.A.3, p. 128 below*

MR(2008)   *Die 26 septembris, Ss. Cosmae et Damiani*

Consérva in nobis. Dómine, munus tuum, et quod, te donánte, pro commemoratióne beatórum mártyrum Cosmæ et Damiáni percépimus, salútem nobis præstet et pacem.

27 September: St Vincent de Paul

Source: MR(1962)

MR(1962)   *Die 19 iulii, S. Vincentii a Paulo, PC*

Cæléstibus, Dómine, refécti sacraméntis: quaesumus; ut, ad evangelizántem paupéribus Fílium tuum imitándum, beáti Vincéntii, sicut exémplis provocámur, ita et patrocíniis adiuvémur.

MR(2008)   *Die 27 septembris, S. Vincentii de Paulo*

Cæléstibus, Dómine, refécti sacraméntis, **súpplices deprecámur**, ut ad imitándum Fílium tuum paupéribus evangelizántem, sicut exémplis beáti Vincéntii provocámur, ita et patrocíniis adiuvémur.

29 September: Ss Michael, Gabriel & Raphael

Source: New composition

MR(2008)   *Die 29 septembris, Ss. Michaelis, Gabrielis et Raphaelis*

Pane cælésti refécti, súpplices te, Dómine, deprecámur, ut, eius fortitúdine roboráti, sub Angelórum tuórum fidéli custódia, fortes, salútis progrediámur in via.

30 SEPTEMBER: ST JEROME

Source: MP 3577*

MP 3577   *Die 30 septembris, S. Hieronymi, PC*

Sancta tua, quae sumpsimus, Domine, intercedente beato Hieronymo, tuorum excitent corda fidelium; ut sacris intenta doctrinis, et intelligant quod sequantur; et sequendo, vitam aeternam apprehendant.

MR(2008)   *Die 30 septembris, S. Hieronymi*

Sancta tua quæ súmpsimus, Dómine, **de** *beáti* Hierónymi **celebritáte lætántes**, tuórum éxcitent corda fidélium, ut, sacris inténta doctrínis, ° intéllegant quod sequántur, et sequéndo vitam **obtíneant** *sempitérnam*.

1 OCTOBER: ST THÉRÈSE OF THE CHILD JESUS

Source: MR 634

MR 634   *Die 3 octobris, S. Teresiae a Iesu Infante, PC*

Illo nos, Dómine, amóris igne cæléste mystérium inflámmet: quo sancta Terésia Virgo tua se tibi pro homínibus caritátis víctimam devóvit.

MR(2008)   *Die 1 octobris, S. Teresiae a Iesu Infante*

Sacraménta quæ súmpsimus, Dómine, *illíus* **in** *nobis* **vim** amóris **accéndant**, quo **beáta** Terésia ° se tibi **addíxit**, *tuámque* **cúpiit miseratiónem** pro **ómnibus impetráre**.

---

* Compare GeV 335 (CO 2556): *Excita, domine, tuorum corda fidelium, ut, sacris intenta doctrinis, et intelligant, quod sequantur, et, sequendo, fideliter apprehendant.*

2 OCTOBER: THE HOLY GUARDIAN ANGELS

Source: MP 3599

MP 3599   *Die 2 octobris, Ss. Angelorum custodum, PC*

Quod tantis, Domine, in vitam aeternam dignaris pascere sacramentis, angelico ministerio dirige in viam iustitiae.

MR(2008)   *Die 2 octobris, Ss. Angelorum custodum*

Quos tantis, Dómine, in vitam ætérnam dignáris páscere sacraméntis, angélico ministério dírige in viam **salútis et pacis**.

4 OCTOBER: ST FRANCIS OF ASSISI

Source: New composition

MR(2008)   *Die 4 octobris, S. Francisci Assisiensis*

Da nobis, quæsumus, Dómine, per hæc sancta quæ súmpsimus, ut, beáti Francísci caritátem zelúmque apostólicum imitántes, tuæ dilectiónis efféctus percipiámus et in salútem ómnium effundámus.

7 OCTOBER: OUR LADY OF THE ROSARY

Source: MP 4300

MP 4300   *Missa de B.M.V. in sabbato, temp. paschali, PC*

Deus, cuius in hoc sacramento mortem annuntiamus; da nobis, per intercessionem beatissimae matris tuae, ut cum ea socii passionum tuarum effecti, consolationis etiam ac gloriae participes esse mereamur.

MR(2008)   *Die 7 octobris, B.M.V. a Rosario*

Quǽsumus, Dómine Deus **noster**, **ut, qui** in hoc sacraménto **Fílii tui** mortem **et resurrectiónem** annuntiámus, ° **eius** sócii passiónum ° effécti, consolatiónis étiam ac glóriæ mereámur esse partícipes.

15 October: St Teresa of Jesus

Source: O.Carm 15/10

O.Carm 15/10   *Die 15 octobris, S. Teresiae, PC*

Subdita tibi familia, quam caelesti pane satiasti, quaesumus, Domine Deus noster: ut, beatae Teresiae intercessione et exemplo, misericordias tuas valeat in aeternum cantare.

MR(2008)   *Die 15 octobris, S. Teresiae a Iesu*

Súbdita tibi família, ° Dómine Deus noster, quam cælésti pane satiásti, **fac ut,** ° exémplo beátæ Terésiæ, misericórdias tuas in ætérnum cantáre **lætétur.**

17 October: St Ignatius of Antioch

Source: MP 2366

MP 2366   *Die 1 februarii, S. Ignatii ep. Antiocheni, PC*

Purifice nos, Domine, coelestis participatio sacramenti; et cum beato Ignatio nihil de his quae videntur desiderantes, tribuat non tantum dici, sed et esse vere Christianos.

MR(2008)   *Die 17 octobris, S. Ignatii Antiocheni*

Refíciat nos, Dómine, **panis** cæléstis °, **quem in** *beáti Ignátii* **natáli suscépimus, ac** tríbuat **nos nómine** et **ópere** esse christiános.

18 OCTOBER: ST LUKE

Source: *See 25 April (St Mark), p. 84 above*

MR(2008)   *Die 18 octobris, S. Lucae*

Præsta, quǽsumus, omnípotens Deus, ut, quod de sancto altári tuo accépimus, nos sanctíficet, et in fide Evangélii, quod beátus Lucas prædicávit, fortes effíciat.

19 OCTOBER: ST PAUL OF THE CROSS

Source: *See Common of Martyrs, I.A.1, p. 127 below*

MR(2008)   *Die 19 octobris, S. Pauli a Cruce*

Deus, qui crucis mystérium in beáto Paulo mirabíliter illustrásti, concéde propítius, ut, ex hoc sacrifício roboráti, Christo fidéles hæreámus, et in Ecclésia ad salútem ómnium operémur

28 OCTOBER: SS SIMON & JUDE

Source: MR 815 (*CO 4200*)

MR 815   *Die 29 novembris, in vig. S. Andrae, PC*

Perceptis, Domine, sacramentis suppliciter exoramus: ut, intercedente beato Andrea Apostolo tuo, quae pro illius veneranda gerimus passione, nobis proficiant ad medalam.

MR(2008)   *Die 28 octobris, Ss. Simonis et Iudae*

Percéptis, Dómine, sacraméntis, *súpplices* **in Spíritu Sancto deprecámur**, ut, **quæ pro** *apostolórum* **Simónis et Iudæ** veneránda gérimus passióne, *nos* **in tua dilectióne consérvent**.

1 NOVEMBER: ALL SAINTS

Source: MP 3798

MP 3798   *Die 1 novembris, Omnium sanctorum, PC*

Mirabilem te, Deus, et unum Sanctum in omnibus Sanctis tuis adorantes, gratiam tuam imploramus; qua, perficientes sanctificationem in timore tuo, ex hac mensa peregrinantium, ad coelestis patriae perenne transeamus.

MR(2008)   *Die 1 novembris, Omnium Sanctorum*

Mirábilem te, Deus, et unum Sanctum in ómnibus Sanctis tuis adorántes, tuam grátiam implorámus, qua, sanctificatiónem in *tui* **amóris plenitúdine consummántes**, ex hac mensa peregrinántium ad cæléstis pátriæ **convívium** transeámus.

2 NOVEMBER: THE COMMEMORATION OF ALL THE FAITHFUL DEPARTED (ALL SOULS) (1)

Source: New composition*

MR(2008)   *Die 2 novembris, In comm. omnium fidelium defunct. (1)*

Præsta, quǽsumus, Dómine, ut fámuli tui defúncti in mansiónem lucis tránseant et pacis, pro quibus paschále celebrávimus sacraméntum.

---

* John 14:2 may have provided some inspiration for the composition of this PC (*In domo Patris mei mansiones multæ sunt; si quominus dixissem vobis: quia vado parare vobis locum*), along with the *Canon Romanus* (*Ipsis, Dómine, et ómnibus in Christo quiescéntibus, locum refrigérii, lucis et pacis, ut indúlgeas, deprecámur*).

2 NOVEMBER: THE COMMEMORATION OF ALL THE FAITHFUL DEPARTED (ALL SOULS) (2)

Source: OV 956 + OV 959

OV 956   *Orat. at matutinum, de resurr. usque in Ascensione, alia*

Christe, Dei filius, <u>qui occisus agnus resurgis in gloriam</u> et habens potestatem magnam, humani generis inluminare dignatus es terram; quo, passionis et resurrectionis tuae pluviis inrigata, te solum sequeretur ad vitam, quae se olim mortis eliserat in ruinam: nostris, quaesumus, precibus favens, dona nobis et resurgendi copiam in actibus bonis, et moriendi efficaciam in operibus pravitatis.

OV 959   *Alia oratio*

Amabiles, Domine, ille satis sunt voces, que te in caelo infatigabili concentu mortem devicisse laudabiliter concinunt, et regnum huius mundi tuum esse fatentur: quaesumus ergo: ut, resurrectionis tuae victoriis recreati, <u>futurae resurrectionis mereamur munere decorari</u>, ut victoria resurrectionis tuae, que laudabilis celebratur in caelis, in terris quoque celebrior ad aeternum lucrum praecinatur in cordibus nostris.

MR(2008)   *Die 2 novembris, In comm. omnium fidelium defunct. (2)*

Sumpto sacraménto Unigéniti tui, <u>qui **pro nobis immolátus resurréxit** in glória</u>, te, Dómine, supplíciter exorámus pro fámulis tuis defúnctis, ut, paschálibus mystériis mundáti, <u>futúræ resurrectiónis ° múnere **gloriéntur**</u>.

2 November: The Commemoration of All the Faithful Departed (All Souls) (3)

Source: GeV 1689 (*CO* 3399)

GeV 1689   *Alia missa in coemeteriis, PC*

Multiplica, domine, super animas famulorum famularumque tuarum misericordiam tuam, et cui donasti baptismi sacramentum, da eis aeternorum plenitudine gaudiorum.

MR(2008)   *Die 2 novembris, In comm. omnium fidelium defunct. (3)*

Multíplica, Dómine, **his sacrifíciis suscéptis**, super ° **fámulos tuos defúnctos** misericórdiam tuam, et, **quibus** donásti baptísmi **grátiam**, da eis æternórum plenitúdinem gaudiórum.

4 November: St Charles Borromeo

Source: MP 3841*

MP 3841   *Die 4 novembris, S. Caroli Borromaei, PC*

Praestent nobis, quaesumus Domine, sacra mysteria quae sumpsimus, eam animi fortitudinem, quae beatum Carolum Sacerdotem tuum reddidit in ministerio fidelem, et in passione victorem.

MR(2008)   *Die 4 novembris, S. Caroli Borromeo*

Præstent nobis, quǽsumus, Dómine, sacra mystéria quæ súmpsimus eam ánimi fortitúdinem, quæ beátum Cárolum ° réddidit in ministério fidélem et in **caritáte ferréntem**.

---

* This oration is almost identical to MP 4008: see Common of Martyrs, I.B.1, p. 129 below.

9 November: Dedication of the Lateran Basilica

Text is the same as Common of the Dedication of a Church, II, p. 121 below.

10 November: St Leo the Great

Source: MR 965 *bis*

MR 965 bis   *Commune Sanct., unius aut plurium Summ. Pont., PC*

Refectióne sancta enutrítam gubérna, quaesumus, Dómine, tuam placátus Ecclésiam: ut, poténti moderatióne dirécta, et increménta libertátis accípiat et in religiónis integritáte persístat.

MR(2008)   *Die 10 novembris, S. Leonis Magni*

Text is the same as the source above.

11 November: St Martin of Tours

Source: MP 2893

MP 2893   *Die 4 iulii, In ord. et transl. S. Martini Turonensis, PC*

Da nobis, Domine, unitatis sacramento refectis, veram in omnibus cum tua voluntate concordiam: ut sicut beatus Martinus totum se tibi sive ad vitam, sive ad mortem subjecti; ita et nos, sive vivamus, sive moriamur, tui esse gloriemur.

MR(2008)   *Die 11 novembris, S. Martini Turonensis*

Da nobis, Dómine, unitátis sacraménto reféctis, **perféctam** in ómnibus cum tua voluntáte concórdiam, ut, sicut beátus Martínus totum se tibi ° subiécit, ita et nos ° esse tui **veráciter** gloriémur.

12 NOVEMBER: ST JOSAPHAT

Source: MR 1067

MR 1067   *Die 14 novembris, S. Iosaphat, PC*

Spritum, Domine, fortitudinis haec nobis tribuat mensa caelestis; quae sancti Iosaphat Martyris tui atque Pontificis vitam pro Ecclesiae honore iugiter aluit ad victoriam.

MR(2008)   *Die 12 novembris, S. Iosaphat*

Spíritum, Dómine, fortitúdinis **et pacis** hæc nobis tríbuat mensa cæléstis, **ut**, sancti Iósaphat ° **exémplo**, vitam **nostram** ad *honórem* **et unitátem** Ecclésiæ **libénter impendámus**.

18 NOVEMBER: DEDICATION OF THE BASILICAS OF SS PETER & PAUL

Source: MR 917 + MR 1043 (*CO* 5389 a + 4763)

MR 917   *Die 6 iulii, in octava Ss. Petri et Pauli, PC*

Protege, <u>Domine, populum tuum</u>: et <u>Apostolorum tuorum Petri et Pauli</u> patrocinio confidentem, perpetua defensione conserva.

MR 1043   *Die 25 ianuarii, in conversione S. Pauli, PC*

Sanctificáti, Dómine, salutári mystério: <u>quaesumus</u>; ut nobis eius non desit orátio, cuius nos <u>donásti patrocínio gubernári</u>.

MR(2008)   *Die 18 novembris, in ded. basilicarum Ss. Petri et Pauli*

<u>Pópulus *tuus*</u>, <u>quǽsumus</u>, <u>Dómine</u>, cælésti pane reféctus, <u>apostolórum °</u> <u>Petri et Pauli</u> commemoratióne lætétur, quorum <u>donásti patrocínio gubernári</u>.

24 NOVEMBER: SS ANDREW DŨNG-LẠC & COMPANIONS[*]

Source: New composition[†]

MR(2008)   *Die 24 novembris, Ss. Andreae Dũng Lạc et sociorum*

Uníus panis alimónia refécti in commemoratióne sanctórum mártyrum, te, Dómine, supplíciter deprecámur, ut, in tua dilectióne unánimes manéntes, patiéntiæ præmium mereámur cónsequi ætérnum.

30 NOVEMBER: ST ANDREW

Source: MP 2091

MP 2091   *Die 30 novembris, S. Andreae, PC*

Roboret nos, Domine, contra voluptatum illecebras sacrae mensae libatio: ut exemplo beati Apostoli tui Andreae crucem nostram quotidie portantes, et cum Christo morientes in cruce, cum ipso regnare mereamur in gloria.

MR(2008)   *Die 30 novembris, S. Andreae*

Róboret nos, Dómine, **sacraménti tui commúnio**, ut, exémplo beáti Andréæ ° apóstoli, ° *Christi* **mortificatiónem feréntes**, cum ipso **vívere** mereámur in glória.

---

[*] This celebration was added to the *editio typica tertia*, so is not in MR(1970) or MR(1975).

[†] The first half of this PC is taken from Common of Martyrs, II.A.2, p. 131 below; the second half appears partly inspired by John 15:9 (*Sicut dilexit me Pater, et ego dilexi vos; manete in dilectione mea*) and partly from Common of Martyrs, I.B.2, p. 130 below.

3 DECEMBER: ST FRANCIS XAVIER

Source: MP 2104

MP 2104   *Die 2 decembris, S. Francisci Xavierii, PC*

Per haec mysteria, quaesumus Domine, eum in nobis accende caritatis ardorem, quem sancto sacerdoti tuo Francisco Xavierio pro salute animarum inspirati: ut digne vocatione nostra ambulantes, promissum bene operantibus mereamur praemium obtinere.

MR(2008)   *Die 3 decembris, S. Francisci Xavier*

° Mystéria **tua**, ° **Deus**, eum in nobis *accéndant* caritátis ardórem, *quo* **beátus** *Francíscus* ° pro animárum salúte **flagrávit**, ut, vocatióne nostra *dígnius* ambulántes, promíssum **bonis** *operáriis* præmium **cum eo consequámur**.

7 DECEMBER: ST AMBROSE

Source: MP 2491

MP 2491   *Die 4 aprilis, S. Ambrosii, PC*

Deus, qui sanctum Pontificem Ambrosium, et fortem ut corriperet, et eloquio suavem ut doceret, esse praestitisti; fac nos suavatatis tuae sapore recreatos, sic eius documentis intendere, ut per custodiam mandatorum tuorum ad caelestia gaudia praeparemur.

MR(2008)   *Die 7 decembris, S. Ambrosii*

Huius sacraménti, Dómine, virtúte roborátos, fac nos beáti *Ambrósii* documéntis **ita profícere**, ut, **viríliter** per **tuas sémitas festinántes**, ad **ætérni** *suavitátem* **convívii** præparémur.

8 December: Immaculate Conception of the B.V.M.

Source: MR 992

MR 992   *Die 8 decembris, in Conceptione Immaculate B.M.V., PC*

Sacraménta quæ súmpsimus, Dómine Deus noster: illíus in nobis culpæ vúlnera réparent; a qua immaculátam beátæ Maríæ Conceptiónem singuláriter præservásti.

MR(2008)   *Die 8 decembris, in Conceptione Immaculata B.M.V.*

Text is the same as the source above.

14 December: St John of the Cross

Source: *See Common of Martyrs, I.A.1, p. 127 below*

MR(2008)   *Die 14 decembris, S. Ioannis a Cruce*

Deus, qui crucis mystérium in beáto Ioánne mirabíliter illustrásti, concéde propítius, ut, ex hoc sacrifício roboráti, Christo fidéles hæreámus, et in Ecclésia ad salútem ómnium operémur.

26 December: St Stephen

Source: GeV 34 (*CO 2753*)

GeV 34   *VII kalendas ianuarii, in nat. sancti Stephani, PC*

Gratiam agimus, domine, multiplicatis circa nos miserationibus tuis, qui et filii tui natiuitatae nos saluas et beati martyris Stephani deprecatione sustentas.

MR(2008)   *Die 26 decembris, S. Stephani*

Grátias ágimus, Dómine, multiplicátis circa nos miseratiónibus tuis, qui et Fílii tui nativitáte nos salvas, et beáti mártyris Stéphani **celebratióne lætíficas**.

27 December: St John

Source: B 155 (*CO* 4569)

B 155   *VI kalendas ianuarii, nat. sancti Iohannis evang.*, SO

Praesta quaesumus omnipotens deus, ut verbum caro factum, quod beatus Iohannes evangelista praedicavit, per hoc sui mysterium habitet semper in nobis.

MR(2008)   *Die 27 decembris, S. Ioannis*

Præsta, quǽsumus, omnípotens Deus, ut Verbum caro factum, quod beátus Ioánnes **apóstolus** prædicávit, per hoc ° mystérium **quod celebrávimus** hábitet semper in nobis.

28 December: The Holy Innocents

Source: GeV 44 (*CO* 192)

GeV 44   *V kalendas ianuarii, in nat. Innocentium, C*

Adiuva nos, domine, quaesumus, eorum deprecatione sanctorum, qui, filium tuum humana necdum voce profitentes, caelesti sunt pro eius nativitate gratia coronati.

MR(2008)   *Die 28 decembris, Ss. Innocentium*

Salvatiónis abundántiam tríbue, Dómine, **fidélibus in eórum festivitáte tua** *sancta* **suméntibus,** qui, Fílium tuum humána necdum voce profiténtes, cælésti sunt grátia pro eius nativitáte coronáti.

COMMONS

COMMON OF THE DEDICATION OF A CHURCH, I

Source: B 1235 (*CO* 508 a)

B 1235   *Orat. et preces in dedicatione ecclesiae, PC*

Benedictionis tuae, quaesumus, Domine, plebs tibi sacra fructus reportet et gaudium, ut, quod in huius festivitatis die corporali servitio exhibuit, spiritaliter se retulisse cognoscat.

MR(2008)   *In anniv. dedicationis, I. In ipsa ecclesia dedicata*

Text is the same as the source above.

COMMON OF THE DEDICATION OF A CHURCH, II

Source: New composition*

MR(2008)   *In anniv. dedicationis, II. Extra ipsam ecclesiam dedicatam*

Deus, qui nobis supérnam Ierúsalem per temporále Ecclésiæ tuæ signum adumbráre voluísti, da, quǽsumus, ut, huius participatióne sacraménti, nos tuæ grátiæ templum effícias, et habitatiónem glóriæ tuæ íngredi concédas.

---

* Revelation 21:10 appears to have provided some inspiration for this PC (*Et sustulit me in spiritu in montem magnum et altum, et ostendit mihi civitatem sanctam Ierusalem descendentem de cælo a Deo*).

COMMON OF THE B.V.M., I. *TEMPUS PER ANNUM* (1)

Source: MR 1075 (*CO* 5542)

MR 1075   *Feria IV Quat. Temp. Pentecostes, PC*

Suméntes, Dómine, cæléstia sacraménta, quaesumus cleméntiam tuam: ut, quod temporáliter gérimus, ætérnis gáudiis consequámur.

MR(2008)   *I. Tempore « per annum », 1*

Suméntes, Dómine, cæléstia sacraménta, quǽsumus cleméntiam tuam, ut, **qui de beátæ Vírginis Maríæ commemoratíone lætámur, eiúsdem Vírginis imitatióne, redemptiónis nostræ mystério digne valeámus famulári.**

COMMON OF THE B.V.M., I. *TEMPUS PER ANNUM* (2)

Text is the same as Saturday after the 2nd Sunday after Pentecost (Immaculate Heart of the Blessed Virgin Mary), p. 88 above.

COMMON OF THE B.V.M., I. *TEMPUS PER ANNUM* (3)*

Source: New composition (*text is the same as CMBMV, 4: Sancta Maria, Dei Genitrix*)

MR(2008)   *I. Tempore « per annum », 3*

Refécti, Dómine, cæléstibus alimóniis, te súpplices exorámus, ut Fílium tuum, ex alma Vírgine natum, quem sacraménto suscépimus, confiteámur verbis et móribus teneámus.

---

* This oration is not in MR(1970) or MR(1975).

COMMON OF THE B.V.M., I. *TEMPUS PER ANNUM* (4)*

Source: Cong. Pass., p. 22

Cong. Pass.   *B.M.V., Mater Sanctae Spei, PC*

Unigeniti Filii tui de Virgine nati pasti deliciis, supplices te, Domine, deprecamur, ut sanctae Spei beatam Matrem devote recolentes, aeternae spei secum participes fieri mereamur.

MR(2008)   *I. Tempore « per annum », 4*

Sumptis, Dómine, **salútis et fídei sacraméntis**, súpplices te deprecámur, ut, ° beátam **Vírginem Maríam** devóte recoléntes, **supérnæ caritátis cum ipsa** partícipes fíeri mereámur.

COMMON OF THE B.V.M., I. *TEMPUS PER ANNUM* (5)*

Source: New composition (*text is the same as CMBMV, 27: B.M.V., Imago et Mater Ecclesiae, III*)

MR(2008)   *I. Tempore « per annum », 5*

Concéde, Dómine, Ecclésiæ tuæ, ut, huius sacraménti virtúte roboráta, sémitas Evangélii alácriter percúrrat, donec beátam pacis visiónem attíngat, qua Virgo María, húmilis ancílla tua, iam frúitur in ætérnum gloriósa.

---

* This oration is not in MR(1970) or MR(1975).

COMMON OF THE B.V.M., I. *TEMPUS PER ANNUM* (6)[*]

Source: New composition (*see CMBMV, 23: B.M.V., Templum Domini*)[†]

MR(2008)   *I. Tempore « per annum »,* 6

Cælésti alimónia nutrítos, fac nos, Dómine, exémplo beátæ Vírginis Maríæ, pura tibi conversatióne servíre, et cum ipsa te sincéris láudibus magnificáre.

COMMON OF THE B.V.M., I. *TEMPUS PER ANNUM* (7)

Source: Cong. Pass., p. 31

Cong. Pass.   *Sancta Maria, ancilla Domini,* PC

Spiritualis alimoniae participes effecti, quaesumus, Domine Deus noster, ut, beatam Virginem imitati, tui experiamur gaudia famulatus, Ecclesiae tuae servientes.

MR(2008)   *I. Tempore « per annum »,* 7

Spirituális alimóniæ partícipes effécti, quǽsumus, Dómine Deus noster, ut, beátam Vírginem **Maríam assídue** imitántes, **et** Ecclésiæ *servítio* **semper inveniámur inténti et** tui experiámur gáudia famulátus.

---

[*] This oration is not in MR(1970) or MR(1975).

[†] The CMBMV text is slightly different: *Cælésti alimónia nutrítos, fac nos, exémplo beátæ Vírginis Maríæ, pura tibi conversatióne servíre, te in frátribus præséntem venerári, te cum ipsa sincéris magnificáre láudibus.*

COMMON OF THE B.V.M., I. *TEMPUS PER ANNUM* (8)*

Source: MR 482 + MR 503

MR 482   *Die 22 augusti, Immaculate Cordis B.M.V., PC*

Divinis refecti muneribus <u>te, Domine, suppliciter</u> exoramus: <u>ut beatae</u> <u>Mariae Virginis</u> intercessione, cuius immaculati Cordis solemnia <u>venerando egimus</u>, a praesentibus periculis liberati, aeternae vitae gaudia consequamur.

MR 503   *PAL, die 27 iunii, B.M.V. de Perpetuo Succursu, C*

Domine Iesu Christe, qui Genitricem tuam Mariam, cuius insignem veneramur imaginem, Matrem nobis dedisti perpetuo succurrere paratam: concede, quaesumus; ut nos, maternam eius opem assidue implorantes, <u>redemptionis tuae fructum perpetuo experiri mereamur</u>.

MR(2008)   *I. Tempore « per annum », 8*

Salutáribus refécti sacraméntis, <u>súpplices te, Dómine</u>, deprecámur, <u>ut</u>, qui memóriam <u>beátæ Vírginis</u> Dei Genetrícis <u>Maríæ venerándo égimus</u>, <u>redemptiónis tuæ fructum perpétuo experíri mereámur</u>.

COMMON OF THE B.V.M., II. ADVENT

Source: New composition (*see CMBMV, 2: B.M.V. in Annuntiatione Domini*)†

MR(2008)   *II. Tempore Adventus*

Mystéria quæ súmpsimus, Dómine Deus noster, misericórdiam tuam in nobis semper osténdant, ut Fílii tui incarnatióne salvémur, qui Genetrícis eius commemoratiónem fidéli mente celebrámus.

---

* In MR(1970) and MR(1975), this PC appears under the heading *Aliae orationes in missis* ("Other Prayers for Masses of the Blessed Virgin Mary").

† CMBMV reads *memóriam* in place of *commemoratiónem*, but otherwise these two texts are identical.

COMMON OF THE B.V.M., III. CHRISTMAS TIME

Source: New composition (*text is the same as CMBMV, 5: B.M.V., Mater Salvatoris*)

MR(2008)   *III. Tempore Nativitatis*

Incarnáti Verbi tui Córpore et Sánguine refécti, quǽsumus, Dómine, ut hæc divína mystéria, quæ in commemoratióne beátæ Vírginis Maríæ lætánter accépimus, eiúsdem Fílii tui divinitátis partícipes nos semper effíciant.

COMMON OF THE B.V.M., IV. EASTER TIME*

Source: IMC 20/01

IMC 20/01   *20 giugno, Messa in onore della consolata, PC*

Paschalibus sacramentis refecti, quaesumus, Domine: ut, qui genetricis Filii tui memoriam recolimus, nuntium resurrectionis quotidie in corpore nostro mortali experientes, pro hominum salute, spe gaudentes, vigiles impendamus curas.

MR(2008)   *IV. Tempore Paschali*

Paschálibus sacraméntis refécti, quǽsumus, Dómine, ut, qui Genetrícis Fílii tui memóriam recólimus, **vitam Iesu in carne** *nostra mortáli* **manifestémus**.

---

* In MR(1970) and MR(1975), the PC for this Mass is *In méntibus nostris, quǽsumus, Dómine*, from 25 March (The Annunciation of the Lord), p. 84 above. The rubrics in MR(2008) also permit the use of the Votive Mass of Our Lady, Queen of Apostles (p. 201 below) to be used as part of the Common of the B.V.M. during Eastertide.

COMMON OF MARTYRS, I. OUTSIDE EASTER TIME, A. SEVERAL MARTYRS (1)

Source: New composition

MR(2008)   *I. Extra temp. paschale, A. Pro pluribus mart., 1*

Deus, qui crucis mystérium in sanctis martýribus tuis mirabíliter illustrásti, concéde propítius, ut, ex hoc sacrifício roboráti, Christo fidéliter hæreámus, et in Ecclésia ad salútem ómnium operémur.

COMMON OF MARTYRS, I. OUTSIDE EASTER TIME, A. SEVERAL MARTYRS (2)

Source: MP 4057

MP 4057   *In nat. plurium Martyrum, temp. paschali, PC*

Nutritos carne Christi tui, Domine, et cum ipso concorporales effectos: da nos, quaesumus, ab eius caritate numquam separari, et sanctorum Martyrum tuorum N. et N. exemplo, in omnibus superare propter eum qui dilexit nos.

MR(2008)   *I. Extra temp. paschale, A. Pro pluribus mart., 2*

Pane cælésti nutrítos et **in** *Christo* **unum corpus** efféctos, da nos, quæsumus, Dómine, ab eius caritáte numquam separári et, sanctórum mártyrum tuórum N. et N. exémplo, propter eum qui diléxit nos **ómnia fórtiter** superáre.

COMMON OF MARTYRS, I. OUTSIDE EASTER TIME, A. SEVERAL MARTYRS (3)

Source: B 1053 (*CO* 812 a)

B 1053   *IV idus augusti, nat. sancti Laurentii, ad missam in die, PC*

Conserva in nobis domine munus tuum, et quod te donate, pro sollemnitate beati martyris tui Laurentii percepimus, et salutem nobis prestet et pacem.

MR(2008)   *I. Extra tempus paschale, A. Pro pluribus mart., 3*

Consérva in nobis, Dómine, munus tuum, et quod, te donánte, pro **festivitáte** *beatórum mártyrum* **N. et N.** percépimus, et salútem nobis præstet et pacem.

COMMON OF MARTYRS, I. OUTSIDE EASTER TIME, A. SEVERAL MARTYRS (4)

Source: Ve 743 (*CO* 671)

Ve 743   *Mense augusti, IV idus, nat. sancti Laurentii, II alia missa, C*

Concede nobis, domine, gratiam tuam in beati Laurentii martyris celebritate multiplicam, ut de tanti agone certaminis discat populus christianus et firma solidari patientia et pia exsultare victoria.

MR(2008)   *I. Extra tempus paschale, A. Pro pluribus mart., 4*

Concéde nobis, Dómine, **per hæc sacraménta cæléstia,** grátiam ° in *beatórum mártyrum* **N. et N.** celebritáte multíplicem, ut de tanti agóne certáminis *discámus* ° et firma solidári patiéntia, et pia exsultáre victória.

COMMON OF MARTYRS, I. OUTSIDE EASTER TIME, A. SEVERAL MARTYRS (5)

Source: MP 3610

MP 3610   *Die 3 octobris, S. Dionysii Areopagitae, PC*

Pastis, Domine, pretioso corpore et sanguine unigeniti Filii tui, da quaesumus, intercedente beato Dionysio Martyre tuo atque Pontifice, perseveranti caritate in te esse, de te vivere, et ad te moveri.

MR(2008)   *I. Extra tempus paschale, A. Pro pluribus mart., 5*

Pasti, Dómine, pretióso Córpore et Sánguine Unigéniti Fílii tui **in commemoratióne** *beatórum mártyrum tuórum* **N. et N., te súpplices deprecámur, ut nobis** peresveránti caritáte in te **manére**, de te vívere, et ad te movéri **concédas.**

COMMON OF MARTYRS, I. OUTSIDE EASTER TIME, B. ONE MARTYR (1)

Source: MP 4008

MP 4008   *In nat. unius Mart. Pont. vel Presb. extra temp. paschale, PC*

Praestent nobis, quaesumus Domine, sacra mysteria quae sumpsimus, eam animi fortitudinem, quae beatum N. sacerdotem tuum reddidit in ministerio fidelem, et in passione victorem.

MR(2008)   *I. Extra tempus paschale, B. Pro uno mart., 1*

Præstent nobis, quǽsumus, Dómine, sacra mystéria quæ súmpsimus eam ánimi fortitúdinem, quæ beátum N. **mártyrem** tuum réddidit in **tuo servítio** fidélem et in passióne victórem.

COMMON OF MARTYRS, I. OUTSIDE EASTER TIME, B. ONE MARTYR (2)

Source: New composition[*]

MR(2008)   *I. Extra tempus paschale, B. Pro uno mart., 2*

Sacris, Dómine, recreáti mystériis, quǽsumus, ut, miram beáti N. constántiam æmulántes, patiéntise prǽmium cónsequi mereámur ætérnum.

COMMON OF MARTYRS, II. DURING EASTER TIME, A. SEVERAL MARTYRS (1)

Source: MP 4021

MP 4021   *In nat. unius Mart. non Pont. extra temp. paschale, PC*

Beati Martyris tui N. caelestem victoriam divino convivio celebrantes; te, Domine, deposcimus, ut panem vitae hic edentibus des vincere, et vincentibus des edere de ligno vitae in paradiso.

MR(2008)   *II. Tempore paschali, A. Pro pluribus mart., 1*

Beatórum mártyrum ° N. **et N.** cæléstem victóriam divino convívio celebrántes, te, Dómine, depóscimus, ut panem vitæ hic *edéntes* des víncere, et *vincéntes* des édere de ligno vitæ in paradíso.

---

[*] This PC, with different vocabulary, appears to be inspired by 1 Corinthians 9:24 (*Nescitis quod hi, qui in stadio currunt, omnes quidem currunt, sed unus accipit bravium? Sic currite, ut comprehendatis*).

COMMON OF MARTYRS, II. DURING EASTER TIME, A. SEVERAL MARTYRS (2)

Source: New composition (see Romans 6:4)

Rom. 6:4

Consepulti ergo sumus cum illo per baptismum in mortem, ut quemadmodum suscitatus est Christus a mortuis per gloriam Patris, ita et nos in novitate vitae ambulemus.

MR(2008)   *II. Tempore paschali, A. Pro pluribus mart., 2*

Uníus panis alimónia refécti, in commemoratióne beatórum mártyrum N. et N. supplíciter te, Dómine, deprecámur, ut nos in tua iúgiter caritáte confírmes, et in novítáte vitæ **concédas** ambuláre.

COMMON OF MARTYRS, II. DURING EASTER TIME, B. ONE MARTYR

Source: New composition

MR(2008)   *II. Tempore paschali, B. Pro uno mart.*

Tua, Dómine, súmpsimus dona cæléstia de hodiérna festivitáte lætántes; præsta, quǽsumus, ut, qui in hoc divíno convívio mortem Fílii tui annuntiámus, eiúsdem resurrectiónis et glóriæ cum sanctis martýribus partícipes esse mereámur

COMMON OF MARTYRS, III. MISSIONARY MARTYRS, A. SEVERAL

Source: MR 98

MR 98   *PAL, die 23 maii, S. Ritae a Cassia, PC*

Cæléstibus, Dómine, pasti delíciis, súpplices te rogámus: ut, intercedénte sancta Rita, caritátis et passiónis tuæ in méntibus nostris signa ferámus, et perpétuæ pacis fructu iúgiter perfruámur.

MR(2008)   *III. Pro missionariis mart., A. Pro pluribus miss. mart.*

Cæléstibus, Dómine, pasti delíciis, súpplices te rogámus, ut, **exémplo beatórum N. et N.**, caritátis et passiónis **Fílii** *tui* in méntibus nostris signa ferámus, et perpétuæ pacis fructu iúgiter perfruámur.

COMMON OF MARTYRS, III. MISSIONARY MARTYRS, B. ONE

Source: MP 2661*

MP 2661   *Die 2 iunii, Ss. mart. Pothini, Blandinae et sociorum, PC*

Deus, cuius virtutis esse cognoscimus, ut sancti Martyres animas suas odiendo diligerent, et perdendo servarent: praesta, ut per huius participationem mysterii, ad tantae fidei exempla sectanda, et eorum beata recordatio nos incitet, et oratio digna perducat.

MR(2008)   *III. Pro missionariis mart., B. Pro uno miss. mart.*

Cæléste convívium celebrántes, te, Dómine, deprecámur, ut nos ad tantæ fídei exémpla sectánda **beáti N.** *mártyris* et ° recordátio íncitet et orátio digna perdúcat.

---

* See also Ve 407 (CO 3975): *Omnipotens sempiterne deus, qui inter innumera beneficia sanctorum tuorum nos sollemnitatibus praecipue consolaris, praesta, quaesumus, ut ad caelestis operis institute et recordatio beata nos incitet et oratio iustorum digna perducat.*

COMMON OF MARTYRS, IV. VIRGIN MARTYR

Source: MP 2146 (*CO* 1369)

MP 2146   *Die 13 decembris, S. Luciae, PC*

Deus, qui beatae Luciae pro gemina virginitatis et martyrii duplicem coronam tua gratia contulisti: da, quaesumus, ut de carne, mundo et diabolo triumphantes, caelestem gloriam consequamur.

MR(2008)   *IV. Pro virgine martyre*

Deus, qui *beátam* **N.** pro gémina virginitátis et martýrii **victória inter Sanctos** *coronásti*, da, quǽsumus, **per huius virtútem sacraménti, ut, omne malum fórtiter superéntes,** cæléstem glóriam consequámur.

COMMON OF MARTYRS, V. FOR A HOLY WOMAN MARTYR

Source: MR 1076 (*CO* 5550)

MR 1076   *Feria IV Quat. Temp. septembris, PC*

Suméntes, Dómine, dona cæléstia, supplíciter deprecámur: ut, quæ sédula servitúte donante te gérimus, dignis sénsibus tuo múnere capiámus.

MR(2008)   *V. Pro sancta muliere martyre*

Suméntes, Dómine, **gáudia sempitérna de participatióne sacraménti, et de memória beátæ N.,** supplíciter deprecámur, ut, quæ sédula servitúte, donánte te, gérimus, dignis sénsibus tuo múnere capiámus.

COMMON OF PASTORS, I. FOR A POPE OR BISHOP (1)

Source: MR 993

MR 993   *Die 13 maii, S. Roberti Bellarmino, PC*

Sacraménta, quæ súmpsimus, Dómine Deus noster, in nobis fóveant caritátis ardórem: quo beátus Robértus veheménter accénsus, pro Ecclésia tua se iúgiter impendébat.

MR(2008)   *I. Pro papa vel pro episcopo, 1*

Sacraménta quæ súmpsimus, Dómine Deus noster, in nobis fóveant caritátis ardórem, quo beátus **N.** veheménter accénsus pro Ecclésia tua se iúgiter impendébat.

COMMON OF PASTORS, I. FOR A POPE OR BISHOP (2)

Source: MR 14

MR 14   *PAL, Pro non martyribus, PC*

Acceptórum múnerum virtus, Dómine Deus, intercedéntibus beátis N. et N., suos in nobis efféctus ímpleat: ut simul et mortális vitæ subsídium cónferat, et gáudium perpétuæ felicitátis obtíneat.

MR(2008)   *I. Pro papa vel pro episcopo, 2*

Acceptórum múnerum virtus, Dómine Deus, **in hac festivitáte** *beáti* N. ° nobis efféctus ímpleat, ut simul et mortális vitæ subsídium cónferat, et gáudium perpétuæ felicitátis obtíneat.

COMMON OF PASTORS, II. FOR A BISHOP (1)

Source: New composition

MR(2008)   *II. Pro episcopo, 1*

Refécti sacris mystériis, Dómine, humíliter deprecámur, ut, beáti N. exémplo, studeámus confitéri quod crédidit, et ópere exercére quod dócuit.

COMMON OF PASTORS, II. FOR A BISHOP (2)

Source: MR 150 (*CO* 847 a)

MR 150   *Die 2 iulii, Ss. Processo et Martiniano, PC*

Córporis sacri et pretiósi Sánguinis repléti libámine, quaesumus, Dómine Deus noster: ut, quod pia devotióne gérimus, certa redemptióne capiámus.

MR(2008)   *II. Pro episcopo, 2*

Córporis sacri et pretiósi Sánguinis **alimónia** repléti, quǽsumus, Dómine Deus noster, ut, quod pia devotióne gérimus, certa redemptióne capiámus.

COMMON OF PASTORS, III. FOR PASTORS, A. SEVERAL

Source: Triplex 2059 (*CO* 5585 c)

Triplex 2059   *V. kalendas iulii, nat. sanctorum Iohannis et Pauli, PC*

Sumpsimus, domine, sanctorum tuorum sollemnis celebrantes, caelestis sacramenta; praesta, quaesumus, ut, quod temporaliter gerimus, aeternis gaudiis consequamur.

MR(2008)   *III. Pro pastoribus, A. Pro pluribus pastoribus*

Súmpsimus, Dómine, sanctórum tuórum **N. et N. memóriam** celebrántes, sacraménta *cæléstia*; præsta, quǽsumus, ut, quod temporáliter gérimus, ætérnis gáudiis consequámur.

Common of Pastors, III. For Pastors, B. One (1)

Source: MR 675

MR 675   *PAL, Commune plurium Confessorum Pont., PC*

Mensa cæléstis, omnípotens Deus, intercedéntibus beatórum N. et N. Pontíficum méritis, supérnas in ómnibus vires firmet et áugeat: ut et fídei donum íntegrum custodiámus, et per osténsum salútis trámitem ambulémus.

MR(2008)   *III. Pro pastoribus, B. Pro uno pastore, 1*

Mensa cæléstis, omnípotens Deus, in ómnibus **festivitátem** *beáti* N. ° **celebrántibus** supérnas vires firmet et áugeat, ut et fídei donum íntegrum custodiámus, et per osténsum salútis trámitem ambulémus.

Common of Pastors, III. For Pastors, B. One (2) *(opt. 1)*

Source: MP 2686

MR 993   *Die 6 iunii, S. Norberti, PC*

Sumpta mysteria, quaesumus, Domine, aeternis nos praeparent gaudiis, quae beatus Pontifex Norbertus fideli dispensatione promeruit.

MR(2008)   *III. Pro pastoribus, B. Pro uno pastore, 2 (prima)*

Sumpta mystéria, quǽsumus, Dómine, ætérnis nos prǽparent gáudiis, quæ beátus **N.** fidéli dispensatióne proméruit.

COMMON OF PASTORS, III. FOR PASTORS, B. ONE (2) (*opt. 2*)

Source: MR 966

MR 966   *PAL, Commune plurium Confessorum Pont., PC*

Refectióne sacra enutrítos, fac nos, omnípotens Deus, vestígiis beatórum N. et N. Pontíficum semper insístere: qui studuérunt pérpeti devotióne te cólere, et indeféssa ómnibus caritáte profícere.

MR(2008)   *III. Pro pastoribus, B. Pro uno pastore, 2 (altera)*

Refectióne sacra enutrítos, fac nos, omnípotens Deus, **exémpla** *beáti* **N. iúgiter sequéntes,** ° te pérpeti devotióne cólere, et indeféssa ómnibus caritáte profícere.

COMMON OF PASTORS, IV. FOUNDERS OF CHURCHES, A. ONE

Source: MR 1082 (*CO* 5579)

MR 1082   *Die 11 augusti, Ss. Tiburtii et Susannae, PC*

Súmpsimus, Dómine, pignus redemptiónis ætérnæ: quod sit nobis, quaesumus, interveniéntibus sanctis Martýribus tuis, vitæ præséntis auxílium páriter et futúræ.

MR(2008)   *IV. Pro fundatoribus Eccl., A. Pro uno fundatore*

Súmpsimus, Dómine, pignus redemptiónis ætérnæ, **beáti N. festivitáte lætántes,** quod sit nobis, quǽsumus, ° vitæ præséntis auxílium páriter et futúræ.

COMMON OF PASTORS, IV. FOUNDERS OF CHURCHES, B. SEVERAL FOUNDERS

Source: MR 1028 + GeV 920 (MR 1028 + *CO* 3225 aA)

MR 1028   *Die 10 maii, S. Antonini, C*

Sancti Antoníni, Dómine, Confessóris tui atque Pontíficis méritis adiuvémur: ut, sicut te in illo mirábilem prædicámus, ita in nos misericórdem fuísse gloriémur.

GeV 920   *III kalendas iulii, in nat. sancti Petri proprie, PC*

Lætíficet nos, domine, munus oblatum, ut sicut in apostolo tuo Petro te mirabile praedicamus, sic per illum tuae sumamus indulgentiae largitatem.

MR(2008)   *IV. Pro fundatoribus Eccl., B. Pro pluribus fundatore*

Lætíficet nos accéptum de altári salutáre tuum, Dómine, in sanctórum N. et N. festivitáte, qua, de tuis benefíciis sollíciti, pretiósa fídei nostræ inítia venerámur, et te in **sanctis tuis** mirábilem prædicámus.

COMMON OF PASTORS, V. FOR MISSIONARIES (1)

Source: MP 2330

MP 2330   *Die 27 ianuarii, S. Iuliani Cenomannensis, PC*

Per huius operationem mysterii, confirma Domine, famulos tuos in fide veritatis, ut eam ubique ore et opera confiteantur, pro qua sanctus Pontifex Iulianus laborare non destitit et mori desideravit.

MR(2008)   *V. Pro missionariis, 1*

° Huius mystérii **virtúte**, confírma, Dómine, fámulos tuos in fide veritátis, ut eam ubíque ore et ópere confiteántur, pro qua **beátus N.** laboráre non déstitit et **vitam suam impéndit**.

Common of Pastors, V. For Missionaries (2)

Source: New composition

MR(2008)   *V. Pro missionariis, 2*

Sacraménta quæ súmpsimus, Dómine Deus noster, illam nobis fidem innútriant, quam et apostólica dócuit prædicátio, et beáti N. sollicitúdo custodívit.

Common of Pastors, V. For Missionaries (3)

Source: MR 1027 (*CO* 5300)

MR 1027   *Dom. infra oct. Ss.mi Cordis Iesu (III post Pent.), PC*

Sancta tua nos, Domine, sumpta vivificent: et misericordiae sempiternae praeparent expiatos.

MR(2008)   *V. Pro missionariis, 3*

Sancta tua nos, Dómine, sumpta vivíficent, **ut, qui beáti N. commemoratióne gaudémus, eius quoque apostólicæ virtútis proficiámus exémplo.**

Common of Doctors, 1

Source: MP 4107

MP 4107   *In natali Doctoris, PC*

Quos Christo pane reficis, eosdem Christo Magistro edoce, Domine; ut interveniente beato N. discant in humilitate veritatem tuam, et eam in caritate fideliter operentur.

MR(2008)   *Commune doctorum Eccl., 1*

Quos Christo réficis pane vivo, eósdem édoce, Dómine, Christo magístro, ut **in festivitáte** *beáti* N. tuam discant ° veritátem, et eam in caritáte ° operéntur.

COMMON OF DOCTORS, 2

Source: MR 87*

MR 87   *Die 14 aprilis, S. Iustini, PC*

Cælésti alimónia refécti, súpplices te, Dómine, deprecámur: ut, beáti Iustíni Mártyris tui mónitis, de accéptis donis semper in gratiárum actióne maneámus.

MR(2008)   *Commune doctorum Eccl., 2*

Cælésti alimónia refécti, súpplices te, Dómine, deprecámur, ut, beáti **N.** mónitis **obsequéntes**, de accéptis donis semper in gratiárum actióne maneámus.

COMMON OF VIRGINS, I. SEVERAL VIRGINS

Source: MR 1084

MR 1084   *PAL, Pro virginis tantum, PC*

Sumpta mystéria, quaesumus, Dómine, suffragántibus beatárum Vírginum N. et N. méritis, íncitent nos iúgiter et illústrent: ut digne advéntum Fílii tui præstolémur, et ad supérnas eius núptias admittámur.

MR(2008)   *I. Pro pluribus virginibus*

Sumpta mystéria, quǽsumus, Dómine, **in hac festivitáte** beatárum vírginum N. et N. °, íncitent nos iúgiter et illústrent, ut digne advéntum Fílii tui præstolémur, et ad supérnas eius núptias admittámur.

---

* See also Ve 1025 (CO 5056 a): *Repleti, domine, muneribus sacris, da, quaesumus, ut in gratiarum semper actione maneamus.*

COMMON OF VIRGINS, II. ONE VIRGIN (1)

Source: MR 476

MR 476 *Feria IV infra hebd. II post oct. Paschae,*
in solemnitate S. Ioseph sponsi B.M.V., PC

Divíni múneris fonte refécti, quaesumus, Dómine Deus noster: ut, sicut nos facis beáti Ioseph protectióne gaudére; ita, eius méritis et intercessióne, cæléstis glóriæ fácias esse partícipes.

MR(2008) *II. Pro una virgine, 1*

Divíni múneris *participatióne* refécti, quǽsumus, Dómine Deus noster, ut, **exémplo** beátæ **N., mortificatiónem Iesu in córpore nostro circumferéntes, tibi soli adhærére studeámus.**

COMMON OF VIRGINS, II. ONE VIRGIN (2)

Source: MR 149

MR 149 *PAL, Pro virginibus tantis, PC*

Córporis et Sánguinis tui sacra libátio, Dómine, intercedéntibus beátis Virgínibus N. et N., ab ómnibus nos cadúcis rebus avértat: ut valeámus tui et sincéra in terris caritáte profícere, et perpétua in cælis visióne gaudére.

MR(2008) *II. Pro una virgine, 2*

Córporis et Sánguinis **Unigéniti** tui sacra **percéptio**, Dómine, ab ómnibus nos cadúcis rebus avértat, ut, **exémplo** beátæ **N. °,** valeámus et sincéra in terris caritáte profícere, et tui perpétua in cælis visióne gaudére.

COMMON OF VIRGINS, II. ONE VIRGIN (3)

Source: New composition

MR(2008)   *II. Pro una virgine, 3*

Cælésti pane refécti, humíliter deprecámur cleméntiam tuam, Dómine, ut, qui de beátæ N. commemoratióne gaudémus, véniam delictórum, sospitátem córporum, gratiámque et glóriam ætérnam consequámur animárum.

COMMON OF HOLY MEN AND WOMEN, I. ALL CATEGORIES OF SAINTS, A. SEVERAL (1)

Source: New composition

MR(2008)   *I. Pro omnibus Sanct. ordinibus, A. Pro pluribus Sanctis, 1*

Omnípotens sempitérne Deus, Pater totíus consolatiónis et pacis, præsta famíliæ tuæ in celebritáte Sanctórum ad laudem tui nóminis congregátæ, ut, per Unigéniti tui sumpta mystéria, pignus accípiat redemptiónis ætérnæ.

COMMON OF HOLY MEN AND WOMEN,
I. ALL CATEGORIES OF SAINTS, A. SEVERAL (2)

Source: MR 719*

MR 87   *Die 12 iulii, Ss. Naboris et Felicis, PC*

Natalíciis Sanctórum tuórum, quǽsumus, Dómine: ut, sacraménti múnere vegetáti, bonis, quibus per tuam grátiam nunc fovémur, perfruámur ætérnis.

MR(2008)   *I. Pro omnibus Sanct. ordinibus, A. Pro pluribus Sanctis, 2*

In natalíciis Sanctórum ° quǽsumus, Dómine, ut, sacraménti múnere vegetáti, bonis, quibus per tuam grátiam nunc fovémur, perfruámur ætérnis.

COMMON OF HOLY MEN AND WOMEN,
I. ALL CATEGORIES OF SAINTS, A. SEVERAL (3)

Text is the same as 19th Sunday per annum, *p. 66 above.*

COMMON OF HOLY MEN AND WOMEN,
I. ALL CATEGORIES OF SAINTS, A. SEVERAL (4)

Source: Ve 151 (*CO* 4813)

Ve 151   *Mense aprilis, XXXVIII alia missa, PC*

Quaesumus, domine deus noster, ut divina mysteria, quae in tuorum commemoratione sanctorum frequentamus actu, subsequamur et sensu.

MR(2008)   *I. Pro omnibus Sanct. ordinibus, A. Pro pluribus Sanctis, 4*

Quǽsumus, Dómine Deus noster, ut divína mystéria, quæ in tuórum commemoratióne Sanctórum frequentámus, **salútem et pacem in nobis operéntur ætérnam.**

---

* See also Ve 167 (*CO* 2452): *Et natalitiis sanctorum, domine, et sacramenti munere vegetati, quaesumus, ut bonis, quibus per tuam gratiam nunc fovemur, perfruamur aeternis.*

Common of Holy Men and Women,
I. All Categories of Saints, B. One (1)

Source: MR 990

MR 990   *Die 18 martii, S. Cyrilli, PC*

Sacraménta Córporis et Sánguinis tui, quæ súmpsimus, Dómine Iesu Christe, beáti Cyrílli Pontíficis précibus, mentes et corda nostra sanctíficent: ut divínæ consórtes natúræ éffici mereámur.

MR(2008)   *I. Pro omnibus Sanct. ordinibus, B. Pro uno Sancto, 1*

Sacraménta ° quæ súmpsimus, Dómine °, **in commemoratióne** beáti **N.** ° mentes et corda nostra sanctíficent, ut divínæ consórtes natúræ éffici mereámur.

Common of Holy Men and Women,
I. All Categories of Saints, B. One (2)

Source: MR 1022 (*CO* 5251 E)

MR 1022   *Die 14 aprilis, Pro Ss. Tiburtio, Valeriano et Maximo, PC*

Sacro múnere satiáti, súpplices te, Dómine, deprecámur: ut, quod débitæ servitútis celebrámus offício, salvatiónis tuæ sentiámus augméntum.

MR(2008)   *I. Pro omnibus Sanct. ordinibus, B. Pro uno Sancto, 2*

Sacro múnere satiáti, súpplices te, Dómine, deprecámur, ut, quod **in festivitáte beáti N.** débitæ servitútis celebrámus offício, salvatiónis tuæ sentiámus augméntum.

COMMON OF HOLY MEN AND WOMEN,
II. FOR MONKS AND RELIGIOUS, A. FOR AN ABBOT[*]

Source: New composition (see Colossians 3:2, 4)

Col. 3:2, 4

Quae sursum sunt sapite, non quae supra terram.

Cum Christus apparuerit, vita vestra, tunc et vos apparebitis cum ipso in gloria.

MR(2008)   *II. Pro monachis et religiosis, A. Pro abbatis*

Huius quod súmpsimus, Dómine, virtúte sacraménti, rénova corda nostra, ut exémplo beáti N. abbátis quæ sursum sunt, non quæ super terram, sapiéntes, cum Christo in glória mereámur apparére.

COMMON OF HOLY MEN AND WOMEN,
II. FOR MONKS AND RELIGIOUS, B. FOR A MONK[*]

Source: Ve 429 (*CO* 279)

Ve 429   *Mense iulii, orat. et preces diurnae, III alia missa, PC*

Annue, quaesumus, domine deus noster, ut per hoc tuae sapientiae sacramentum circumspecta moderatione vivamus.

MR(2008)   *II. Pro monachis et religiosis, B. Pro monacho*

Annue, quǽsumus, Dómine, Deus noster, ut, **beáti N. fulti præsídio**, per hoc tuæ sapiéntiæ sacraméntum **æqua** moderatióne vivámus.

---

[*] This oration is not in MR(1970) or MR(1975).

COMMON OF HOLY MEN AND WOMEN,
II. FOR MONKS AND RELIGIOUS, C. FOR A NUN[*]

Source: New composition

MR(2008)   *II. Pro monachis et religiosis, C. Pro moniali*

Salutáribus, Dómine, fóntibus recreáti, te súpplices exorámus, ut, beátæ N. intercessióne, Christo in dies intímius adhæréntes, in eius regno grátiæ mereámur esse consórtes.

COMMON OF HOLY MEN AND WOMEN,
II. FOR MONKS AND RELIGIOUS, D. FOR RELIGIOUS (1)

Source: MP 4145

MP 4145   *In nat. abbatum, monach., coenobit. et anachoretarum, PC*

Per huius virtutem Sacramenti, quaesumus Domine, tribue nobis beati N. exemplo iugiter in tua dilectione proficere: et opus bonum, quod coepisti in nobis, ipse perficias usque in diem Christi Iesu.

MR(2008)   *II. Pro monachis et religiosis, D. Pro religiosis, 1*

Per huius virtútem sacrménti, quǽsumus, Dómine, ° beáti N. exémplo, **deduc nos** iúgiter in tua dilectióne °, et opus bonum quod cœpísti in nobis ° pérfice usque in diem Christi Iesu.

---

[*] This oration is not in MR(1970) or MR(1975).

COMMON OF HOLY MEN AND WOMEN,
II. FOR MONKS AND RELIGIOUS, D. FOR RELIGIOUS (1)

Source: New composition (see Matthew 6:33; Ephesians 2:15b)

Mt. 6:33

Quaerite autem primum regnum Dei et iustitiam eius, et haec omnia adicientur vobis.

*Eph. 2:15b**

Ut duos condat in semetipso in unum novum hominem, faciens pacem.

MR(2008)   *II. Pro monachis et religiosis, D. Pro religiosis, 2*

Quǽsumus, omnípotens Deus, ut, qui huius sacraménti munímur virtúte, exémplo beáti N., discámus te super ómnia semper inquírere, et novi hóminis formam in hoc sǽculo portáre.

---

* In connection with this passage, see also 2 Corinthians 5:17 (*Si qua ergo in Christo nova creatura, vetera transierunt: ecce facta sunt omnia nova*).

Common of Holy Men and Women,
III. For Those who Practiced Works of Mercy (*opt. 1*)

Source: MP(1841), p. 549

MP(1841)   *Die 19 maii, S. Yvonis, PC*

Sacris mysteriis refectos, da nos, Deus, beati Yvonis Presbyteri exempla sectari, qui indefessa te pietate coluit, et populis immensa caritate profuit.

MR(2008)   *III. Pro iis qui opera misericordia exercuerunt (prima)*

Sacris mystériis reféctos, da nos, **quǽsumus, Dómine,** beáti **N.** exémpla sectári, qui te indeféssa pietáte cóluit, et *pópulo* **tuo** imménsa prófuit caritáte.

Common of Holy Men and Women,
III. For Those who Practiced Works of Mercy (*opt. 2*)

Source: MR 889

MR 889   *Die 20 octobris, S. Ioannis Cantii, PC*

Pretiósi Córporis et Sánguinis tui, Dómine, pasti delíciis, tuam súpplices deprecámur cleméntiam: ut, sancti Ioánnis Confessóris tui méritis et exémplis, eiúsdem caritátis imitatóres effécti, consórtes simus et glóriæ.

MR(2008)   *III. Pro iis qui opera misericordia exercuerunt (altera)*

Sacraménti salutáris, Dómine, pasti delíciis, tuam súpplices deprecámur **pietátem,** ut, **beáti N.** ° caritátis imitatóres effécti, consórtes simus et glóriæ.

COMMON OF HOLY MEN AND WOMEN, IV. FOR EDUCATORS

Source: MR 1139 + Vatican II, *Lumen gentium* 41

MR 1139   *PAL, Plurium Conf. non Pont., PC*

Tríbuat nobis, omnípotens Deus, suffragántibus beatórum N. et N. Confessórum tuórum précibus, reféctio sacra subsídium: ut et castitátis mundítiam observémus in córpore, et lumen veritátis exhibeámus in ópere.

Lum. gent.   *Cap. IV: De laicis, n. 41*

Ita enim exemplum indefessi et generosi amoris omnibus praebent, fraternitatem caritatis aedificant, et foecunditatis Matris Ecclesiae testes et cooperatores exsistunt...

MR(2008)   *IV. Pro educatoribus*

Tríbuat nobis, omnípotens Deus, reféctio sancta subsídium, ut, exémplo *beáti N.,* et *fraternitátis caritátem* et lumen veritátis **in corde** exhibeámus **et** ópere.

COMMON OF HOLY MEN AND WOMEN, V. FOR HOLY WOMEN (1)

Source: MR 478

MR 478   *PAL, Pro neque Martyribus neque Virginibus, PC*

Divíni operátio sacraménti, omnípotens Deus, suffragántibus beatárum N. et N. méritis, illúminet nos páriter et inflámmet: ut et sanctis iúgiter desidériis ferveámus, et bonis opéribus abundémus.

MR(2008)   *V. Pro sanctis mulieribus, 1*

Divíni operátio sacraménti, omnípotens Deus, **in hac festivitáte** *beátæ* N. ° illúminet nos páriter et inflámmet, ut et sanctis iúgiter desidériis ferveámus, et bonis opéribus abundémus.

COMMON OF HOLY MEN AND WOMEN, V. FOR HOLY WOMEN (2)

Source: MR 975 (*CO* 5072)

MR 975   *Dom. VI post Pentecosten, PC*

Repléti sumus, Dómine, munéribus tuis: tríbue, quaesumus; ut eórum et mundémur efféctu, et muniámur auxílio.

MR(2008)   *V. Pro sanctis mulieribus, 2*

Repléti sumus, Dómine, munéribus tuis, **quæ in celebritáte beátæ N. percépimus;** tríbue, quǽsumus, ut eórum et mundémur efféctu, et muniámur auxílio.

RITUAL MASSES

I. Conferral of the Sacraments of Christian Initiation, 1. For the Election or Enrollment of Names

Text is the same as Thursday in Week 4 of Lent, p. 35 above.

I. Conferral of the Sacraments of Christian Initiation, 2. For the Scrutinies, A. First Scrutiny

Source: GeV 198 (*CO* 127)

GeV 198   *Dom. III Quadrag., quae pro scrutino primo, PC*

Adesto, domine, quaesumus, nostri redemptionis affectibus, ut quos sacramentis aeternitatis instities, eosdem protegas dignanter aptandos.

MR(2008)   *I. In conferendis Sacramentis initiationis Christianae,*
                    2. In scrutiniis peragendis, A. In primo scrutino

Adésto, Dómine, quǽsumus, ° redemptiónis **efféctibus**, ut, quos sacraméntis æternitátis instítues, eósdem prótegas dignánter aptándos.

I. Conferral of the Sacraments of Christian Initiation, 2. For the Scrutinies, B. Second Scrutiny

Source: GeV 227 (*CO* 5941)

GeV 227   *Dom. IV Quadrag., quae pro scrutino secundo, PC*

Tu semper, quaesumus, domine, tuam attolle benignus familiam, tu dispone correctam, tu propitius tuere subiectam, tu gubnera perpetua bonitate salvandam.

MR(2008)   *I. In conferendis Sacramentis initiationis Christianae,*
                    2. In scrutiniis peragendis, B. In secondo scrutino

Text is the same as the source above.

I. Conferral of the Sacraments of Christian Initiation, 2. For the Scrutinies, C. Third Scrutiny

Source: GeV 256 (*CO* 788)

GeV 256   *Dom. V Quadrag., quae pro scrutino tertio, PC*

Concurrat, domine, quaesumus, populus tuus et toto tibi corde subiectus obtineat, ut ab omni perturbatione securus et salvationis suae gaudia promptus exerceat et pro regenerandis benignos exoret.

MR(2008)   *I. In conferendis Sacramentis initiationis Christianae,*
                    2. In scrutiniis peragendis, C. In tertio scrutino

Text is the same as the source above.

I. Conferral of the Sacraments of Christian Initiation, 3. For the Conferral of Baptism (A)

Source: New composition

MR(2008)   *I. In conferendis Sacramentis initiationis Christianae,*
                    3. In conferendo Baptismate, A

Præsta, quǽsumus, Dómine, ut, Carnis et Sánguinis Fílii tui prǽditi sacraménto, in communióne Spíritus eius fratrúmque dilectióne ita crescámus, quátenus ad plenam Córporis Christi mensúram caritáte vívida dilatémur.

I. CONFERRAL OF THE SACRAMENTS OF CHRISTIAN INITIATION, 3. FOR THE CONFERRAL OF BAPTISM (B)

Source: New composition

MR(2008) *I. In conferendis Sacramentis initiationis Christianae, 3. In conferendo Baptismate, B*

Præclárum, Dómine, mortis et resurrectiónis Fílii tui mystérium, quod annuntiávimus, celebrándo, fac, ut, per huius sacraménti virtútem, étiam vivéndo fateámur.

I. CONFERRAL OF THE SACRAMENTS OF CHRISTIAN INITIATION, 4. FOR THE CONFERRAL OF CONFIRMATION (A)

Source: New composition

MR(2008) *I. In conferendis Sacramentis initiationis Christianae, 4. In conferenda Confirmatione, A*

Spíritu Sancto, Dómine, perúnctos tuíque Fílii sacraménto nutrítos tua in pósterum benedictióne proséquere, ut, ómnibus adversitátibus superátis, Ecclésiam tuam sanctitáte lætíficent, eiúsque in mundo increménta suis opéribus et caritáte promóveant.

I. CONFERRAL OF THE SACRAMENTS OF CHRISTIAN INITIATION, 4. FOR THE CONFERRAL OF CONFIRMATION (B)

Source: New composition

MR(2008) *I. In conferendis Sacramentis initiationis Christianae, 4. In conferenda Confirmatione, B*

Quos tui Spíritus, Dómine, cumulásti munéribus, tuíque auxísti Unigéniti nutriménto, fac étiam in plenitúdine legis instrúctos, ut coram mundo tuæ libertátem adoptiónis iúgiter maniféstent, et prophéticum tui pópuli munus sua váleant sanctitáte præbére.

I. Conferral of the Sacraments of Christian Initiation, 4. For the Conferral of Confirmation (C)

Source: *See 2nd Sunday* per annum, *p. 59 above*

MR(2008)   *I. In conferendis Sacramentis initiationis Christianae, 4. In conferenda Confirmatione, C*

Spíritum nobis, Dómine, tuæ caritátis infúnde, ut, quos uno pane cælésti satiásti, una fácias pietáte concórdes.

II. For the Conferral of the Anointing of the Sick

Text is the same as Masses and Prayers for Various Needs and Occasions, III.45, p. 188 below.

III. For the Administering of Viaticum

Source: New composition

MR(2008)   *III. Ad ministrandum Viaticum*

Dómine, qui es salus ætérna in te credéntium, præsta, quǽsumus, ut fámulus tuus N., cælésti pane potúque reféctus, in regnum lúminis et vitæ secúrus pervéniat.

IV. For the Conferral of Holy Orders

NB: In MR(1970), the PC is taken, depending on the Order being conferred, from one of the Masses for Various Needs and Occasions for Bishops, Priests, or Ministers. In MR(1975) and MR(2002), the PC orations in the list below are specifically assigned.

1. For the Ordination of a Bishop

Option 1 is used if the newly-ordained Bishop presides at the Liturgy of the Eucharist. Option 2 is used if the principle ordaining Bishop presides.

A. Ordination of One Bishop (1): *See 21st Sunday per annum, p. 67 above*

A. Ordination of One Bishop (2): *See VNO, I.3, p. 167 below*

B. Ordination of Several Bishops (1): *Same as IV.1.A (1)*

B. Ordination of Several Bishops (2): *Same as IV.1.A (2), but in the plural*

2. For the Ordination of Priests

A. Ordination of Several Priests: *See VNO, I.6, p. 169 below*

B. Ordination of One Priest: *Same as IV.2.A*

3. For the Ordination of Deacons

A. Ordination of Several Deacons: *See VNO, I.8, p. 171 below*

B. Ordination of One Deacon: *Same as IV.3.A, but in the singular*

4. For the Ordination of Priests and Deacons in the Same Celebration

Same as IV.3.A

V. For the Celebration of Marriage (A)

Source: MR 936 + MR 1069 (*CO* 4858 + 5521 a)

MR 936   *Missa votivae, Pro sponso et sponsa, PC*

Quaesumus, omnípotens Deus: <u>instittúa providéntiæ tuæ pió favóre comitáre; ut, quos legítima societáte connéctis</u>, longaeva pace custódias.

MR 1069   *Feria VI post Cineres*

Spiritum nobis, <u>Domine</u>, tuae caritatis infunde: ut, quos <u>uno pane caelsti satiasti, tua facias pietate concordes</u>.

MR(2008)   *V. In celebratione Matrimonii, A*

Huius, <u>Dómine</u>, sacrifícii virtúte, <u>instituta providéntiæ tuæ pio favóre comitáre, ut, quos</u> **sancta** <u>societáte</u> **iunxísti** (et <u>uno pane</u> ° unóque cálice <u>satiásti</u>), una étiam <u>fácias</u> **caritáte** <u>concórdes</u>.

V. For the Celebration of Marriage (B)

Source: New composition

MR(2008)   *V. In celebratione Matrimonii, B*

Mensæ tuæ partícipes effécti, quæsumus, Dómine, ut, qui nuptiárum iungúntur sacraménto, tibi semper adhǽreant, et tuum homínibus nomen annúntient.

V. For the Celebration of Marriage (C)

Source: New composition

MR(2008)   *V. In celebratione Matrimonii, C*

Concéde, quæsumus, omnípotens Deus, ut accépti virtus sacraménti in his fámulis tuis sumat augméntum, et hóstiæ quam obtúlimus a nobis ómnibus percipiátur efféctus.

VI. FOR THE BLESSING OF AN ABBOT OR ABBESS[*]

Source: New composition (see *Regula Sancti Benedicti*)

RB, Prol:21, 49; 57:9

Succinctis ergo fide vel observantia bonorum actuum lumbis nostris, <u>per ducatum evangelii pergamus itinera eius</u>, ut mereamur eum qui nos vocavit in regnum suum videre.

Processu vero conversationis et fidei, dilatato corde inenarrabili dilectionis dulcedine <u>curritur via mandatorum Dei</u>.

[U]t <u>in omnibus glorificetur</u> Deus.

MR(2008)   *VI. In benedictione Abbatis vel Abbatissae*

Fámiliam tuam, Dómine, réspice propítius, et nos, qui mystérium fídei celebrávimus, <u>fac per sémitas Evangélii indesinénter cúrrere</u>, <u>in ómnibus te glorificántes</u>.

VII. FOR THE CONSECRATION OF VIRGINS

Source: New composition

MR(2008)   *VII. In consecratione Virginum*

Repléti, Dómine, munéribus sacris, súpplices deprecámur, ut famulárum tuárum N. et N. conversátio et humánæ societátis proféctui constánter fáveat, et ad Ecclésiæ increméntum indesinénter profíciat.

---

[*] This PC is the same for the blessing of an Abbot (formulary 1) and of an Abbess (formulary 2).

160

VIII. For Religious Profession, 1. First Profession

Source: New composition

MR(2008)   *VIII. In professione religiosa, 1. In prima professione*

Lætíficent nos, Dómine, sumpta mystéria et præsta, ut, eórum virtúte, hi fámuli tui inchoáta religiónis múnera fidéliter adímpleant et líberam tibi exhíbeant servitútem.

VIII. For Religious Profession, 2. Perpetual Profession (A)

Source: New composition

MR(2008)   *VIII. In professione religiosa, 2. In professione perpetua, A*

Divínis mystériis veneránter assúmptis, te, Dómine, súpplices deprecámur, ut hos fámulos tuos, sacra tibi oblatióne devínctos, et Sancti Spíritus igne succéndas et Fílio tuo perénni iungas consórtio.

VIII. For Religious Profession, 2. Perpetual Profession (B)

Source: New composition

MR(2008)   *VIII. In professione religiosa, 2. In professione perpetua, B*

Lætíficet nos, Dómine, confirmáti propósiti hodiérna sollémnitas ac divíni sacraménti veneránda percéptio, et concéde propítius, ut gemínátum devotiónis munus famulórum tuórum péctora in Ecclésiæ hominúmque servítium veheménti caritáte compéllat.

VIII. For Religious Profession, 3. Renewal of Vows

Source: New composition

MR(2008)   *VIII. In professione religiosa, 3. In renovatione votorum*

Sumptis, Dómine, cæléstibus sacraméntis, súpplices te rogámus, ut hi fámuli tui, qui, supérna grátia tantum confísi, árdua renovárunt propósita, Christi virtúte roboréntur et Sancti Spíritus muniántur præsídio.

IX. For the Institution of Lectors and Acolytes

Text is the same as Masses and Prayers for Various Needs and Occasions, I.8, p. 171 below.

X. For the Dedication of a Church and Altar, 1. Dedication of a Church

Source: Fulda 2145 (*CO* 3398)

Fulda 2145   *In anniv. dedicationis ecclesiae, PC*

Multiplica, domine, quaesumus, per haec sancta, quae sumpsimus, veritatem tuam in animabus nostris, ut te in templo sancto iugiter adoremus et in conspectu tuo cum sanctis angelis gloriemur.

MR(2008)   *X. In ded. Ecclesiae et Altaris, 1. In ded. Ecclesiae*

Multíplica, Dómine, quǽsumus, per hæc sancta quæ súmpsimus, veritátem tuam in **méntibus** nostris, ut te in templo sancto iúgiter adorémus, et in conspéctu tuo cum **ómnibus** Sanctis ° gloriémur.

X. For the Dedication of a Church and Altar,
2. Dedication of an Altar

Source: New composition

MR(2008)   *X. In ded. Ecclesiae et Altaris, 2. In ded. Altaris*

Da nobis, Dómine, tuis semper altáribus inhærére, ubi sacrifícii sacraméntum celebrátur, ut, fide et caritáte coniúncti, dum Christo refícimur, in Christum transformémur.

MASSES AND PRAYERS FOR
VARIOUS NEEDS AND OCCASIONS

I. For Holy Church, 1. For the Church (A)

Source: New composition*

MR(2008)   *1. Pro Ecclesia, A*

Deus, qui tuis Ecclésiam iúgiter pascis et róboras sacraméntis, concéde nobis mensa cælésti reféctis, ut, caritátis tuæ documéntis obsequéndo, ferméntum vivíficans et salútis instruméntum humáno efficiámur consórtio.

I. For Holy Church, 1. For the Church (B)

Source: New composition†

MR(2008)   *1. Pro Ecclesia, B*

Sacraménto Fílii tui recreáti, te, Dómine, deprecámur, ut Ecclésiæ tuæ operatiónem fecúndes, qua salutáris mystérii plenitúdinem paupéribus contínuo revélas, quos ad tui regni præcípuam vocásti portiónem.

---

* This second half of this PC appears to take inspiration from Vatican II, *Gaudium et spes*, 40: *Ita Ecclesia, insimul « coetus adspectabilis et communitas spiritualis », una cum tota humanitate incedit eamdemque cum mundo sortem terrenam experitur, ac tamquam fermentum et veluti anima societatis humanae in Christo renovandae et in familiam Dei transformandae exsistit* (see also the Collect for VNO, I.1.B, which directly cites this).

† This last part of this PC would seem to be inspired by Matthew 5:3 (*Beati pauperes spiritu: quoniam ipsorum est regnum cælorum*).

I. For Holy Church, 1. For the Church (C)

Source: New composition

MR(2008)   *1. Pro Ecclesia, C*

Deus, qui mirábili sacraménto Ecclésiæ fortitúdinem tríbuis et solámen, da pópulo tuo per hæc sancta Christo adhærére, ut, temporálibus munéribus quæ gerit, tuum in libertáte regnum ædíficet ætérnum.

I. For Holy Church, 1. For the Church (D)

Source: *See 10 November: St Leo the Great, p. 113 above.*

MR(2008)   *1. Pro Ecclesia, D*

Refectióne sancta enutrítam, gubérna, quæsumus, Dómine, tuam placátus Ecclésiam, ut, poténti moderatióne recta, et increménta libertátis accípiat, et in religiónis integritáte persístat.

I. For Holy Church, 1. For the Church, E. Particular Church

Source: MP 4867

MP 4867   *Ad diversa, 8. Pro Ecclesia Parisiensi, PC*

Vigeat in hac Ecclesia tua, Domine, et usque in finem perseveret fidei integritatis, morum sanctitas, sincera pietas, et munda religio: et quam Filii corpore, et verbo tuo pascere non desinis, eam quoque tuis non cesses gubernare praesidiis.

MR(2008)   *1. Pro Ecclesia, E. Pro Ecclesia particulari*

Vígeat in hac Ecclésia tua, Dómine, et usque in finem persevéret fídei intégritas, morum sánctitas, **fratérna cáritas** et munda relígio, et, quam Fílii tui Córpore et verbo tuo páscere non désinis, eam quoque tuis non cesses gubernáre præsídiis.

I. For Holy Church, 2. For the Pope

Source: MP 4864

MP 4864   *Ad diversa, 7. Pro Papa, PC*

Haec nos, quaesumus Domine, divini sacramenti perceptio protegat: et famulum tuum N. quem Ecclesiae tuae praeesse voluisti, una cum commisso sibi grege salvet semper et muniat.

MR(2008)   *2. Pro Papa*

Mensæ cæléstis partícipes effécti, súpplices te, Dómine, **deprecámur, ut, huius virtúte mystérii,** *Ecclésiam tuam* **in unitáte et caritáte confírmes,** et fámulum tuum N., **cui pastorále munus tradidísti,** una cum commísso sibi grege salves semper et múnias.

I. For Holy Church, 3. For the Bishop

Source: MP 4870

MP 4870   *Ad diversa, 9. Pro domino Archiepiscopo, PC*

Huius, Domine, virtute mysterii, in famulo tuo N. Pontifice nostro gratiae tuae dona multiplica: ut et tibi digne persolvat sacerdotale ministerium, et fidelia dispensationis aeterna praemia consequatur.

MR(2008)   *3. Pro Episcopo*

Huius, Dómine, virtúte mystérii, in fámulo tuo N. **epíscopo** nostro grátiæ tuæ dona multíplica, ut et tibi digne persólvat **pastorále** ministérium, et fidélis dispensatiónis ætérna præmia consequátur.

I. For Holy Church, 4. For the Election of a Pope/Bishop

Source: MR 890

MR 890   *Missa votivae, Pro eligendo Summo Pontifice, PC*

Pretiosi corporis et sanguinis tui nos, Domine, sacramento refectos, mirifica tuae maiestatis gratia de ipsius summi Pontificis concessione laetificet: qui et plebe tuam virtutibus instruat, et fidelium mentes spiritualium aromatum odore perfundat.

MR(2008)   *4. Pro eligendo Papa vel Episcopo*

Reféctos, Dómine, ° Córporis et Sánguinis **Unigéniti** tui **salubérrimo** sacraménto, nos mirífica tuæ maiestátis grátia de **illíus pastóris** concessióne lætíficet, qui et *plebem* tuam virtútibus ínstruat, et fidélium mentes **evangélica veritáte** perfúndat.

I. For Holy Church, 5. For a Council/Synod

Source: Fulda 1798 (*CO* 918)

Fulda 1798   *Missa pro synodo, PC*

Da nobis, misericors deus, ut sancta tua, quae sumpsimus, nos in tua voluntate confirment et veritatis ubique praedicatores efficiant.

MR(2008)   *5. Pro concilio vel synodo*

Da °, quǽsumus, miséricors Deus, ut sancta ° quæ súmpsimus **fámulos tuos** in **veritáte** confírment, et **honórem tui nóminis illos fáciant exquírere**.

I. FOR HOLY CHURCH, 6. FOR PRIESTS

Source: MR 788 + MR 1177 (*CO* 3980 + MR 1177)

MR 788   *Orat. diversae, Pro seipso Sacerdote, PC*
Omnípotens sempitérne Deus, qui me peccatórem sacris altáribus astáre
voluísti, et sancti nóminis tui laudáre poténtiam: concéde propítius, per
huius sacraménti mystérium, meórum mihi véniam peccatórum; ut tuæ
maiestáti digne mérear famulári.

MR 1177   *Missa votivae, D.N.I.C. summi et aeterni Sacerdotis, PC*
Vivíficet nos, quaesumus, Dómine, divína quam obtúlimus et súmpsimus
hóstia: ut, perpétua tibi caritáte coniúncti, fructum, qui semper máneat,
afferámus.

MR(2008)   *6. Pro Sacerdotibus*
Sacerdótes tuos, Dómine, et omnes **fámulos tuos** vivíficet divína, quam
obtúlimus et súmpsimus, hóstia, ut, perpétua tibi caritáte coniúncti, digne
famulári tuæ *mereántur* maiestáti.

I. FOR HOLY CHURCH, 7. FOR THE PRIEST HIMSELF,
A. ESPECIALLY FOR A PRIEST WITH THE CARE OF SOULS

Source: MP 5008 (*CO* 3874)

MP 5008   *56. Pro seipso Pastore seu eccl. Rectore, PC*
Omnipotens sempiterne Deus, origo cunctarum perfectioque virtutum, da
nobis quaesumus, huius sanctificatione mysterii, et exercere quae recta
sunt, et praedicare quae vera: ut instructionem gratiae tuae fidelibus, et
agendo praebeamus, et docendo.

MR(2008)   *7. Pro seipso Sac., A. Praes. pro sac. curam anim. gerente*
Omnípotens sempitérne Deus, orígo cunctárum perfectióque virtútum, da
mihi, quǽsumus, huius **participatióne** mystérii, et exercére quæ recta sunt
et prædicáre quæ vera, ut instructiónem grátiæ tuæ fidélibus et agéndo
prǽbeam et docéndo.

I. For Holy Church, 7. For the Priest Himself (B)

Source: New composition*

MR(2008)   *7. Pro seipso Sacerdote, B*

Pane cælésti confirmátum et novi testaménti cálice congaudéntem, fac me, Pater sancte, tibi servíre fidéliter, et in salútem hóminum vitam fórtiter devotéque consúmere.

I. For Holy Church, 7. For the Priest Himself, C. On the Anniversary of his Ordination

Source: Ve 999 (CO 78)†

Ve 999   *Mense septembris, in nat. episcop., VI alia missa, SO*

Ad gloriam, domine, tui nominis annua festa repetentes sacerdotalis exordii, hostiam tibi laudis offerimus, suppliciter exorantes, ut cuius ministerii vice tibi servimus immeriti, suffragiis eius reddamur accepti.

MR(2008)   *7. Pro seipso Sacerdote, C. In anniv. propriae ordinationis*

Ad glóriam, Dómine, tui nóminis ánnua festa répetens sacerdotális exórdii, **mystérium fídei lætánter celebrávi, ut in veritáte hoc sim, quod in sacrifício mýstice tractávi.**

---

* There are a number of possible biblical inspirations for the second half of this PC: e.g., 2 Corinthians 12:15a (*Ego autem libentissime impendam et superimpendar ipse pro animabus vestris*); Philippians 2:7a (*sed semetipsum exinanivit formam servi accipiens*). See also Vatican II, *Presbyterorum ordinis*, 15: [L]*ibentissime impendentes et superimpendentes seipsos in quocumque munere etiam humiliori et pauperiori quod ipsis concreditur.*

† The second half of this PC may have been inspired by Vatican II, *Presbyterorum ordinis*, 13: *Ut Sacrorum ministri, praesertim in Sacrificio Missae, Presbyteri personam specialiter gerunt Christi, qui seipsum ad sanctificandos homines victimam dedit; ideoque invitantur ut quod tractant imitentur, quatenus mortis Dominicae mysterium celebrantes, membra sua a vitiis et concupiscentiis mortificare procurent.*

I. For Holy Church, 8. For Ministers of the Church

Source: New composition

MR(2008)   *8. Pro ministris Ecclesiae*

Concéde fámulis tuis, Dómine, cælésti cibo potúque replétis, ut, ad glóriam tuam et salútem credéntium procurándam, fidéles inveniántur Evangélii, sacramentórum caritatísque minístri.

I. For Holy Church, 9. For Vocations to Holy Orders

Source: New composition*

MR(2008)   *9. Pro vocationibus ad Sacros Ordines*

Pane mensæ cæléstis refécti, te, Dómine, deprecámur, ut, per hoc sacraméntum caritátis, illa sémina maturéscant, quæ magna in agrum Ecclésiæ tuæ largitáte dispérgis, quátenus multi sorte sibi éligant tibi in frátribus ministráre.

---

* This PC may have taken inspiration from Vatican II, *Presbyterorum ordinis*, 22: *Gaudet vero Sacrosancta Synodus quod terra Evangelii semine inseminata nunc multis in locis fructificat sub ductu Spiritus Domini, qui replet orbem terrarum, quique in multorum cordibus sacerdotum atque fidelium spiritum vere missionalem excitavit.*

172

I. For Holy Church, 10. For the Laity

Source: New composition*

MR(2008)   *10. Pro laicis*

De plenitúdine grátiæ tuæ suméntes, quæsumus, Dómine, ut, eucharístici convívii fortitúdine roboráti, fidéles tui, quos rebus sæculáribus déditos esse voluísti, strénui sint evangélicæ testes veritátis, et Ecclésiam tuam in rebus temporálibus præséntem iúgiter reddant et actuósam.

I. For Holy Church, 11. On Anniversaries of Marriage, A. On any Anniversary

Source: New composition

MR(2008)   *11. In anniv. Matrimonii, A. In anniversario*

Supérno cibo potúque reféctis, Dómine, his fámulis tuis in gáudio et caritáte corda diláta, ut sit eórum domus sedes honestátis et pacis, et ómnibus ad consolatiónes páteat caritátis.

---

* This PC would appear to take inspiration from Vatican II, *Lumen gentium*, 31, and *Apostolicam actuositatem*, 2:

    LG, 31: *Laicorum est, ex vocatione propria, res temporales gerendo et secundum Deum ordinando, regnum Dei quaerere… Ibi a Deo vocantur, ut suum proprium munus exercendo, spiritu evangelico ducti, fermenti instar ad mundi sanctificationem velut ab intra conferant, sicque praeprimis testimonio vitae suae, fide, spe et caritate fulgentes, Christum aliis manifestent.*

    AA, 2: *Cum vero laicorum statui hoc sit proprium ut in medio mundi negotiorumque saecularium vitam agant, ipsi a Deo vocantur ut, spiritu christiano ferventes, fermenti instar in mundo apostolatum suum exerceant.*

I. For Holy Church, 11. On Anniversaries of Marriage, B. On the Twenty-Fifth Anniversary

Source: New composition

MR(2008)   *11. In anniv. Matrimonii, B. In XXV anniversario*

Deus, qui ad mensam famíliæ tuæ hos cóniuges N. et N. (cum líberis et amícis) propítius admisísti, da eis fórtiter et alácriter in mútuam communiónem sic prógredi, ut usque ad cæléste convívium, tuo múnere, coniungántur.

I. For Holy Church, 11. On Anniversaries of Marriage, C. On the Fiftieth Anniversary

Source: New composition

MR(2008)   *11. In anniv. Matrimonii, C. In L anniversario*

Mensæ tuæ pasti delíciis, te, Dómine, deprecámur, ut hos cóniuges N. et N. in sancta senectúte custódias, donec ambos, plenos diérum, ad tuum admíttas cæléste convívium.

I. For Holy Church, 12. For the Family

Source: *See Holy Family (Sunday in the Octave of Christmas), p. 15 above*

MR(2008)   *12. Pro familia*

Quos cæléstibus réficis sacraméntis, fac, clementíssime Pater, sanctæ Famíliæ Unigéniti tui exémpla iúgiter imitári, ut, post ærúmnas sǽculi, eius consórtium consequántur ætérnum.

I. For Holy Church, 13. For Religious (A)

Source: MP 5029

MP 5029   *63. Pro congregatione, vel ordine religioso, PC*

Servos tuos, Domine, congregatos in nomine tuo et de uno pane participantes, da unanimes considerare invicem, ut provocationem caritatis et bonorum operum: ut eorum sancta conversatione, Christi bonus odor ubique diffundatur.

MR(2008)   *13. Pro Religiosis, A*

Servos tuos, Dómine, in **amóre** tuo congregátos et de uno pane participántes, da unánimes consideráre ínvicem **in** provocatiónem caritátis et bonórum óperum, ut eórum sancta conversatióne Christi **testes veri** ubíque **exhibeántur.**

I. For Holy Church, 13. For Religious, B. On the Twenty-Fifth or Fiftieth Anniversary of Profession

Source: New composition

MR(2008)   *13. Pro Religiosis, B. In XXV vel L anniv. prof. religiosae*

Súmpsimus, Dómine, Corpus et Sánguinem Fílii tui, quæ in iucúnda celebratióne huius anniversárii contulísti; concéde, quǽsumus, ut frater noster (soror nostra) N., cælésti pane potúque reféctus (refécta), incépti itíneris ad te ducéntis felícem progréssum obtíneat.

I. For Holy Church, 14. For Vocations to Religious Life (*opt. 1*)

Source: New composition

MR(2008)   *14. Pro vocationibus ad vitam Religiosam (prima)*

Fámulos tuos, Dómine, spiritáli cibo potúque confírma, ut, evangélicæ semper vocatióni fidéles, vivam ubíque Fílii tui imáginem repræséntent.

I. For Holy Church, 14. For Vocations to Religious Life (*opt. 2*)*

Source: MR(1962)†

MR(1962)   *17. Ad vocationes religiosas petendas et fovendas, PC*

Huius, Domine, virtute sacramenti, da nobis, quaesumus, perseverantem in tua voluntate famulatum, ut in diebus nostris, et merito et numero, familia tibi serviens augeatur.

MR(2008)   *14. Pro vocationibus ad vitam Religiosam (altera)*

Huius, Dómine, virtúte sacraménti, da nobis, quǽsumus, perseverántem in tua voluntáte famulátum, ut **tuam caritátem mundo testári et bona quæ sola non amittúntur valeámus fórtiter inquírere.**

---

* The rubrics of MR(2008) stipulate that this PC is to be used by a Religious Priest.

† The second half of this PC may have been inspired by Vatican II, *Perfectae caritatis*, 25: *Religiosi ergo omnes fidei integritate, caritate erga Deum et proximum, amore crucis necnon spe futurae gloriae, Christi bonum nuntium in toto mundo diffundant, ut testimonium eorum ab omnibus conspiciatur et Pater noster, qui in caelis est, glorificetur.*

I. For Holy Church, 15. For Promoting Harmony

Source: MP 4855 (*CO* 4368)

MP 4855   4. *Pro pace et unitate Ecclesiae, PC*

Sumpsimus, Domine sacramentum bonitatis, signum unitatis et vinculum caritatis: praesta nobis, quaesumus, sancta unanimitate in domo tua viventibus, pacem habere quam tradimus, pacem servare quam sumimus.

MR(2008)   15. *Pro concordia fovenda*

Súmpsimus, Dómine, sacraméntum **unitátis**; ° præsta nobis, quǽsumus, sancta unanimitáte in domo tua vivéntibus, pacem habére quam trádimus, pacem serváre quam súmimus.

I. For Holy Church, 16. For Reconciliation*

Source: New composition†

MR(2008)   16. *Pro reconciliatione*

Sacraméntum Fílii tui, quod súmpsimus, quǽsumus, Dómine, vires nostras adáugeat, ut, ex hoc unitátis mystério, válidum hauriámus amórem et ubique tuæ pacis operatóres efficiámur.

I. For Holy Church, 17. For the Unity of Christians (A)

Text is the same as 11th Sunday per annum, *p. 63 above.*

---

* This PC is not in MR(1970).

† This PC may have been inspired by Vatican II, *Ad gentes*, 21: *Iungantur concivibus suis sincera caritate, ut in eorum conversatione appareat novum vinculum unitatis et solidarietatis universalis, quae ex mysterio Christi hauritur.*

I. For Holy Church, 17. For the Unity of Christians (B)

Source: *See 2nd Sunday* per annum, *p. 59 above*

MR(2008)   *17. Pro unitate Christianorum, B*

Spíritum nobis, Dómine, tuæ caritátis infúnde, ut, huius sacrifícii virtúte, una fácias in te credéntes pietáte concórdes.

I. For Holy Church, 17. For the Unity of Christians (C)

Source: GeV 625 (*CO* 1192)

GeV 625   *In vigilia Pentecostes, alia, C*

Deus, cuius spiritu totum corpus ecclesiae multiplicatur et regitur, conserva in nova familiae tuae progenie sanctificationis gratiam, quam dedisti, ut corpore et mente renovati in unitatem fidei ferventes tibi domine servire mereantur.

MR(2008)   *17. Pro unitate Christianorum, C*

Sacraménta Christi tui suméntes, quæsumus, Dómine, **ut in** *Ecclésia* **tua** sanctificatiónis grátiam **rénoves** quam dedísti, et **omnes qui christiáno gloriántur nómine** in unitáte fídei ° tibi servíre mereántur.

I. For Holy Church, 18. For the Evangelization of Peoples (A)

Text is the same as 4th Sunday per annum, *p. 60 above.*

I. For Holy Church, 18. For the
Evangelization of Peoples (B)

Source: New composition

MR(2008)   *18. Pro evangelizatione populorum, B*

Sanctíficet nos, quǽsumus. Dómine, mensæ tuæ participátio, et præsta, ut, quam Unigénitus tuus in cruce operátus est salútem, omnes gentes per Ecclésiæ tuæ sacraméntum gratánter accípiant.

I. For Holy Church, 19. For Persecuted Christians

Source: New composition (see Luke 14:27; 1 Peter 4:16; 2 Peter 1:12)

Lk. 14:27

Et, qui non baiulat crucem suam et venit post me, non potest esse meus discipulus.

1 Pet. 4:16

Si autem [patiatur] ut christianus, non erubescat, glorificet autem Deum in isto nomine.

2 Pet. 1:12

Propter quod incipiam vos semper commonere de his, et quidem scientes et confirmatos in praesenti veritate.

MR(2008)   *19. Pro christianae persecutione vexatis*

Per huius sacraménti virtútem fámulos tuos, Dómine, in veritáte confírma, et fidélibus tuis in tribulatióne pósitis concéde, ut, crucem sibi post Fílium tuum baiulántes, christiáno nómine iúgiter váleant inter advérsa gloriári.

I. For Holy Church, 20. For a Spiritual/Pastoral Gathering

Source: MP 3478

MP 3478   *Die 18 septembris, S. Ioannis Chrysostomi, PC*

Da nobis, misericors Deus, interveniente beato Joanne Chrysostomo Pontifice, ut tremenda mysteria quae sumpsimus, nos in tua caritate confirment, et constantes veritatis defensores efficiant.

MR(2008)   *17. Pro unitate Christianorum, C*

Da nobis, miséricors Deus, ° ut **sancta** quæ súmpsimus **et** nos in tua **voluntáte** confírment, et **testes ubíque** veritátis effíciant.

II. For Civil Needs, 25. Beginning of the Civil Year

Source: GeV 248 (*CO* 109)

GeV 248   *Feria VI hebd. IV Quadrag., PC*

Adesto, domine, populis qui sacra mysteria contingerunt, ut nullis periculis affligantur, qui te protectore confidunt.

MR(2008)   *25. Initio anni civilis*

Adésto, Dómine, pópulis, qui sacra mystéria contigérunt, ut **in toto decúrsu huius anni** nullis perículis affligántur, qui **in tua semper** protectióne confídunt.

II. FOR CIVIL NEEDS, 26. SANCTIFICATION OF HUMAN LABOUR (A)

Source: New composition

MR(2008)   *26. Pro humano labore sanctificando, A*

Unitátis et caritátis mensæ partícipes effécti, rogámus, Dómine, cleméntiam tuam, ut, per ópera quæ nobis implénda commisísti, et vitam sustentémus terrénam, et regnum tuum ædificémus fidéntes.

II. FOR CIVIL NEEDS, 26. SANCTIFICATION OF HUMAN LABOUR (B)

Source: MR 577 (*CO 2779*)

MR 577   *Orat. diversae, temporis famis, PC*

Gubérna, quaesumus, Dómine, temporálibus aliméntis: quos dignáris ætérnis informáre mystériis.

MR(2008)   *26. Pro humano labore sanctificando, B*

Gubérna, quǽsumus, Dómine, temporálibus **adiuméntis** quos dignáris ætérnis **recreáre** mystériis.

II. FOR CIVIL NEEDS, 27. AT SEED TIME (A)

Source: New composition (see Acts 17:28)

Acts 17:28

In ipso enim vivimus et movemur et sumus, sicut et quidam vestrum poetarum dixerunt: « Ipsius enim et genus sumus ».

MR(2008)   *27. In agris conserendis, A*

Qui tuis nos, Dómine, réficis sacraméntis, mánuum nostrárum adésto labóribus, ut, qui in te vívimus, movémur et sumus, terræ semínibus benedictióne concéssa de segétibus multiplicátis nutriámur.

II. FOR CIVIL NEEDS, 27. AT SEED TIME (B)

Source: MP 4969

MR 4969   *43. Pro fructibus terris, PC*

Largire fidelibus tuis, omnipotens Deus, congruam terrae fructum ubertatem; quibus temporaliter enutriti, ad aeterna bona capessenda, spiritualibus incrementis proficiant.

MR(2008)   *27. In agris conserendis, B*

Concéde fidélibus tuis, omnípotens Deus, cóngruam terræ frúctuum **largitátem**, quibus temporáliter enutríti, spiritálibus **quoque** profícient increméntis, **ut, quorum in hoc sacraménto pignus accepérunt,** bona **consequántur** ætérna.

II. FOR CIVIL NEEDS, 28. AFTER THE HARVEST

Source: MP 4686

MR 4969   *44. Pro collectos terrae fructus, PC*

Da, quaesumus Domine, ut de perceptis terrae fructibus hoc salutari gratias exhibentes, eodem operante in nobis, bona potiora consequi mereamur.

MR(2008)   *28. Post collectos fructus terrae*

Da, quǽsumus, Dómine, ut de percéptis terræ frúctibus hoc salutári **mystério tibi** grátias exhibéntes, eódem operánte in nobis, bona potióra cónsequi mereámur.

II. FOR CIVIL NEEDS, 29. FOR THE PROGRESS OF PEOPLES

Source: New composition (see Vatican II, *Gaudium et spes*, 72)

GS 72   *Cap. III, sectio II*

Quicumque Christo obediens, primum quaerit Regnum Dei, inde validiorem ac puriorem amorem suscipit, ad omnes fratres suos adiuvandos et ad opus iustitiae, inspirante caritate, perficiendum.

MR(2008)   *29. Pro populorum progressione*

Uno pane refécti, quo humánam famíliam iúgiter instáuras, quǽsumus. Dómine, ut, ex unitátis participatióne saraménti, válidum et purum hauriámus amórem ad progrediéntes pópulos iuvándos, et ad opus iustítiæ, inspiránte caritáte, perficiéndum.

II. FOR CIVIL NEEDS, 30. PRESERVATION OF PEACE & JUSTICE (A)

Source: New composition

MR(2008)   *30. Pro pace et iustitia servanda, A*

Largíre nobis, quǽsumus, Dómine, spíritum caritátis, ut, Córpore et Sánguine Unigéniti tui vegetáti, pacem inter omnes, quam ipse relíquit, efficáciter nutriámus.

II. For Civil Needs, 31. In Time of War/Civil Disturbance

Source: New composition*

MR(2008)   *31. Tempore belli vel eversionis*

Uno pane, qui cor hóminis confírmat, suáviter satiátis, da nobis, Dómine, et belli furóres superáre felíciter, et tuam amóris ac iustítiæ legem fírmiter custodíre.

II. For Civil Needs, 32. For Refugees/Exiles

Source: New composition

MR(2008)   *32. Pro profugis et exsulibus*

Dómine, qui nos uno pane et uno cálice refecísti, da nobis humanitátem in ádvenas ac derelíctos sincéro corde sectári, ut omnes in terra vivéntium congregári dénique mereámur.

---

* This PC appears influenced by Vatican II, *Gaudium et spes*, 77: *Ideo Concilium veram et nobilissimam pacis rationem illustrans, belli immanitate damnata, christianos ferventer evocare intendit ut, auxiliante Christo auctore pacis, cum omnibus hominibus ad pacem in iustitia et amore inter eos firmandam et ad instrumenta pacis apparanda cooperentur.*

II. FOR CIVIL NEEDS, 33. IN TIME OF FAMINE/FOR THOSE SUFFERING HUNGER (A)

Source: New composition (see John 6:51a)

Jn. 6:51a

Ego sum panis vivus, qui de caelo descendi.

MR(2008)   *33. Tempore famis vel pro fame laborantibus, A*

Deus, Pater omnípotens, súpplices te rogámus, ut panis vivus, qui de cælo descéndit, ad fratres ínopes nos róboret sublevándos.

II. FOR CIVIL NEEDS, 33. IN TIME OF FAMINE/FOR THOSE SUFFERING HUNGER (B)

Source: New composition

MR(2008)   *33. Tempore famis vel pro fame laborantibus, B*

Qui cibum cæléstem. Dómine, a tua largitáte suscépimus, quæsumus, ut spem nobis et robur sic cónferat ad labórem, ut efficáciter nostris fratrúmque necessitátibus subveníre possímus.

III. For Various Occasions, 38. Forgiveness of Sins (A)

Source: MR 835 + MR 762 (*CO* 4381 b + 3837)

MR 835   *Missa votivae, Pro remissione peccatorum, PC*

<u>Praesta nobis</u>, aeterne Salvator: <u>ut percipientes hoc munere veniam peccatorum, deinceps peccata vitemus</u>.

MR 762   *Dom. infra octavam Ascensionis, C*

Omnipotens sempiterne Deus: fac nos tibi semper et devotam gerere voluntatem; <u>et maiestati tuae sincero corde servire</u>.

MR(2008)   *38. Pro remissione peccatorum, A*

<u>Præsta nobis</u>, miséricors Deus, <u>ut, percipiéntes hoc múnere véniam peccatórum</u>, **illa** deínceps *vitáre* tua grátia valeámus, <u>et ° tibi sincéro corde servíre</u>.

III. For Various Occasions, 38. Forgiveness of Sins (B)[*]

Source: MR 574 (*CO* 2747)

MR 574   *Orat. diversae, Pro petitione lacrimarum, PC[†]*

Gratiam Spiritus Sancti, Domine Deus, cordibus nostris clementer infunde: quae nos gemitibus lacrimarum efficiat maculas nostrorum diluere peccatorum; atque optatae nobis, te largiente, indulgentiae praestet effectum.

MR(2008)   *38. Pro remissione peccatorum, B*

Tui, Dómine, **sacraménti veneránda percéptio fáciat** nos gemítibus lacrimárum ° máculas nostrórum dilúere peccatórum atque optátæ nobis, te largiénte, indulgéntiæ præstet efféctum.

---

[*] This PC is not in MR(1970) or MR(1975).

[†] In MR(1962), this title of this Mass is *Ad petendam compunctionem cordis*.

III. For Various Occasions, 39. For Chastity[*]

Source: MR 484 + MR 878 (*CO* 2264 + 4374)

MR 484   *Orat. diversae, Ad postulandam contintentiam, PC*

Domine, adiutor et protector noster, adiuva nos: et refloreat cor et caro nostra vigore pudicitiae, et castimoniae novitate; ut per hoc sacrificium, quod tuae obtulimus pietati, ab omnibus tentationibus emundemur.

MR 878   *Feria II post Dom III Quadrag., PC*

Praesta, quaesumus, omnipotens et misericors Deus: ut, quod ore contingimus, pura mente capiamus.

MR(2008)   *39. Ad postulandam continentiam*

Percépta nobis sacraménta, quæ súmpsimus, Dómine, reflóreat cor et caro nostra vigóre pudicítiæ et castimóniæ novitáte, ut, quod ore contíngimus, pura mente capiámus.

III. For Various Occasions, 40. For Charity

Source: New composition

MR(2008)   *40. Ad postulandam caritatem*

Quos uno pane cælésti satiásti, quæsumus. Dómine, ut Sancti Spíritus grátia perfúndas, et abundánter refícias perféctæ dulcédine caritátis.

---

[*] This PC is not in MR(1970) or MR(1975).

III. For Various Occasions, 41. For Relatives and Friends

Source: MR 156 (*CO* 887)

MR 156   *Orat. diversae, Pro omni gradu Ecclesiae, SO*

Da famulis tuis, Domine, indulgentiam peccatorum, consolationem vitae, gubernationem perpetuam: ut, tibi servientes, ad tuam iugiter misericordiam pervenire mereantur.

MR(2008)   *41. Pro familiaribus et amicis*

Te quǽsumus, Dómine, **suméntes divína mystéria,** ut fámulis tuis, **quibus dedísti in nos caritátem,** indulgéntiam **tríbuas** peccatórum, consolatiónem vitæ *gubernationémque* perpétuam, **quátenus nos omnes,** tibi **unánimes** serviéntes, **ante fáciem** tuam **congaudéntes** perveníre mereámur.

III. For Various Occasions, 42. For our Oppressors

Source: MP 5014

MP 5014   *Orat. diversae, 58. Pro inimicis, aut persequentibus, PC*

Per haec pacis nostrae mysteria da nos, Deus, cum his, qui oderunt pacem, esse pacificos: et eos, qui nobis adversantur, tibi gratos effice, nobisque placatos.

MR(2008)   *42. Pro affligentibus nos*

Per hæc pacis nostræ mystéria, da nos, Deus, cum ° **ómnibus** esse pacíficos, et eos qui nobis adversántur tibi gratos *efficere*, nobísque placátos.

III. FOR VARIOUS OCCASIONS, 43. FOR THOSE HELD IN CAPTIVITY

Source: MP 5053

MP 5053   *Orat. diversae, 71. Pro captivis, aut detentis in carcere, PC*

Sumpto, Domine, nostrae pretio libertatis, tuam pro captivis imploramus clementiam; ut et a corporis vinculis solvantur, et liberati a peccato, servi fiant iustitiae.

MR(2008)   *43. Pro captivitate detentis*

° Nostræ libertátis *prétium* **recoléntes**, tuam, Dómine, pro **frátribus nostris** implorámus cleméntiam, ut ° a ° vínculis solvántur, et ° servi fiant iustítiæ **tuæ**.

III. FOR VARIOUS OCCASIONS, 45. FOR THE SICK

Source: MR 234 (*CO* 1259)

MR 234   *Missa votivae, pro infirmis, PC*

Deus, infirmitátis humánæ singuláre præsídium: auxílii tui super infírmos fámulos tuos osténde virtútem; ut, ope misericórdiæ tuæ adiúti, Ecclésiæ tuæ sanctæ incólumes repræsentári mereántur.

MR(2008)   *45. Pro infirmis*

Text is the same as the source above.

III. For Various Occasions, 46. For the Dying

Source: MR 926

MR 926   *Missa votivae, pro infirmo qui proximus est morti, PC*

Quaesumus clementiam tuam, omnipotens Deus, ut per huius virtutem sacramenti famulum tuum gratia tua confirmare digneris: ut in hora mortis eius non praevaleat contra eum adversarius; sed cum Angelis tuis transitum habere mereatur ad vitam.

MR(2008)   *46. Pro morientibus*

° Per huius, **Dómine,** sacraménti virtútem, fámulum tuum **dignáre** *cleménter* tua grátia **sustinére,** ut in hora mortis contra **se inimícum** prævalére non **vídeat,** sed cum Angelis tuis tránsitum habére mereátur ad vitam.

III. For Various Occasions, 47. Grace of a Happy Death

Source: New composition

MR(2008)   *47. Ad postulandam gratiam bene moriendi*

Immortalitátis pígnora, Dómine, per hæc mystéria consecúti, pro nostræ mortis éxito pietátis tuæ auxílium súpplices implorámus, ut, inimíci superátis insídiis, in sinu glóriæ tuæ reficiámur ætérnæ.

III. For Various Occasions, 48. In Any Need (A)[*]

Text is the same as Monday in Week 1 of Lent, p. 25 above

---

[*] This Mass formulary is not in MR(1970) or MR(1975).

III. For Various Occasions, 48. In Any Need (B)

Source: New composition

MR(2008)   *48. In quacumque necessitate, B*

Te súpplices, Dómine, exorámus, ut, dápibus recreáti munitíque divínis, et futúros labóres fórtiter ággredi valeámus, et fratres in pressúra pósitos impénsius confirmémus.

III. For Various Occasions, 48. In Any Need (C)

Source: MR 1142 (*CO* 5934)

MR 1142   *Orat. diversae, Pro quacumque tribulatione, PC*

Tribulatiónem nostram, quaesumus, Dómine, propítius réspice: et iram tuæ indignatiónis, quam iuste merémur, avérte.

MR(2008)   *48. In quacumque necessitate, C*

Tribulatiónem nostram, quǽsumus, Dómine, propítius réspice, et iram tuæ indignatiónis, quam **pro peccátis nostris** iuste merémur, **per passiónem Fílii tui, propitiátus** avérte.

III. For Various Occasions, 49. For Giving Thanks to God (A)

Source: New composition

MR(2008)   *49. Pro gratiis Deo reddendis, A*

Omnípotens Deus, qui per hunc panem vitæ fámulos tuos et peccáti vínculo liberáre et vires eórum dignáris tua pietáte refícere, da nobis in spem glóriæ sine intermissióne profícere.

III. FOR VARIOUS OCCASIONS, 49. FOR GIVING THANKS TO GOD (B)

Source: New composition

MR(2008)   *49. Pro gratiis Deo reddendis, B*

Deus, qui nobis in cibum spiritálem reddidísti Fílii tui sacraméntum salutáre, quod tibi in actiónem obtúlimus gratiárum, da nobis ita virtútis et gáudii munéribus confirmári, ut tibi servíre devótius et nova benefícia cónsequi mereámur.

VOTIVE MASSES

1. The Most Holy Trinity

Text is the same as Trinity Sunday, p. 75 above.

2. The Mercy of God*

Source: New composition

MR(2008)   *2. De Dei misericordia*

Concéde nobis, miséricors Deus, ut Córpore et Sánguine Fílii tui enutríti, fiduciáliter e misericórdiæ fóntibus hauriámus et in fratres magis magísque misericórdes nosmetípsos præbeámus.

3. Our Lord Jesus Christ, Eternal High Priest†

Source: MP 4364

MP 4364   *Missa votivae, De Ss. Sacramento, PC*

Quaesumus, Domine, ut huius participatione sacrificii quod in tui commemorationem offerri praecepisti, nos ipsos tecum holacaustum facias sempiternum.

MR(2008)   *3. De D.N.I.C. Summo et Aeterno Sacerdote*

Quǽsumus, Dómine, ut, huius participatióne sacrifícii, quod in **sui** commemoratiónem **Fílius tuus præcépit** offérri, *nosmetípsos* **cum illo oblatiónem** fácias **tibi** sempitérnam.

---

* This PC is not in MR(1970) or MR(1975).

† In MR(1970) and MR(1975), this is the Votive Mass of the Most Holy Eucharist (B), with the option of celebrating it as a Votive Mass of O.L.J.C., Eternal High Priest.

4. The Mystery of the Holy Cross

Text is the same as 14 September: Exaltation of the Holy Cross, p. 102 above.

5. The Most Holy Eucharist

Source: LMS 1378 (*CO* 6501)

LMS 1378   *Ad orationem Dominicam*

Accepturi, fratres carissimi, intra mortalia uiscera celeste sacrificium, et intra cubiculum humani pectoris hospitem Deum, mundemus conscientias nostras ab omni labe uitiorum: ut nihil sit in nobis subdolum et superbum, sed in humilitatis studium et caritatis assensum per escam et sanguinem Domini corporis fraternitas copuletur, ut cum magna fiducia dicere mereamur.

MR(2008)   *5. De Ss.ma Eucharistia*

Sanctíficet nos, quǽsumus, Dómine, mensæ cæléstis participátio, ut, per ° Corpus et Sánguinem **Christi**, fratérnitas **cuncta** copulétur.

6. The Most Holy Name of Jesus

Source: MP 4340

MP 4340   *Missa votivae, De Ss. nomine Iesu, PC*

Praesta, quaesumus, misericors Deus, ut in his tremendis mysteriis Dominum nostrum Jesum Christum dignis obsequiis veneremur, in cuius nomine omne genu flecti voluisti.

MR(2008)   *6. De Ss.mo nomine Iesu*

Tua nobis, quǽsumus, **Dómine, miseratióne concéde**, ut in his **sacris** mystériis Dóminum ° Iesum ° dignis obséquiis venerémur, in cuius nómine voluísti omne genu flecti, **omnésque hómines inveníre salútem**.

7. THE MOST PRECIOUS BLOOS OF OUR LORD JESUS CHRIST (*opt. 1*)

Source: MR 21*

MR 21   *Missa votivae, De Ss. nomine Iesu, PC*

Ad sacram, Domine, mensam admissi, hausimus aquas in gaudio de fontibus Salvatoris: sanguis eius fiat nobis, quaesumus, fons aquae in vitam aeternam salientis.

MR(2008)   *7. De Pretiosissimo Sanguine D.N.I.C (prima)*

Cibo refécti, Dómine, **potúque salútis,** Salvatóris **nostri,** quǽsumus, **semper Sánguine perfundámur, qui** fons aquæ nobis fiat in vitam saliéntis ætérnam.

7. THE MOST PRECIOUS BLOOS OF OUR LORD JESUS CHRIST (*opt. 2*)

Source: MP 4993

MP 4993   *Dom. proxima post S. Petri ad Vincula, in suscep. S. Crucis, PC*

Refecti cibo potuque coelesti, quaesumus omnipotens Deus, ut ab hostium nos defendas formidine, quos redemisti pretioso sanguine Filii tui Domine nostri Jesu Christi.

MR(2008)   *7. De Pretiosissimo Sanguine D.N.I.C (altera)*

Refécti cibo potúque cælésti, quǽsumus, omnípotens Deus, ut ab hóstium ° deféndas formídine, quos pretióso Fílii tui Sánguine redemísti °.

---

* See also John 4:14 (*sed aqua quam ego dabo ei, fiet in eo fons aquæ salientis in vitam æternam*).

8. The Most Sacred Heart of Jesus

Source: MP 4470

MP 4470   *Missa de Ss. Corde D.N.I.C., temp. Septuag. et Quadrag., PC*

Quos pretiosi corporis ac sanguinis tui, Domine, participes effecisti; praesta, ut divini Cordis tui passionibus communicantes in terris, ejusdem gaudiis perfrui mereamur in coelis.

MR(2008)   *8. De Ss. Corde Iesu*

° Tui **sacraménti caritátis** partícipes *effécti*, **cleméntiam tuam,** Dómine, **supplíciter implorámus**, ut **Christo conformémur** in terris, **et** *eius* **glóriæ consórtes fíeri** mereámur in cælis.

9. The Holy Spirit (A)

Source: MR 1034 (*CO* 5351 b)

MR 1034   *Sabbato in vig. Pentecostes, PC*

Sancti Spiritus, Domine, corda nostra mundet infusio: et sui roris intima aspersione foecundet.

MR(2008)   *9. De Spiritu Sancto, A*

Text is the same as the source above, with the exception of the slight variation in spelling of fecundet.

9. The Holy Spirit (B)

Source: Ve 870 (*CO* 2283)

Ve 870   *Mense septembris, orat. et preces mensis septimi, II alia missa, PC*

Domine deus noster, qui nos vegetare dignatus es caelestibus alimentis: suavitatem verbi tui penetralibus nostri cordis infunde; ut quae temporali devotione percepimus, sempiterno munere capiamus.

MR(2008)   *9. De Sancto Spiritu, B*

Dómine Deus noster, qui nos vegetáre dignátus es cæléstibus aliméntis, suavitátem **Spíritus** tui penetrálibus nostri cordis infúnde, ut, quæ temporáli devotióne percépimus, sempitérno múnere capiámus.

9. The Holy Spirit (C)

Text is the same as Pentecost Vigil, p. 56 above.

10. The Blessed Virgin Mary (A)

Any Mass from the Common of the Blessed Virgin Mary (see pp. 122-126 above) is used, in accordance with the various times of the year.

10. The Blessed Virgin Mary,
B. Our Lady, Mother of the Church

Source: New composition (= *CMBMV, 25.I, Imago et Mater Ecclesiae*)

MR(2008)   *10. De B.M.V., B. De beata Maria Ecclesiae Matre*

Sumpto, Dómine, pígnore redemptiónis et vitæ, súpplices adprecámur, ut Ecclésia tua, matérna Vírginis ope, et Evangélii præcónio univérsas gentes erúdiat et Spíritus effusióne orbem terrárum adímpleat.

10. THE BLESSED VIRGIN MARY, C. MOST HOLY NAME OF MARY*

Source: Soc.M 12/09 + MR 336 (Soc.M 12/09 + CO 1582)

Soc.M 12/09   *Die 12 septembris, Ss.mi nominis Mariae, PC*

Tribue nobis, quaesumus, Domine, quos ad verbi et sacramenti mensam
roborasti, ut, beatae Mariae vestigiis inhaerentes ignoti simus et quasi
occulti in hoc mundo et ita in nobis Christus ipse hominibus appareat.

MR 336   *Dom. III post Pascha, C*

Deus, qui errantibus, ut in viam possint redire iustitiae, veritatis tuae
lumen ostendis: da cunctis qui christiana professione censentur, et illa
respuere, quae huic inimica sunt nomini; et ea quae sunt apta, sectari.

MR(2008)   *10. De B.M.V., C. De sanctissimo Nomine Mariae*

Tríbue nobis, quæsumus, Dómine, quos ad verbi et sacraménti mensam
roborásti, ut, beátæ Maríæ ductu et patrocínio, et illa respuámus, quæ
christiáno inimíca sunt nómini et ea, quæ sunt apta, sectémur.

---

* This PC is identical to that of CMBMV, 21, *Sanctum nomen B.M.V.*

10. The Blessed Virgin Mary, D. Our Lady, Queen of Apostles

Source: SAC, p. 6*

SAC   *B.M.V. regina Apostolorum, PC*

Sumptis salutis nostrae subsidiis in festivitate beatae Mariae Virginis ac Reginae Apostolorum, te Domine, deprecamur, ut in tua voluntate servitioque hominum perseverans, populus tuus semper proficiat ad salutem.

MR(2008)   *10. De B.M.V., D. Regina Apostolorum*

Súmptis, Domine, salútis nostræ subsídiis in **memória** beátæ Maríæ Vírginis, Apostolórum regínæ, te **súpplices**, deprecámur, ut in tua voluntáte **et in** hóminum *servítio* persevérans, pópulus tuus semper profíciat ad salútem.

11. The Holy Angels

Source: *See 29 September, Ss Michael, Gabriel & Raphael, p. 105 above.*

MR(2008)   *11. De sanctis Angelis*

Pane cælésti reféacti, súpplices te, Dómine, deprecámur, ut, eius fortitúdine roboráti, sub Angelórum fidéli custódia, fortes, salútis progrediámur in via.

12. St John the Baptist

Text is the same as 24 June, Vigil of the Nativity of St John the Baptist, p. 90 above.

---

* See CMBMV, 18, *B.M.V., Regina Apostolorum*, which has minor differences to MR(2008): *Sumptis salútis nostræ subsídiis... te, Dómine, deprecámur...*

13. St Joseph

Source: New composition (see Matthew 1:19)

Mt. 1:19

Ioseph autem <u>vir</u> eius, cum esset <u>iustus</u> et nollet eam traducere, voluit occulte dimittere eam.

MR(2008)   *13. De S. Ioseph*

His recreáti, Dómine, vivíficis sacraméntis, in iustítia tibi semper et sanctitáte vivámus, beáti Ioseph exémplo et intercessióne, qui magnis tuis perficiéndis mystériis <u>vir iustus</u> et obœ́diens ministrávit.

14. All the Holy Apostles

Source: MP 4423*

MP 4423   *Missa votivae de S. Apostolis omnibus, extra temp. paschali, PC*

Fac nos, Deus, cum exultatione et simplicitate cordis, perseverare in doctrina Apostolorum et communicatione fractionis panis et orationibus.

MR(2008)   *14. De omnibus sanctis Apostolis*

Fac nos, Deus, cum exsultatióne et simplicitáte cordis perseveráre in doctrína Apostolórum, **in** fractióne panis communicántes et oratiónibus.

15. Ss Peter & Paul, Apostles

Text is the same as 29 June, Vigil of Ss Peter & Paul, p. 92 above.

---

* See also Acts 2:42 (*Erant autem perseverantes in doctrina Apostolorum, et communicatione fractionis panis, et orationibus*).

16. St Peter, Apostle

Source: New composition (see John 6:68)*

Jn. 6:68

Respondit ei Simon Petrus: « Domine, ad quem ibimus? <u>Verba vitae aeternae habes</u> ».

MR(2008)   *16. De S. Petro*

Ad convívium, Dómine, salútis admíssi, beáti Petri apóstoli memóriam veterántes, gratánter expóscimus, ut Fílio tuo, <u>qui solus verba vitæ habet</u>, iúgiter hæreámus, quátenus oves gregis tui fidéles ad páscua felíciter deducámur ætérna.

17. St Paul, Apostle

Source: New composition (see Philippians 1:21; Romans 8:35a)

Phil. 1:21

Mihi enim <u>vivere Christus est</u> et mori lucrum.

Rom. 8:35a

Quis nos <u>separabit a caritate</u> Christi?

MR(2008)   *17. De S. Paulo*

Córporis et Sánguinis Fílii tui, Dómine, communióne reféctis, concéde, ut ipse <u>Christus sit nobis vívere</u>, nihílque ab eius nos <u>séparet caritáte</u>, et, beáto monénte Apóstolo, in dilectióne cum frátribus ambulémus.

---

* Verse 69 in the Clementine Vulgate.

18. One Holy Apostle[*]

Source: *See Common of Pastors, IV.A, p. 137 above*

MR(2008)   *18. De quovis S. Apostolo*

Súmpsimus, Dómine, pignus salútis ætérnæ, memóriam beáti N. apóstoli celebrántes, quod sit nobis, quǽsumus, vitæ præséntis auxílium páriter et futúræ.

19. All Saints

Source: MP 4471

MP 4471   *Missa votiva, de uno vel pluribus Sanctis, PC*

Deus, qui nos uno pane reficis, et una spe sustentas; tua nos pariter gratia corrobora: ut omnes cum sanctis tuis unum in Christo Corpus, et unus spiritus; cum ipsis ad gloriam in eodem Christo resurgamus.

MR(2008)   *19. De omnibus Sanctis*

Deus, qui nos uno pane réficis et una spe susténtas, tua nos páriter grátia corróbora, ut omnes, cum Sanctis tuis unum in Christo corpus et unus spíritus, ad glóriam cum *ipso* ° resurgámus.

---

[*] The rubrics of MR(2008) stipulate that, normally, the Mass of the particular Apostle is said; e.g. to celebrate a Votive Mass of St Barnabas, one would use the texts that are assigned to his feast day on 11 June. However, if the Apostle is honored together with another (e.g. 3 May, Ss Philip & James), and the texts of that Mass are not considered appropriate, then this Votive Mass is used.

MASSES FOR THE DEAD

I. For the Funeral, A. Outside Easter Time

Source: St Peter Chrysologus, *Sermon* 68

S. Pet. Chrys.   *Sermo 68 (PL 52:395)*

Sed quotidianum et in diem vult <u>nos in sacramento sui corporis panis viaticum postulare</u>, ut hoc ad perpetuam diem <u>et ipsam Christi perveniamus ad mensam</u>, ut unde hic hustum sumpsimus inde ibi plenitudinem totasque satieates capiamus.

MR(2008)   *I. In exsequiis, A. Extra tempus paschale*

Dómine Deus, cuius Fílius <u>in sacraménto Córporis sui viáticum **nobis** relíquit</u>, concéde propítius, ut per hoc frater noster N. **ad** ipsam Christi <u>*pervéniat* mensam</u> **ætérnam**.

I. For the Funeral, B. Outside Easter Time

Source: MR(1962) (*CO* 4342 b)

MR(1962)   *In die obitus seu depositionis defunct., PC*

Præsta, quaesumus, omnípotens Deus, ut ánima fámuli tui N. (fámulæ tuæ N.), quæ hódie de hoc saeculo migrávit, his sacrifíciis purgáta et a peccátis expedíta, indulgéntiam páriter et réquiem cápiat sempitérnam.

MR(2008)   *I. In exsequiis, B. Extra tempus paschale*

Præsta, quǽsumus, omnípotens Deus, ut ° *fámulus tuus* N., *qui* (hódie) de hoc sǽculo migrávit, his sacrifíciis *purgátus* et a peccátis *expedítus*, **resurrectiónis suscípiat gáudia** *sempitérna*.

I. For the Funeral, C. During Easter Time

Soucre: *See 2 November, All Souls (1st Mass), p. 110 above.*

MR(2008)   *I. In exsequiis, C. Tempore paschali*

Præsta, quǽsumus, Dómine, ut fámulus tuus N. in mansiónem lucis tránseat et pacis, pro quo paschále celebrávimus sacraméntum.

I. For the Funeral, D. Other Prayers

Source: *See 2 November, All Souls (2nd Mass), p. 111 above.*

MR(2008)   *I. In exsequiis, D. Aliae orationes*

Sumpto sacraménto Unigéniti tui, qui pro nobis immolátus resurréxit in glória, te, Dómine, suppliciter exorámus pro fámulo tuo N., ut, paschálibus mystériis mundátus, futúræ resurrectiónis múnere gloriétur.

I. For the Funeral, E. Funeral of a Baptised Child (1)

Source: New composition

MR(2008)   *I. In exsequiis, E. In exsequiis parvuli baptizati, 1*

Córporis, Dómine, et Sánguinis Fílii tui communióne percépta, te fidéliter deprecámur, ut, quos in spem vitæ ætérnæ sacris dignátus es nutríre mystériis, in huius tríbuas vitæ mæróribus confortári.

I. For the Funeral, E. Funeral of a Baptised Child (2)

Source: New composition

MR(2008)   *I. In exsequiis, E. In exsequiis parvuli baptizati, 2*

Divíno múnere satiáti, te, Dómine, deprecámur, ut, qui hunc infántem ad mensam tríbuís regni cæléstis acctúmbere, eándem et nos participáre concédas.

I. For the Funeral, F. Funeral of a Child Who Died before Baptism

Text is the same as Masses for the Dead, I.E.1, p. 208 above.

II. On the Anniversary, A. Outside Easter Time

Source: Ve 55 + OV 884 (*CO* 5249 + OV 884)

Ve 55   *Mense aprilis, XVII alia missa, PC*

<u>Sacris reparati mysteriis, suppliciter exoramus</u>, ut intervenientibus sanctis tuis, apprehendamus rebus effectu, quod actionibus celebramus affectu.

OV 884   *De Resurrectione, III feria, item in eodem die, ad Vesperum*

Omnipotens Deus pater, qui die tertio ab infidelium cordibus, quasi ab inferioribus salsis aquis aridam, id est populum fontem fidei sitientem, segregare dignatus es: da nobis, ut, ab infidelium laqueis segregati, resurrectionem filii tui praedicemus indubii; ut, qui tertio ab inferis suscitatus est die, trina nos virtutem copulatione resuscitet, quo fide, spe, et caritate robusti, de <u>aeterno resurrectionis mereamur munere consolari</u>.

MR(2008)   *II. In anniversario, A. Extra tempus paschale*

<u>Sacris reparáti mystériis</u>, **te, Dómine,** <u>supplíciter exorámus</u>, ut fámulus tuus N., a delíctis ómnibus emundátus, <u>ætérno resurrectiónis múnere</u> **ditári** <u>mereátur</u>.

II. On the Anniversary, B. Outside Easter Time

Source: MR 1117 (CO 5754)

MR 1117   *Missa defunct., in die tertio, septimo et trigesimo dep., PC*

Súscipe, Dómine, preces nostras pro ánima fámuli tui N. (fámulæ tuæ N.): ut, si quæ ei máculæ de terrénis contágiis adhæsérunt, remissiónis tuæ misericórdia deleántur.

MR(2008)   *II. In anniversario, B. Extra tempus paschale*

Précibus nostris **et sacrifíciis**, Dómine, pro ánima fámuli tui N. **benígne** suscéptis, **te súpplices deprecámur,** ut, si quæ ei máculæ **peccáti** adhæsérunt, remissiónis tuæ misericórdia deleántur.

II. On the Anniversary, C. During Easter Time

See 2 November, All Souls (2nd Mass), p. 111 above; text is the same as Masses for the Dead, I.D, p. 208 above.

II. On the Anniversary, D. Other Prayers

Source: Ve 34 + OV 465 (*CO* 5068 + OV 465)

Ve 34   *Mense aprilis, XIII alia missa, PC*

Repleti substantia reparationis et vitae quaesumus, domine deus noster, ut per ea, quae nobis munera dignaris praebere caelestia, per haec eadem tribues nos inherere caelestibus.

OV 465   *In die fructuosi, alia*

Domine Iesu Christe, cuius potentia sancti martyres tui rotantem ignis impetum extinxerunt, et iustitiam operanti sunt: peccatoribus nobis favorem tuae pietatis indulge; ut per fidem, qua sancta regna vicerunt, per eam nos peccatores caeleste mereamur obtinere consortium.

MR(2008)   *II. In anniversario, D. Aliae orationes in anniversario*

Repléti **alimónia** reparatiónis et vitæ, quǽsumus, Dómine, ut per eam frater noster N., **ab ómnibus** *peccátis* **emundátus, ad** cæléste **váleat transíre** consórtium.

I. For the Funeral, E. Other Prayers

Source: MR 887 (*CO* 4459)

MR 877   *Die 2 novembris, Comm. omn. fid. defunct., ad tertiam Missae, PC*

Præsta, quaesumus, omnípotens et miséricors Deus: ut ánimæ famulórum famularúmque tuárum, pro quibus hoc sacrifícium laudis tuæ obtúlimus maiestáti; per huius virtútem sacraménti a peccátis ómnibus expiátæ, lucis perpétuæ, te miseránte, recípiant beatitúdinem.

MR(2008)   *II. In anniversario, E. Aliae orationes in anniversario*

Præsta, quǽsumus, omnípotens ° Deus, ut *ánima fámuli tui* **N.**, pro **qua** hoc sacrifícium ° tuæ obtúlimus maiestáti, per huius virtútem sacraménti a peccátis omnibus expiáta, lucis perpétuæ, te miseránte, recípiat beatitúdinem.

III. Various Commemorations, A. For One Deceased Person (1)

Source: Ve 1323 + OV 934 (*CO* 5014 + OV 934)

Ve 1323   *Mense decembris, in ieiunio mensis decimi, IV alia missa, PC*

<u>Refecti vitalibus alimentis quaesumus domine</u>: quod tempore nostrae mortalitatis exsequimur, immortalitatis tuae munere consequamur.

OV 934   *Alia*

Laetatur ecce, Domine, Hierusalem fidelis in victoriam crucis et potentiam salvatoris: fac ergo; ut et diligentes eam in eius pace consistant, et recedentes ab ea ad eius amplexum quandoque perveniant; ut, ablato luctu, de resurrectionis aeternae gaudiis consorti, <u>in eius pace mereamur sine fine constitui</u>.

MR(2008)   *III. In variis commemorationibus, A. Pro uno defuncto, 1*

<u>Vitálibus refécti **sacraméntis**, **quǽsumus, Dómine**</u>, ut ánima fratris nostri N., quam testament tui partícipem effecísti, huius mystérii purificáta virtúte, <u>in pace **Christi** sine fine **lætétur**</u>.

III. Various Commemorations, A. For One Deceased Person (2)

Source: MR 654 (*CO* 3192 b)

MR 654   *Orat. diversae pro defunct., 10. Pro una defunct., PC*

Invéniat, quaesumus, Dómine, ánima fámulæ tuæ N. lucis ætérnæ consórtium: cuius perpétuæ misericórdiæ consecúta est sacraméntum.

MR(2008)   *III. In variis commemorationibus, A. Pro uno defuncto, 2*

Prosit, quǽsumus, Dómine, *ánimæ fámuli tui* N. **sacrifícium Ecclésiæ tuæ, ut, cum Sanctis tuis, Christi** consórtium invéniat, cuius ° misericórdiæ *consecútus* est sacraméntum.

III. VARIOUS COMMEMORATIONS, A. FOR ONE DECEASED PERSON (3)

Source: Ve 537 (*CO* 5559)

Ve 537   *Mense iulii, orat. et preces diurnae, XXI alia missa, PC*

Sumentes dona caelestia, gratias tibi referimus, sancte pater, omnipotens aeterne deus.

MR(2008)   *III. In variis commemorationibus, A. Pro uno defuncto, 3*

Suméntes dona cæléstia, grátias tibi, **Dómine**, reférimus, **humíliter deprecántes, ut ánima fámuli tui N., per Fílii tui passiónem a peccatórum vínculis absolúta, felíciter váleat ad te perveníre.**

III. VARIOUS COMMEMORATIONS, A. FOR ONE DECEASED PERSON (4)

Source: Ve 441 + MR 302 (*CO* 4971 + 1467)

Ve 441   *Mense iulii, orat. et preces diurnae, V alia missa, PC*

Recreati sacri muneris gustu, quaesumus, domine: non indigne sumentibus nobis vertatur ad poenam, sed fideliter libantibus prosit ad veniam.

MR 302   *PAL, 1 augusti, S. Petri ad Vincula, C*

Deus, qui beatum Petrum Apostolum, a vinculis absolutum, illaesum abire fecisti: nostrorum, quaesumus, absolve vincula peccatorum; et omnia mala a nobis propitiatus exclude.

MR(2008)   *III. In variis commemorationibus, A. Pro uno defuncto, 4*

Recreáti sacri múneris **alimónia**, quǽsumus, Dómine, ut frater noster N., **mortis** *vínculis absolútus*, resurrectiónis Fílii tui participatióne lætétur.

III. Various Commemorations, A. For One Deceased Person (5)

Source: Ve 335 + OV 1081 (*CO* 228 + OV 1081)

Ve 335   *Mense iunii, in nat. apost. Petri et Pauli, XVII alia missa, PC*

Aeternae pignus vitae capientes humiliter imploramus, ut, apostolicis fulti patrociniis, quod in imagine gerimus sacramenti, manifesta perceptione sumamus.

OV 1081   *De festivitate S. Ioannis, alia*

Domine Iesu Christe, qui non solum in nativitate praecursoris tui Iohannis multos gaudere et exultare denuntias, sed ipsum quoque Iohannem gaudium et exultationem futurum esse significas; ut, qui te in mundo magnificis vocibus nuntiaret, ab ipso matris utero sanctificatus procederet: sanctificationis tuae nos indue libertate, ut Spiritu sancto repleti, mundialium curarum fasce deposito, angelorum mereamur adunari consortio.

MR(2008)   *III. In variis commemorationibus, A. Pro uno defuncto, 5*

Ætérnæ pignus vitæ capiéntes, te, **Dómine**, humíliter implorámus pro ánima fámuli tui N., ut, mortálibus néxibus expedíta, **redemptórum possit** adunári consórtio.

III. Various Commemorations,
B. For Several Deceased/All the Dead (1)

Text is the same as 2 November, All Souls (3rd Mass), p. 112 above.

III. Various Commemorations,
B. For Several Deceased/All the Dead (2)

Source: Fulda 2584 (*CO* 2246)

Fulda 2584   *Item missa pro defunctis, PC*

Divina libantes sacramenta, concede, quaesumus, omnipotens deus, ut haec eadem nobis proficiant ad salutem et animabus, pro quibus tuam deprecamur clementiam, prosint ad indulgentiam.

MR(2008)   *III. In variis comm., B. Pro pluribus vel pro omn. defunct., 2*

Divína **participántes mystéria**, ° quǽsumus, omnípotens Deus, ut hæc éadem nobis profíciant ad salútem, et animábus **famulórum tuórum**, pro quibus tuam deprecámur cleméntiam, prosint ad **véniam**.

III. Various Commemorations,
B. For Several Deceased/All the Dead (3)

Source: Gell 2931 (*CO* 5571)

Gell 2931   *Missa pro defuncto de cuius anima dubitatur, PC*

Sumpsimus, domine, corporis et sanguis tui remedia, obsecrantes maiestatis tuae clementiam, ut et viventibus sint tutela et defunctis obtineant veniam.

MR(2008)   *III. In variis comm., B. Pro pluribus vel pro omn. defunct., 3*

Súmpsimus, Dómine, **redemptiónis sacraménta**, tuam cleméntiam obsecrántes °, ut, **te miseránte, nobis** vivéntibus *tutélam*, et **nostris** defúnctis véniam **sempitérnam** obtíneant.

III. Various Commemorations,
B. For Several Deceased/All the Dead (4)

Source: MR 52 (*CO* 260)

MR 52   *Die 2 novembris, In comm. omn. fid. def., ad primam Missae, PC*

Animábus, quaesumus, Dómine, famulórum famularúmque tuárum orátio profíciat supplicántium: ut eas et a peccátis ómnibus éxuas, et tuæ redemptiónis fácias esse partícipes.

MR(2008)   *III. In variis comm., B. Pro pluribus vel pro omn. defunct., 4*

Animábus famulórum ° **tuórum**, quǽsumus, Dómine, orátio profíciat supplicántium, ut *eos*, **his sacrifíciis,** et a peccátis ómnibus éxuas, et **ætérnæ salvatiónis** fácias esse partícipes.

III. Various Commemorations,
B. For Several Deceased/All the Dead (5)*

Source: New composition (see Romans 8:11)

Rom. 8:11

Quod si Spiritus eius, qui suscitavit Iesum a mortuis, habitat in vobis, qui suscitavit Christum a mortuis, vivificabit et mortalia corpora vestra per inhabitantem Spiritum suum in vobis.

MR(2008)   *III. In variis comm., B. Pro pluribus vel pro omn. defunct., 5*

Exáudi, Deus, tuos sacraménto salútis fílios enutrítos, et, qui Christum Unigénitum tuum per Sanctum Spíritum e mórtuis suscitásti, fidélibus tuis (N. et N.) immortalitátis et vitæ concéde lætítiam.

---

* This PC is not in MR(1970) or MR(1975).

III. Various Commemorations,
B. For Several Deceased/All the Dead (6)

Source: MR 654 (*CO* 3192 a)

MR 654   *Orat. diversae pro defunct., Pro una defuncta, PC*

Invéniat, quaesumus, Dómine, ánima fámulæ tuæ N. lucis ætérnæ consórtium: cuius perpétuæ misericórdiæ consecúta est sacraméntum.

MR(2008)   *III. In variis comm., B. Pro pluribus vel pro omn. defunct., 6*

Invéniant, quǽsumus, Dómine, ° *fámuli tui,* **omnésque in Christo quiescéntes,** lucis ætérnæ consórtium, **qui, in hac luce pósiti, tuum** *consecúti sunt* sacraméntum.

III. Various Commemorations,
B. For Several Deceased/All the Dead (7)

Source: MR 835 + Leofric 267 (*CO* 4381 b + 5618)

MR 835   *Missa votivae, Pro remissione peccatorum, PC*

Praesta nobis, aeterne Salvator: ut percipientes hoc munere veniam peccatorum, deinceps peccata vitemus.

Leofric 267   *Pro rege, PC*

Sumptis, domine, caelestibus sacramentis, quaesumus clementiam tuam, ut famulum tuum regem nostrum illum cum suis omnibus respicere digneris pietatisque tuae donis ab omnibus purges peccatis et a cunctis imminentibus periculis tuearis.

MR(2008)   *III. In variis comm., B. Pro pluribus vel pro omn. defunct., 7*

Sumptis, Dómine, cæléstibus sacraméntis, tuam cleméntiam **humíliter deprecámur,** ut *fámuli tui,* percipiéntes hoc múnere véniam peccatórum, regnum tuum introíre, teque in ætérnum mereántur collaudáre.

III. Various Commemorations,
B. For Several Deceased/All the Dead (8)

Source: GeV 1637 (CO 4469)

GeV 1637   *Alia missa pro episcopo defuncto, PC*

Praesta, quaesumus, omnipotens deus, ut anima famuli tui illius episcopi in congregatione iustorum aeternae beatitudinis iubeas esse consortem.

MR(2008)   *III. In variis comm., B. Pro pluribus vel pro omn. defunct., 8*

Præsta, quǽsumus, omnípotens Deus, ut ° *fámulos tuos* °, **per huius sacraménti virtútem,** in congregatióne iustórum ætérnæ beatitúdinis iúbeas esse consórtes.

III. Various Commemorations,
B. For Several Deceased/All the Dead (9)

Source: MR 923 (CO 4788)

MR 923   *Orat. diversae, 35. Pro vivis et defunctis, PC*

Puríficent nos, quaesumus, omnípotens et miséricors Deus, sacraménta quæ súmpsimus: et, intercedéntibus ómnibus Sanctis tuis, præsta; ut hoc tuum sacraméntum non sit nobis reátus ad pœnam, sed intercéssio salutáris ad véniam: sit ablútio scélerum, sit fortitúdo fragílium, sit contra ómnia mundi perícula firmaméntum: sit vivórum atque mortuórum fidélium remíssio ómnium delictórum.

MR(2008)   *III. In variis comm., B. Pro pluribus vel pro omn. defunct., 9*

Puríficent nos, quǽsumus, omnípotens et miséricors Deus, sacraménta quæ súmpsimus, et ° præsta, ut hoc ° **sacrifícium** ° sit nobis ° intercéssio ° ad véniam, ° sit fortitúdo fragílium, sit ° **in** *perículis* firmaméntum, sit *vivis* atque **defúnctis** remíssio ómnium **peccatórum, et pignus redemptiónis ætérnæ.**

IV. VARIOUS PRAYERS FOR THE DEAD, 1. FOR A POPE (A)

Source: New composition (see Vatican II, *Lumen gentium*, 18)

Lum. gent., 18   *Cap. III*

Ut vero Episcopatus ipse unus et indivisus esset, beatum Petrum ceteris Apostolis praeposuit in ipsoque instituit perpetuum ac <u>visibile unitatis</u> fidei et communionis principium et <u>fundamentum</u>.

MR(2008)   *IV. Orat. diversae pro defunctis, 1. Pro papa, A*

Divínæ tuæ communiónis refécti sacraméntis, quǽsumus, Dómine, ut fámulus tuus Papa N., quem Ecclésiæ tuæ <u>visíbile</u> voluísti <u>fundaméntum</u> <u>unitátis</u> in terris, beatitúdini gregis tui felíciter aggregétur.

IV. VARIOUS PRAYERS FOR THE DEAD, 1. FOR A POPE (B)

Source: New composition

MR(2008)   *IV. Orat. diversae pro defunctis, 1. Pro papa, B*

Caritátis tuæ, Dómine, suméntes sacra subsídia, quǽsumus, ut fámulus tuus Papa N. misericórdiam tuam in Sanctórum glória perpétuo colláudet, qui fidélis éxstitit mysteriórum tuórum dispensátor in terris.

IV. Various Prayers for the Dead, 1. For a Pope (C)

Source: New composition (see Luke 22:32)*

Lk. 22:32

Ego autem rogavi pro te, ut non deficiat fides tua. Et tu, aliquando conversus, <u>confirma fratres tuos</u>.

MR(2008)   *IV. Orat. diversae pro defunctis, 1. Pro papa, C*

Ad mensam ætérni accedéntes convívii, misericórdiam tuam, Dómine, pro ánima fámuli tui Papæ N. supplíciter implorámus, ut veritátis possessióne tandem congáudeat, <u>in qua pópulum tuum fídenter confirmávit</u>.

IV. Various Prayers for the Dead, 2. For a Bishop,
A. For a Diocesan Bishop

Source: MR 909 (*CO* 4734)

MR 909   *In Missis quot. defunct., Pro defunct. Ep. seu Sacerdotis, PC*

Prosit, quaesumus, Dómine, animábus famulórum tuórum N. et N. Pontíficum (Sacerdótum) misericórdiæ tuæ imploráta cleméntia: ut eius, in quo speravérunt et credidérunt, ætérnum cápiant, te miseránte, consórtium.

MR(2008)   *IV. Orat. diversae pro defunctis, 2. Pro episcopo, A*

Prosit, quǽsumus, Dómine, *ánimæ fámuli tui* N. **epíscopi** misericórdiæ tuæ imploráta cleméntia, ut **Christi**, in quo *sperávit* et **quem prædicávit**, ætérnum cápiat, **his sacrifíciis**, consórtium.

---

* See also Vatican II, *Lumen gentium*, 25: *Qua quidem infallibilitate Romanus Pontifex, Collegii Episcoporum Caput, vi muneris sui gaudet, quando, ut supremus omnium christifidelium pastor et doctor, qui fratres suos in fide confirmat (cf. Lc 22:32), doctrinam de fide vel moribus definitivo actu proclamat.*

IV. VARIOUS PRAYERS FOR THE DEAD, 2. FOR A BISHOP, B. FOR ANOTHER BISHOP

Source: MP 4717

MP 4717   *In die obitus et in depositione Pontificis aut Presbyteri, PC*

Quaesumus, omnipotens et misericors Deus, ut famulum tuum N. quem in terris pro Christo legatione fungi tribuisti, his emendatum sacrificiis, concedere facias in caelestibus cum eodem Christo Jesu Domino nostro.

MR(2008)   *IV. Orat. diversae pro defunctis, 2. Pro episcopo, B*

Quæsumus, omnípotens et miséricors Deus, ut fámulum tuum N. **epíscopum (*vel* cardinálem),** quem in terris pro Christo legatióne fungi tribuísti, his emundátum sacrifíciis, consedére fácias in cæléstibus cum **ipso** °.

IV. VARIOUS PRAYERS FOR THE DEAD, 3. FOR A PRIEST (A)

Source: MP(1841)

MP(1841)   *In die obitus et in depositione Pontificis aut Presbyteri, PC*

Sumptis salutaribus sacramentis, imploramus clementiam tuam, omnipotens Deus, ut famulum tuum N. sacerdotem, quem fecisti mysteriorum tuorum dispensatorem in terris, eorum facias in coelis aperta veritate nutriri.

MR(2008)   *IV. Orat. diversae pro defunctis, 3. Pro sacerdote, A*

Sumptis salutáribus sacraméntis, implorámus, ° Deus, cleméntiam tuam, ut fámulum tuum N. sacerdótem, quem fecísti mysteriórum tuórum dispensatórem in terris, eórum fácias in cælis apérta veritáte nutríri.

IV. Various Prayers for the Dead, 3. For a Priest (B)

Source: GeV 1640 (*CO* 740)

GeV 1640   *Alia missa pro sacerdote sive abbate, SO*

Concede, quasumus, omnipotens deus, ut anima famuli tui illius abbatis atque sacerdotis per haec sancta misteria in tuo conspectu semper clara consistat, que fideliter ministravit.

MR(2008)   *IV. Orat. diversae pro defunctis, 3. Pro sacerdote, B*

Mensæ cæléstis alimónia refécti, te, Dómine, suppliciter exorámus, ut, huius virtúte sacrifícii, ánima fámuli tui **N.** ° sacerdótis **ante** conspéctum *tuum* semper **exsúltet,** qui **in Ecclésia tua** fidéliter ministrávit.

IV. Various Prayers for the Dead, 4. For a Deacon

Source: New composition

MR(2008)   *IV. Orat. diversae pro defunctis, 4. Pro diacono*

Munéribus sacris repléti, te, Dómine, humíliter deprecámur, ut per hoc sacrifícium fámulum tuum N. diáconum, quem inter servos Ecclésiæ tuæ vocásti, a mortis vínculis absolútum, cum iis qui bene ministravérunt partem recípere et in gáudium tuum intráre benígne concédas.

IV. VARIOUS PRAYERS FOR THE DEAD, 11. FOR THE PRIEST'S PARENTS

Source: MR 106 (*CO* 560)

MR 106   *Orat. diversae pro defunctis, Pro patre et matre, PC*

Cæléstis participátio sacraménti, quaesumus, Dómine, animábus patris et matris meæ (paréntum nostrórum) réquiem et lucem obtíneat perpétuam: meque (nosque) cum illis grátia tua corónet ætérna.

MR(2008)   *IV. Orat. diversae pro defunctis, 11. Pro parentibus*

Cæléstis participátio sacraménti, quǽsumus, Dómine, patri et matri meæ (*paréntibus nostris*) réquiem et lucem obtíneat perpétuam, meque (nosque) cum illis **glória** tua **sátiet sempitérna**.

IV. VARIOUS PRAYERS FOR THE DEAD,
12. FOR RELATIVES, FRIENDS AND BENEFACTORS

Source: MR 877 (*CO* 4459)

MR 877   *Die 2 novembris, In comm. omn. fid. def., ad tertiam Missam, PC*

Præsta, quaesumus, omnípotens et miséricors Deus: ut ánimæ famulórum famularúmque tuárum, pro quibus hoc sacrifícium laudis tuæ obtúlimus maiestáti; per huius virtútem sacraménti a peccátis ómnibus expiátæ, lucis perpétuæ, te miseránte, recípiant beatitúdinem.

MR(2008)   *IV. Orat. diversae pro defunctis,*
12. Pro defunctis fratribus propinquis, et benefactoribus

Præsta, quǽsumus, omnípotens et miséricors Deus, ut ánimæ **fratrum, propinquórum et benefactórum nostrórum**, pro quibus hoc sacrifícium laudis tuæ obtúlimus maiestáti, per huius virtútem sacraménti a peccátis ómnibus expiátæ, lucis perpétuæ, te miseránte, recípiant beatitúdinem.

APPENDICES

Note: alterations in word order are not counted for the purposes of deciding whether or not a source has been edited before its inclusion in the 2008 *Missale Romanum*.

Day	Source(s)	CO / Pref	Edited
Sunday 1 Advent	Ve 173 + 1053	901 + 4718	
Sunday 2 Advent	MR 970	5044 b	Yes
Sunday 3 Advent	MR 639	3076 b	No
Sunday 4 Advent	Ve 741 + A 507	CO 5579 + Pref 543	
Mon of Adv (bef 17 Dec)	= Sunday 1 Advent		
Tue of Adv (bef 17 Dec)	= Sunday 2 Advent		
Wed of Adv (bef 17 Dec)	= Sunday 3 Advent		
Thu of Adv (bef 17 Dec)	= Sunday 1 Advent		
Fri of Adv (bef 17 Dec)	= Sunday 2 Advent		
Sat of Adv (bef 17 Dec)	= Sunday 3 Advent		
17 December	GeV 1134	263	Yes
18 December	MR 1135	5845	Yes
19 December	A 1589 + Ve 1313	Pref 1415 + Pref 1390	
20 December	Gell 1887	4946 b	Yes
21 December	Ve 1305	5499	Yes
22 December	Ve 1341	6783	Yes
23 December	GeV 996	528	Yes
24 December	MR 177	927	Yes
Christmas (Vigil)	MR 169	904	No
Christmas (Night)	MR 164	935 a	Yes
Christmas (Dawn)	OV 216		Yes
Christmas (Day)	MR 858	4365	Yes
Holy Family	MR 956		Yes
5th Day in Christmas Oct	Ve 1067	1022 aA	Yes
6th Day in Christmas Oct	Ve 1256	1919	No
7th Day in Christmas Oct	Ve 1299	2242	No
Mary, Mother of God	GeV 1252	3220	Yes
2nd Sun aft Christmas	MR 812	5708	Yes
Epiphany (Vigil)	GeV 61	4061	Yes
Epiphany (Day)	MR 92	524	No
Baptism of the Lord	New		
Monday in Christmas	= 5th Day in Xmas Oct		
Tuesday in Christmas	= 6th Day in Xmas Oct		
Wednesday in Christmas	= 7th Day in Xmas Oct		
Thursday in Christmas	= 5th Day in Xmas Oct		

Day	Source(s)	CO / Pref	Edited
Friday in Christmas	= 6th Day in Xmas Oct		
Saturday in Christmas	= 7th Day in Xmas Oct		
Ash Wednesday	MR 814	4194 B	No
Thursday aft Ash Wed	MR 104	554	Yes
Friday aft Ash Wed	Ve 868 + 1255	CO 3153 + Pref 1445	
Saturday aft Ash Wed	MR 107	562	No
Sunday 1 Lent	A 320	Pref 501	Yes
Monday 1 Lent	MR 1063	5471	No
Tuesday 1 Lent	MR 604	2912	No
Wednesday 1 Lent	GeV 782	1921	No
Thursday 1 Lent	MR 928	4831	No
Friday 1 Lent	MR 1160	6001	No
Saturday 1 Lent	GeV 132	4224	No
Sunday 2 Lent	GeV 213	4209	Yes
Monday 2 Lent	MR 588	2841	Yes
Tuesday 2 Lent	MR 989	5134 a	Yes
Wednesday 2 Lent	Ve 484	4827	No
Thursday 2 Lent	MR 583	2828	No
Friday 2 Lent	MR 551	2586	No
Saturday 2 Lent	MR 996	5152	Yes
Sunday 3 Lent	Ve 23	5562	Yes
Monday 3 Lent	MR 1159	6000	No
Tuesday 3 Lent	MR 1178	6101 b	No
Wednesday 3 Lent	MR 1048	5394 A	No
Thursday 3 Lent	GeV 161	2938	Yes
Friday 3 Lent	Ve 1121	3334	No
Saturday 3 Lent	MR 172	919	No
Sunday 4 Lent	MR 358	1721	No
Monday 4 Lent	Ve 1078	5298	Yes
Tuesday 4 Lent	MR 920	4775	No
Wednesday 4 Lent	MR 95	533	No
Thursday 4 Lent	MR 922	4784	No
Friday 4 Lent	MR(1962)	4455 b	No
Saturday 4 Lent	MR 1151	5962 c	No
Sunday 5 Lent	MR 942	4889	No
Monday 5 Lent	Ve 556	5165 a	Yes
Tuesday 5 Lent	MR 188	1023 a	Yes
Wednesday 5 Lent	GeV 1241 + MR 85	374 + 519	
Thursday 5 Lent	Ve 507	5456	No
Friday 5 Lent	MR 1086	5614 D	Yes
Saturday 5 Lent	Ve 525	3283	Yes

Day	Source(s)	CO / Pref	Edited
Palm Sunday	MR 243 + MR 1022	1319 + 5251	
Monday in Holy Wk	GeV 282	6086 b	No
Tuesday in Holy Wk	= *Thursday 5 Lent*		
Wednesday in Holy Wk	MR 662	3243	No
Maundy Thu (Chrism)	MR 1103 + MR 83	5693 bc + MR 83	
Maundy Thu (Supper)	Go 214	698	Yes
Good Friday	MR(1962)	3910	Yes
Easter Vigil	MP 1313	5521 b	No
Easter Sunday	B 564	4223	Yes
Easter Monday	GeV 498 + 503	2580 + 3287	
Easter Tuesday	GeV 530	2527	No
Easter Wednesday	MR 4	10	Yes
Easter Thursday	MR 531	2482	No
Easter Friday	GeV 532	5502	Yes
Easter Saturday	MR 985 + S. Leo, *Sermo 71, 6*	5125 + S. Leo	
Sunday 2 Easter	MR 133	754 a	No
Saturday 2 Easter	MR 1083	5583	Yes
Sunday 3 Easter	= *Easter Sat*		
Sunday 4 Easter	GeV 272	2774	Yes
Sunday 5 Easter	MR 36 + Ve 1297	126 a + *Pref* 1320	
Sunday 6 Easter	GeV 467	3888	Yes
Ascension (Vigil)	MP 1495		Yes
Ascension (Day)	Ve 185 + Ve 689	5924 + 3972	
Sunday 7 Easter	Ve 174	2505	No
Monday 2, 4, 6 Easter	= *Easter Sat*		
Tuesday 2, 4, 6 Easter	= *Easter Thu*		
Wednesday 2, 4, 6 Easter	= *Sun 5 Easter*		
Thursday 2, 4, [6]* Easter	= *Sun 6 Easter*		
Friday 2, 4, 6 Easter	= *Easter Fri*		
Saturday 2, 4, 6 Easter	= *Sat 2 Easter*		
Monday 3, 5 Easter	= *Sun 6 Easter*		
Tuesday 3, 5 Easter	= *Easter Sat*		
Wednesday 3, 5 Easter	= *Easter Thu*		
Thursday 3, 5 Easter	= *Sun 5 Easter*		
Friday 3, 5 Easter	= *Sat 2 Easter*		
Saturday 3, 5 Easter	= *Easter Fri*		
Monday 7 Easter	= *Sun 5 Easter*		
Tuesday 7 Easter	= *Sat 2 Easter*		
Wednesday 7 Easter	Ve 924	2749	Yes

---

* Week 6 in regions where Ascension is transferred to the 7th Sunday of Easter.

Day	Source(s)	CO / Pref	Edited
Thursday 7 Easter	B 917	4193	No
Friday 7 Easter	Ve 208 + Ve 969	1180 + 1921	
Saturday 7 Easter	Ve 250	267	Yes
Pentecost (Vigil)	B 775	2837	No
Pentecost (Day)	Ve 491 + LMS	1480 + 2398 a	
Week 1 *per annum*	MR 1103	5693 b	No
Sunday 2 *per annum*	MR 1069	5521 a	Yes
Sunday 3 *per annum*	MR 840	4384	No
Sunday 4 *per annum*	MR 959	4979 B	No
Sunday 5 *per annum*	OP 27/04 + Jn. 15:16		
Sunday 6 *per annum*	MR 97	536	No
Sunday 7 *per annum*	MR 940	4887	Yes
Sunday 8 *per annum*	= *Thursday 5 Lent*		
Sunday 9 *per annum*	MP 1768		Yes
Sunday 10 *per annum*	MR 1146	5953 a	No
Sunday 11 *per annum*	MR 597	2889	Yes
Sunday 12 *per annum*	MR 150	5182	Yes
Sunday 13 *per annum*	MR 1177		No
Sunday 14 *per annum*	MR 1136	5854 b	No
Sunday 15 *per annum*	MR 1090	5641	No
Sunday 16 *per annum*	= *Sunday 5 Easter*		
Sunday 17 *per annum*	OP 28/04		Yes
Sunday 18 *per annum*	MR 955	4941	No
Sunday 19 *per annum*	MR 1000	5166	No
Sunday 20 *per annum*	MP 4470		Yes
Sunday 21 *per annum*	MR 822	4279	No
Sunday 22 *per annum*	New		
Sunday 23 *per annum*	MP 425		Yes
Sunday 24 *per annum*	MR 677	3335	Yes
Sunday 25 *per annum*	MR 958	2938	Yes
Sunday 26 *per annum*	MP 1782		No
Sunday 27 *per annum*	S. Leo, *Sermo 63, 7*		
Sunday 28 *per annum*	= *Saturday 5 Lent*		
Sunday 29 *per annum*	Ve 982	2703	Yes
Sunday 30 *per annum*	MR 817	4219	No
Sunday 31 *per annum*	MR 63	357	Yes
Sunday 32 *per annum*	MR 576 + Go 541	2770 + 240	
Sunday 33 *per annum*	= *Saturday 2 Easter*		
Week 34 *per annum*	MR 947	4828 b	Yes
Trinity Sunday	MR 897	4657	No
Corpus Christi	MR 552	2597	No

Day	Source(s)	CO / Pref	Edited
Sacred Heart	New		
Christ the King	MR 637		Yes
Ss Basil & Gregory (2 Jan)	= *Com: Pastors III.B.1*		
Holy Name of Jesus (3 Jan)	MR 741		Yes
St Anthony (17 Jan)	New		
St Francis (24 Jan)	MR(1962)		No
Conv. of St Paul (25 Jan)	= *Com: Pastors, I.1*		
Ss Timothy & Titus (26 Jan)	= *Com: Pastors, V.2*		
Candlemas (2 Feb)	MP 2384		Yes
Ss Cyril & Methodius (14 Feb)	New		
Chair of St Peter (22 Feb)	Ve 552 + S. Aug., *Tr. Io. 26, 17*	2763 a + S. Aug.	
Ss Perpetua & Felicity (7 Mar)	= *Com: Martyrs, V*		
St Joseph (19 Mar)	MR 35	160	Yes
Annunciation (25 Mar)	MR 641	3094	No
St Mark (25 Apr)	MR 871 + MP 3692	4460 + MP	
St Catherine (29 Apr)	MR 45		Yes
St Joseph the Worker (1 May)	MR 98		Yes
St Athanasius (2 May)	MP 2573		Yes
Ss Philip & James (3 May)	MP 2563		Yes
St Matthias (14 May)	MP 2432		Yes
St Philip Neri (26 May)	= *Sun 6 per annum*		
Visitation of BVM (31 May)	MP 2883		Yes
Immac. Heart of BVM	New		
St Justin (1 Jun)	= *Com: Doctors, 2*		
Ss Charles et al (3 Jun)	MP 2913		Yes
St Barnabas (11 Jun)	Ve 335	228	Yes
St Aloysius (21 Jun)	MR 48		Yes
Nat. of St John (24 Jun) (Vigil)	MR 73	423 b	Yes
Nat. of St John (24 Jun) (Day)	MR 1074	5540	Yes
St Irenaeus (28 Jun)	MP 2831		Yes
Ss Peter & Paul (29 Jun) (Vigil)	MP 2840		Yes
Ss Peter & Paul (29 Jun) (Day)	MP 2711		Yes
St Thomas (3 Jul)	MP 2161		Yes
St Benedict (11 Jul)	New		

Day	Source(s)	CO / Pref	Edited
St Mary Magdalene (22 Jul)	MP 2987		Yes
St James (25 Jul)	MR 71	459	No
Ss Joachin & Anne (26 Jul)	MP 3048		Yes
St Martha (29 Jul)	= Com: Virgins, II.2		
St Ignatius Loyola (31 Jul)	MR 663		Yes
St Alphonsus (1 Aug)	MR 282		Yes
Transfiguration (6 Aug)	MP 3144		No
St Dominic (8 Aug)	MP 3128		Yes
St Lawrence (10 Aug)	= Com: HM&W, I.B.2		
St Maximilian Kolbe (14 Aug)	OFM 14/08		Yes
Assumption (15 Aug) (Vigil)	MR 676	3328	Yes
Assumption (15 Aug) (Day)	MR 1087		Yes
St Bernard (20 Aug)	O.Cist 20/08		Yes
St Pius X (21 Aug)	MR(1962)		Yes
Queenship of BVM (22 Aug)	MR 67		Yes
St Bartholomew (24 Aug)	= Com: Pastors, IV.A		
St Augustine (28 Aug)	S. Aug., Sermo 57, 7		
Passion of St John (20 Aug)	MR 142	792	Yes
St Gregory (3 Sep)	= Com: Doctors, 1		
Nat. of BVM (8 Sep)	New		
Holy Name of Mary (12 Sep)	Triplex 271	506 b	Yes
St John Chrysostom (13 Sep)	MP 3478		Yes
Holy Cross (14 Sep)	MR 967 + MR 438	5040 + 2032	
Our Lady of Sorrows (15 Sep)	New (see Col. 1:24)		
Ss Cornelius & Cyprian (16 Sep)	MP 3457		Yes
Ss Andrew et al (20 Sep)	New (see Com: Martyrs, I.A.1)		
St Matthew (21 Sep)	MP 3497		Yes
Ss Cosmas & Damien (26 Sep)	= Com: Martyrs, I.A.3		
St Vincent (27 Sep)	MR(1962)		Yes
Ss Michael, Gabriel & Raphael (29 Sep)	New		
St Jerome (30 Sep)	MP 3557	[see 2556]	Yes
St Thérèse (1 Oct)	MR 634		Yes
Holy Guardian Angels (2 Oct)	MP 3599		Yes

Day	Source(s)	CO / Pref	Edited
St Francis (4 Oct)	New		
Our Lady of the Rosary (7 Oct)	MP 4300		Yes
St Teresa (15 Oct)	O.Carm 15/10		Yes
St Ignatius (17 Oct)	MP 2366		Yes
St Luke (18 Oct)	= 25 April		
St Paul of the Cross (19 Oct)	= Com: Martyrs, I.A.1		
Ss Simon & Jude (28 Oct)	MR 815	4200	Yes
All Saints (1 Nov)	MP 3798		Yes
All Souls (2 Nov) (1)	New		
All Souls (2 Nov) (2)	OV 956 + 959		
All Souls (2 Nov) (3)	GeV 1689	3399	Yes
St Charles (4 Nov)	MP 3841		Yes
Ded. of Lateran Basilica (9 Nov)	= Com: Ded. Church, II		
St Leo (10 Nov)	MR 965 bis		No
St Martin (11 Nov)	MP 2893		Yes
St Josephat (12 Nov)	MR 1067		Yes
Ded. Basilicas of Ss Peter & Paul (18 Nov)	MR 917 + 1043	5389 a + 4763	
Ss Andrew Dung-Lac et al (24 Nov)	New (see Com:Martyrs II.A.2 & I.B.2; Jn. 15:9)		
St Andrew (30 Nov)	MP 2091		Yes
St Francis Xavier (3 Dec)	MP 2104		Yes
St Ambrose (7 Dec)	MP 2491		Yes
Immac. Concep. (8 Dec)	MR 902		No
St John of the Cross (14 Dec)	= Com: Martyrs, I.A.1		
St Stephen (26 Dec)	GeV 34	2753	Yes
St John (27 Dec)	B 155	4569	Yes
Holy Innocents (28 Dec)	GeV 44	192	Yes
Com: Ded. Church I	B 1235	508 a	No
Com: Ded. Church II	New (see Rev. 21:10)		
Com: BVM, per annum I	MR 1075	5542	Yes
Com: BVM, per annum II	= Immac. Heart BVM		
Com: BVM, per annum III	New (see CMBMV, 4)		
Com: BVM, per annum IV	Cong. Pass., p. 22		Yes
Com: BVM, per annum V	New (see CMBMV, 27)		
Com: BVM, per annum VI	New (see CMBMV, 23)		
Com: BVM, per annum VII	Cong. Pass., p. 31		Yes
Com: BVM, per annum VIII	MR 482 + 503		
Com: BVM, Advent	New (see CMBMV, 2)		

Day	Source(s)	CO / Pref	Edited
Com: BVM, Christmas	New (see CMBMV, 5)		
Com: BVM, Easter	IMC 20/01		Yes
Com: Martyrs, I.A.1	New		
Com: Martyrs, I.A.2	MP 4057		Yes
Com: Martyrs, I.A.3	B 1053	812 a	Yes
Com: Martyrs, I.A.4	Ve 743	671	Yes
Com: Martyrs, I.A.5	MP 3610		Yes
Com: Martyrs, I.B.1	MP 4008		Yes
Com: Martyrs, I.B.2	New		
Com: Martyrs, II.A.1	MP 4021		No
Com: Martyrs, II.A.2	New (see Rom. 6:4)		
Com: Martyrs, II.B	New		
Com: Martyrs, III.A	MR 98		Yes
Com: Martyrs, III.B	MP 2661		Yes
Com: Martyrs, IV	MP 2146	1369	Yes
Com: Martyrs, V	MR 1076	5550	Yes
Com: Pastors, I.1	MR 993		Yes
Com: Pastors, I.2	MR 14		Yes
Com: Pastors, II.1	New		
Com: Pastors, II.2	MR 150	847 a	Yes
Com: Pastors, III.A	Triplex 2059	5585 c	Yes
Com: Pastors, III.B.1	MR 675		Yes
Com: Pastors, III.B.2 (1)	MP 2686		No
Com: Pastors, III.B.2 (2)	MR 966		Yes
Com: Pastors, IV.A	MR 1082	5579	Yes
Com: Pastors, IV.B	MR 1028 + GeV 920	MR + 3552 aA	
Com: Pastors, V.1	MP 2330		Yes
Com: Pastors, V.2	New		
Com: Pastors, V.3	MR 1027	5300	Yes
Com: Doctors, 1	MP 4107		Yes
Com: Doctors, 2	MR 87		Yes
Com: Virgins, I	MR 1084		Yes
Com: Virgins, II.1	MR 476		Yes
Com: Virgins, II.2	MR 149		Yes
Com: Virgins, II.3	New		
Com: HM&W, I.A.1	New		
Com: HM&W, I.A.2	MR 719	[see 2452]	No
Com: HM&W, I.A.3	= Sun 19 per annum		
Com: HM&W, I.A.4	Ve 151	4813	Yes
Com: HM&W, I.B.1	MR 990	-	Yes
Com: HM&W, I.B.2	MR 1022	5251 E	Yes

Day	Source(s)	CO / Pref	Edited
Com: HM&W, II.A	New (*see Col. 3:2, 4*)		
Com: HM&W, II.B	Ve 429	279	Yes
Com: HM&W, II.C	New		
Com: HM&W, II.D.1	MP 4145	-	Yes
Com: HM&W, II.D.2	New (*see Mt. 6:33; Eph. 2:15b*)		
Com: HM&W, III (1)	MP(1841), p. 549	-	Yes
Com: HM&W, III (2)	MR 889	-	Yes
Com: HM&W, IV	MR 1139 + LG 41	-	
Com: HM&W, V.1	MR 478	-	Yes
Com: HM&W, V.2	MR 975	5072	Yes
Ritual, I.1	= *Thursday 4 Lent*		
Ritual, I.2.A	GeV 198	127	Yes
Ritual, I.2.B	GeV 227	5941	No
Ritual, I.2.C	GeV 256	788	No
Ritual, I.3.A	New		
Ritual, I.3.B	New		
Ritual, I.4.A	New		
Ritual, I.4.B	New		
Ritual, I.4.C	= *2nd Sun per annum*		
Ritual, II	= *VNO, III.45*		
Ritual, III	New		
Ritual, IV.1.A (1)	= *Sun 21 per annum*		
Ritual, IV.1.A (2)	= *VNO, I.3*		
Ritual, IV.1.B (1)	= *Sun 21 per annum* [pl.]		
Ritual, IV.1.B (2)	= *VNO, I.3* [pl.]		
Ritual, IV.2.A	= *VNO, I.6*		
Ritual, IV.2.B	= *VNO, I.6*		
Ritual, IV.3.A	= *VNO, I.8*		
Ritual, IV.3.B	= *VNO, I.8* [masc. sing.]		
Ritual, IV.4	= *VNO, I.8*		
Ritual, V.A	MR 936 + 1069	4858 + 5521 a	
Ritual, V.B	New		
Ritual, V.C	New		
Ritual, VI.1	New (*see. RB Prol:21, 49; 57:9*)		
Ritual, VI.2	= *Ritual, VI.1*		
Ritual, VII	New		
Ritual, VIII.1	New		
Ritual, VIII.2.A	New		
Ritual, VIII.2.B	New		
Ritual, VIII.3	New		
Ritual, IX	= *VNO, I.8*		

Day	Source(s)	CO / Pref	Edited
Ritual, X.1	Fulda 2145	3398	Yes
Ritual, X.2	New		
VNO, I.1.A	New (see GS 40)		
VNO, I.1.B	New (see Mt. 5:3)		
VNO, I.1.C	New		
VNO, I.1.D	= 10 November		
VNO, I.1.E	MP 4867		Yes
VNO, I.2	MP 4864		Yes
VNO, I.3	MP 4870		Yes
VNO, I.4	MR 890		Yes
VNO, I.5	Fulda 1798	918	Yes
VNO, I.6	MR 788 + 1177	3980 + MR 1177	
VNO, I.7.A	MP 5008	3874	Yes
VNO, I.7.B	New (see 2 Cor. 12:15a; Phil. 2:7a; PO 15)		
VNO, I.7.C	Ve 999 (see PO 13)	78	Yes
VNO, I.8	New		
VNO, I.9	New (see PO 22)		
VNO, I.10	New (see LG 31, AA 2)		
VNO, I.11.A	New		
VNO, I.11.B	New		
VNO, I.11.C	New		
VNO, I.12	= Holy Family		
VNO, I.13.A	MP 5029		Yes
VNO, I.13.B	New		
VNO, I.14.1	New		
VNO, I.14.2	MR(1962) + PC 25		
VNO, I.15	MP 4855	4368	Yes
VNO, I.16	New (see AG 21)		
VNO, I.17.A	= Sunday 11 per annum		
VNO, I.17.B	= Sunday 2 per annum		
VNO, I.17.C	GeV 625	1192	Yes
VNO, I.18.A	= Sunday 4 per annum		
VNO, I.18.B	New		
VNO, I.19	New (see Lk. 14:27; 1 Pet. 4:16; 2 Pet. 1:12)		
VNO, I.20	MP 3478		Yes
VNO, II.25	GeV 248	109	Yes
VNO, II.26.A	New		
VNO, II.26.B	MR 577	2779	Yes
VNO, II.27.A	New (see Acts 17:28)		

Day	Source(s)	CO / Pref	Edited
VNO, II.27.B	MP 4969		Yes
VNO, II.28	MP 4686		Yes
VNO, II.29	New (see GS 72)		
VNO, II.30.A	New		
VNO, II.31	New (see GS 77)		
VNO, II.32	New		
VNO, II.33.A	New (see Jn. 6:51a)		
VNO, II.33.B	New		
VNO, III.38.A	MR 835 + 762	4381 b + 3837	
VNO, III.38.B	MR 574	2747	Yes
VNO, III.39	MR 484 + 878	2264 + 4374	
VNO, III.40	New		
VNO, III.41	MR 156	887	Yes
VNO, III.42	MP 5014		Yes
VNO, III.43	MP 5053		Yes
VNO, III.45	MR 234	1259	No
VNO, III.46	MR 926		Yes
VNO, III.47	New		
VNO, III.48.A	= Monday 1 Lent		
VNO, III.48.B	New		
VNO, III.48.C	MR 1142	5934	Yes
VNO, III.49.A	New		
VNO, III.49.B	New		
Votive, 1	= Trinity Sunday		
Votive, 2	New		
Votive, 3	MP 4364		Yes
Votive, 4	= 14 September		
Votive, 5	LMS 1378	6501	Yes
Votive, 6	MP 4340		Yes
Votive, 7.1	MR 21		Yes
Votive, 7.2	MP 4993		Yes
Votive, 8	MP 4470		Yes
Votive, 9.A	MR 1034	5351 b	No*
Votive, 9.B	Ve 870	2283	Yes
Votive, 9.C	= Pentecost (Vigil)		
Votive, 10.A	= Com: BVM		
Votive, 10.B	New (see CMBMV, 25.I)		
Votive, 10.C	Soc.M 12/09 + MR 336	Soc.M + 1582	
Votive, 10.D	SAC, p. 6		No

---

* Except for a slight spelling variation that does not change the grammar.

Day	Source(s)	CO / Pref	Edited
Votive, 11	= 29 September		
Votive, 12	= 24 June		
Votive, 13	New (see Mt. 1:19)		
Votive, 14	MP 4423		No
Votive, 15	= 29 June		
Votive, 16	New (see Jn. 6:68)		
Votive, 17	New (see Phil. 1:21; Rom. 8:35a)		
Votive, 18	= Com: Pastors, IV.A		
Votive, 19	MP 4471		Yes
Defunct, I.A	S. Pet. Chrys.		
Defunct, I.B	MR(1962)	4342 b	Yes
Defunct, I.C	= 2 November (1)		
Defunct, I.D	= 2 November (2)		
Defunct, I.E.1	New		
Defunct, I.E.2	New		
Defunct, I.F	= Defunct, I.E.1		
Defunct, II.A	Ve 55 + OV 884	5249 + OV	
Defunct, II.B	MR 1117	5754	Yes
Defunct, II.C	= 2nd November (2)		
Defunct, II.D	Ve 34 + OV 465	5068 + OV	
Defunct, II.E	MR 877	4459	Yes
Defunct, III.A.1	Ve 1323 + OV 934	5014 + OV	
Defunct, III.A.2	MR 654	3192 b	Yes
Defunct, III.A.3	Ve 537	5559	Yes
Defunct, III.A.4	Ve 441 + MR 302	4971 + 1467	
Defunct, III.A.5	Ve 335 + OV 1081	228 + OV	
Defunct, III.B.1	= 2nd November (3)		
Defunct, III.B.2	Fulda 2584	2246	Yes
Defunct, III.B.3	Gell 2931	5571	Yes
Defunct, III.B.4	MR 52	260	Yes
Defunct, III.B.5	New (see Rom. 8:11)		
Defunct, III.B.6	MR 654	3192 a	Yes
Defunct, III.B.7	MR 835 + Leofric 267	4381 b + 5618	
Defunct, III.B.8	GeV 1637	4469	Yes
Defunct, III.B.9	MR 923	4788	Yes
Defunct, IV.1.A	New (see LG 18)		
Defunct, IV.1.B	New		
Defunct, IV.1.C	New (see Lk. 22:32; LG 25)		
Defunct, IV.2.A	MR 909	4734	Yes
Defunct, IV.2.B	MP 4717		Yes

Day	Source(s)	CO / Pref	Edited
Defunct, IV.3.A	MP(1841)		Yes
Defunct, IV.3.B	GeV 1640	740	Yes
Defunct, IV.4	New		
Defunct, IV.11	MR 106	560	Yes
Defunct, IV.12	MR 877	4459	Yes

Appendix 2: Statistics

Note: The following statistics have been compiled using the <u>382</u> unique post-communion prayers in the 2008 *Missale Romanum*. Duplicates and very similar prayers have not been counted; for a list of these, see Appendix 4, pp. 255-260 below.

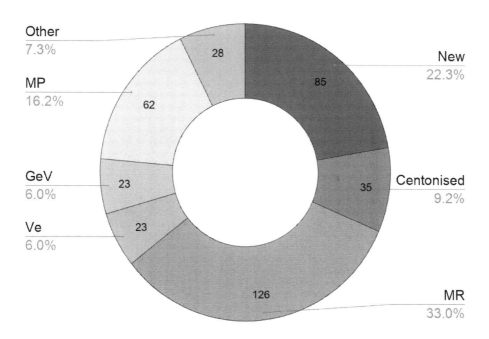

Figure 1: Sources of the Post-Communion Prayers in MR(2008)
(*382 unique prayers*)

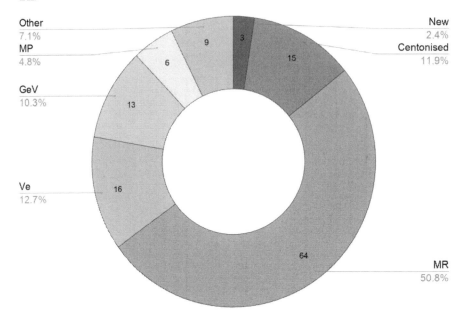

Figure 2: Sources of the Post-Communion Prayers
of the Proper of Time in MR(2008) (*126 prayers*)

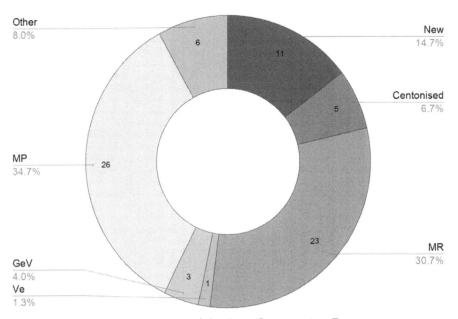

Figure 3: Sources of the Post-Communion Prayers
of the Proper of Saints in MR(2008) (*75 prayers*)

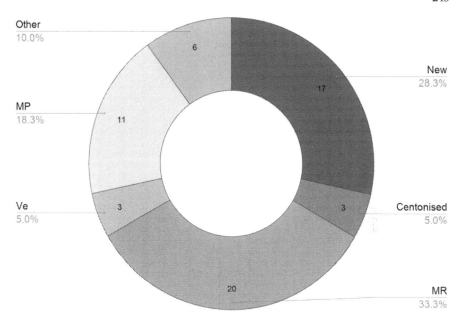

Figure 4: Sources of the Post-Communion Prayers
of the Commons in MR(2008) (*60 prayers*)

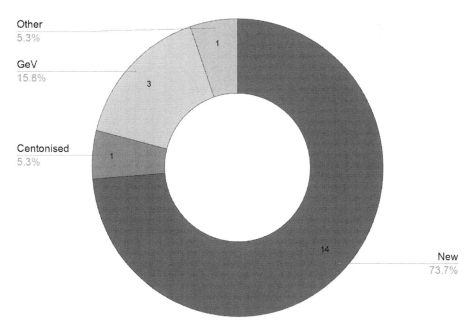

Figure 5: Sources of the Post-Communion Prayers
of the Ritual Masses in MR(2008) (*19 prayers*)

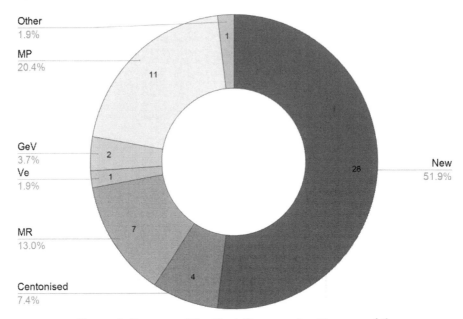

Figure 6: Sources of the Post-Communion Prayers of the
Masses for Various Needs & Occasions in MR(2008) (*54 prayers*)

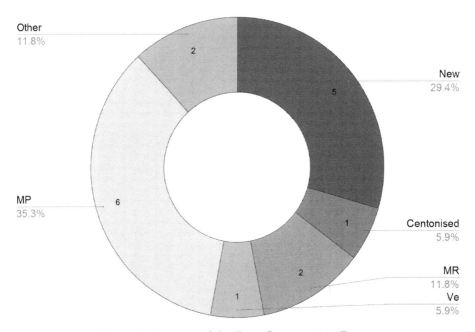

Figure 7: Sources of the Post-Communion Prayers
of the Votive Masses in MR(2008) (*17 prayers*)

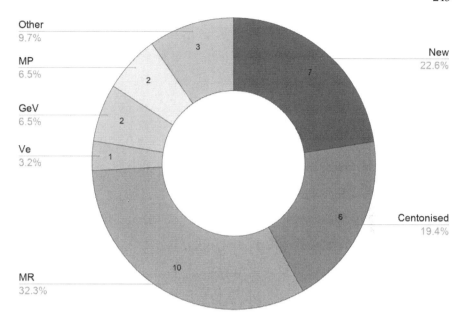

Figure 8: Sources of the Post-Communion Prayers of the
Funeral Masses in MR(2008) (*31 prayers*)

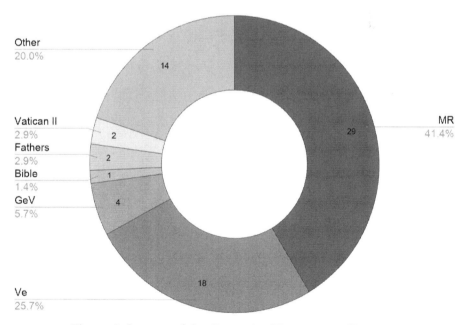

Figure 9: Sources of the Centonised Prayers in MR(2008)
(*35 prayers, 70 source texts*)

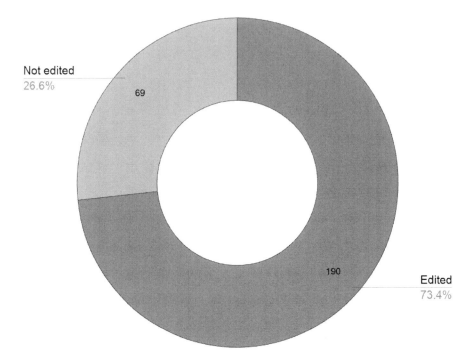

Figure 10: Edited Prayers in MR(2008)
(*excludes new compositions and centonised prayers*)

Figure 11: Table of Post-Communion Sources of MR(2008)

	New	Cent.	MR	Ve	GeV	MP	Other															
							A	B	Cong. Pass.	Fulda	Gell	Go	IMC	LMS	O.Carm	O.Cist	OFM	OP	OV	SAC	Triplex	Fathers
Adv	-	3	4	2	2	-	-	-	-	-	1	-	-	-	-	-	-	-	-	-	-	-
Xmas	1	-	6	3	2	-	-	-	-	-	-	-	-	-	-	-	-	-	1	-	-	-
Lent	-	4	27	7	5	-	1	-	-	-	-	1	-	-	-	-	-	-	-	-	-	-
Easter	-	6	4	3	4	2	-	3	-	-	-	-	-	-	-	-	-	-	-	-	-	-
TPA	2	2	23	1	-	4	-	-	-	-	-	-	-	-	-	-	-	1	-	-	-	1
Prop. of Ss.	11	5	23	1	3	26	-	1	-	-	-	-	-	-	1	1	1	-	-	-	1	1
Commons	17	3	20	3	-	11	-	2	2	-	-	-	1	-	-	-	-	-	-	-	1	-
Ritual	14	1	-	-	3	-	-	-	-	1	-	-	-	-	-	-	-	-	-	-	-	-
VNO	28	4	7	1	2	11	-	-	-	1	-	-	-	-	-	-	-	-	-	-	-	-
Votive	5	1	2	1	-	6	-	-	-	-	-	-	-	1	-	-	-	-	-	1	-	-
Defunct.	7	6	10	1	2	2	-	-	-	1	1	-	-	-	-	-	-	-	-	-	-	1
TOTAL	85	35	126	23	23	62	1	6	2	3	2	1	1	1	1	1	1	1	1	1	1	3

Adv–TPA grouped under **Proper of Time**.

Appendix 3: List of Saints in the General Roman Calendar lacking proper Post-Communions

The *General Instruction of the Roman Missal*, n. 363, states that:

> On Memorials of Saints, the proper Collect is said or, if this is lacking, one from an appropriate Common. As to the Prayer over the Offerings and the Prayer after Communion, unless these are proper, they may be taken either from the Common or from the weekday of the current time of year.

Note also that the rubrics of MR(2008) allow the use of Masses contained in section I ("For All Categories of Saints") of the Common of Holy Men and Women to be used if desired.*

This list is accurate as of October, 2020.

January
7, St Raymond of Penyafort: Pastors (III.B.1-2)
13, St Hilary: Pastors (II.1-2) *or* Doctors (1-2)
20, St Fabian: Martyrs (I.B.1-2) *or* Pastors (I.1-2)
20, St Sebastian: Martyrs (I.B.1-2)
21, St Agnes: Martyrs (IV) *or* Virgins (II.1-3)
22, St Vincent: Martyrs (I.B.1-2)
27, St Angela Merici: Virgins (II.1-3) *or* HM&W (IV)
28, St Thomas Aquinas: Doctors (1-2) *or* Pastors (III.B.1-2)
31, St John Bosco: Pastors (III.B.1-2) *or* HM&W (IV)

February
3, St Blaise: Martyrs (I.B.1-2) *or* Pastors (II.1-2)
3, St Ansgar: Pastors (V.1-3 *or* II.1-2)
5, St Agatha: Martyrs (IV) *or* Virgins (II.1-3)
6, Ss Paul Miki & Companions: Martyrs (I.A.1-5)
8, St Jerome Emiliani: HM&W (IV)
8, St Josephine Bakhita: Virgins (II.1-3)
10, St Scholastica: Virgins (II.1-3) *or* HM&W (Nun)
11, Our Lady of Lourdes: BVM (I.1-8)
17, Seven Holy Founders of the Servite Order: HM&W (II.D.1-2)
21, St Peter Damian: Doctors, 1-2 or Pastors (II.1-2)
23, St Polycarp: Martyrs (I.B.1-2) or Pastors (II.1-2)

---

* Note also that MR(2008) does not specifically assign the fomularies "For Founders of Churches" (Common of Pastors, IV.A-B) to any Masses in the Proper of Saints.

March

4, St Casimir: HM&W (I.B.1-2)

8, St John of God: HM&W (II.D.1-2 *or* III)

9, St Frances of Rome: HM&W (V.1-2 *or* II.D.1-2)

17, St Patrick: Pastors (V.1-3 *or* II.1-2)

18, St Cyril of Jerusalem: Pastors (II.1-2) *or* Doctors (1-2)

23, St Turibius of Mogrovejo: Pastors (II.1-2)

April

2, St Francis of Paola: HM&W (II.D.1-2)

4, St Isidore: Pastors (II.1-2) *or* Doctors (1-2)

5, St Vincent Ferrer: Pastors (V.1-3)

7, St John Baptist de la Salle: Pastors (III.B.1-2) *or* HM&W (IV)

11, St Stanislaus: Martyrs (I.B.1-2/II.B)* *or* Pastors (II.1-2)

13, St Martin I: Martyrs (I.B.1-2/II.B)* *or* Pastors (I.1-2)

21, St Anselm: Pastors (II.1-2) *or* Doctors (1-2)

23, St George: Martyrs (II.B)

23, St Adalbert: Martyrs (II.B) *or* Pastors (II.1-2)

24, St Fidelis of Sigmaringen: Martyrs (II.B) or Pastors (III.B.1-2)

28, St Peter Chanel: Martyrs (II.B) or Pastors (V.1-3)

28, St Louis Grignion de Montfort: Pastors (III.B.1-2)

30, St Pius V: Pastors (I.1-2)

May

12, Ss Nereus & Achilleus: Martyrs (I.A.1-5/II.A.1-2)*

12, St Pancras: Martyrs (I.B.1-2/II.B)*

13, Our Lady of Fatima: BVM (I.1-8/IV)*

18, St John I: Martyrs (I.B.1-2/II.B)* *or* Pastors (I.1-2)

20, St Bernardine of Siena: Pastors (V.1-3) or HM&W (II.D.1-2)

21, St Christopher Magallanes & Companions: Martyrs (I.A.1-5/II.A.1-2)*

22, St Rita of Cascia: HM&W (II.D.1-2)

25, St Bede the Venerable: Doctors (1-2) *or* HM&W (II.B)

25, St Gregory VII: Pastors (I.1-2)

25, St Mary Magdalene de' Pazzi: Virgins (II.1-3) *or* HM&W (II.D.1-2)

27, St Augustine of Canterbury: Pastors (V.1-3 or II.1-2)

29, St Paul VI: Pastors (I.1-2)

Monday after Pentecost: B.V.M., Mother of the Church (Votive, 10.B)

---

* Depending on whether this celebration falls in Eastertide or outside Eastertide.

June

2, Ss Marcellinus & Peter: Martyrs (I.A.1-5/II.A.1-2)*

5, St Boniface: Martyrs (I.B.1-2/II.B)* *or* Pastors (V.1-3)

6, St Norbert: Pastors (II.1-2) *or* HM&W (II.D.1-2)

9, St Ephrem: Doctors (1-2)

13, St Anthony of Padua: Pastors (III.B.1-2)† *or* Doctors (1-2) *or* HM&W (II.D.1-2)

19, St Romuald: HM&W (Abbot)

22, St Paulinus of Nola: Pastors (II.1-2)

22, Ss John Fisher & Thomas More: Martyrs (I.A.1-5)

27, St Cyril of Alexandria: Pastors (II.1-2) *or* Doctors (1-2)

30, The First Martyrs of Holy Roman Church: Martyrs (I.A.1-5)

July

4, St Elizabeth of Portugal: HM&W (III)

5, St Anthony Zaccaria: Pastors (III.B.1-2)† *or* HM&W (IV or II.D.1-2)

6, St Maria Goretti: Martyrs (IV) *or* Virgins (II.1-3)

9, St Augustine Zhao Rong & Companions: Martyrs (I.A.1-5)

13, St Henry: HM&W (I.B.1-2)

14, St Camillus de Lellis: HM&W (III)

15, St Bonaventure: Pastors (II.1-2) *or* Doctors (1-2)

16, Our Lady of Mount Carmel: BVM

20, St Apollinaris: Martyrs (I.B.1-2) *or* Pastors (II.1-2)

21, St Lawrence of Brindisi: Pastors (III.B.1-2)† *or* Doctors (1-2) *or* HM&W (II.D.1-2)

24, St Sharbel Makhlūf: Pastors (III.B.1-2) *or* HM&W (Monk)

30, St Peter Chrysologus: Pastors (II.1-2) *or* Doctors (1-2)

August

2, St Eusebius of Vercelli: Pastors (II.1-2)

2, St Peter Julian Eymard: HM&W (II.D.1-2) *or* Pastors (III.B.1-2)

4, St John Vianney: Pastors (III.B.1-2)

5, Dedication of the Basilica of St Mary Major: BVM (I.1-8)

7, St Sixtus II & Companions: Martyrs (I.A.1-5)

7, St Cajetan: Pastors (III.B.1-2) *or* HM&W (II.D.1-2)

11, St Clare: Virgins (II.1-3) *or* HM&W (II.C)

12, St Jane Frances de Chantal: HM&W (II.D.1-2)

---

* Depending on whether this celebration falls in Eastertide or outside Eastertide.

† MR(2008) just reads *De Communi pastorum*, with no further delineation.

13, Ss Pontian & Hippolytus: Martyrs (I.A.1-5) *or* Pastors (III.A)*
16, St Stephen of Hungary: HM&W (I.B.1-2)
19, St John Eudes: Pastors (III.B.1-2) *or* HM&W (II.D.1-2)
23, St Rose of Lima: Virgins (II.1-3)
25, St Louis: HM&W (I.B.1-2)
25, St Joseph Calasanz: HM&W (IV) *or* Pastors (III.B.1-2)
27, St Monica: HM&W (V.1-2)

September

9, St Peter Claver: Pastors (III.B.1-2) *or* HM&W (III)
17, St Robert Bellarmine: Pastors (II.1-2) *or* Doctors (1-2)
19, St Januarius: Martyrs (I.B.1-2) *or* Pastors (II.1-2)
23, St Pius of Pieltrelcina: Pastors (III.B.1-2) *or* HM&W (II.D.1-2)
28, St Wenceslaus: Martyrs (I.B.1-2)
28, Ss Lawrence Ruiz & Companions: Martyrs (I.A.1-5)

October

5, St Faustina Kowalska: Virgins (II.1-3) *or* HM&W (II.D.1-2)
6, St Bruno: HM&W (II.B) *or* Pastors (III.B.1-2)
9, Ss Denis & Companions: Martyrs (I.A.1-5)
9, St John Leonardi: Pastors (V.1-3) *or* HM&W (III)
11, St John XXIII: Pastors (I.1-2)
14, St Callistus I: Martyrs (I.B.1-2) *or* Pastors (I.1-2)
16, St Hedwig: HM&W (II.D.1-2 *or* V)
16, St Margaret Mary Alacoque: Virgins (II.1-3)
19, Ss John de Brébeuf, Isaac Jogues & Companions: Martyrs (III.A)
22, St John Paul II: Pastors (I.1-2)
23, St John of Capistrano: Pastors (V.1-3) *or* HM&W (II.D.1-2)
24, St Anthony Mary Claret: Pastors (V.1-3 *or* II.1-2)

November

3, St Martin de Porres: HM&W (II.D.1-2)
15, St Albert the Great: Pastors (II.1-2) *or* Doctors (1-2)
16, St Margaret of Scotland: HM&W (III)
16, St Gertrude: Virgins (II.1-3)† *or* HM&W (II.C)
17, St Elizabeth of Hungary: HM&W (III)

---

* MR(2008) just reads *De Communi pastorum*, with no further delineation.

† MR(2008) just reads *De Communi virgini*, with no further delineation.

21, Presentation of the Blessed Virgin Mary: BVM (I.1-8)

22, St Cecilia: Martyrs (IV) *or* Virgins (II.1-3)

23, St Clement I: Martyrs (I.B.1-2) *or* Pastors (I.1-2)

23, St Columban: Pastors (V.1-3) *or* HM&W (II.A)

25, St Catherine of Alexandria: Martyrs (IV) *or* Virgins (II.1-3)

December

4, St John Damascene: Pastors (III.B.1-2) *or* Doctors (1-2)

6, St Nicholas: Pastors (II.1-2)

9, St Juan Diego Cuauhtlatoatzin: HM&W (I.B.1-2)

10, Our Lady of Loreto: BVM (II)

11, St Damasus I: Pastors (I.1-2)

12, Our Lady of Guadalupe: BVM (II)

13, St Lucy: Martyrs (IV) *or* Virgins (II.1-3)

21, St Peter Canisius: Pastors (III.B.1-2)* *or* Doctors (1-2)

23, St John of Kanty: Pastors (III.B.1-2)* *or* HM&W (III)

29, St Thomas Beckett: Martyrs (I.B.1-2) *or* Pastors (II.1-2)

31, St Sylvester I: Pastors (I.1-2)

As well as the above Masses in the Proper of Saints, there are a number of Masses for Various Needs and Occasions and Masses for the Dead where only a Collect is provided, and both the SO and PC need to be taken from another suitable Mass or the Mass of the day:

MASSES FOR VARIOUS NEEDS AND OCCASIONS

II. For Civil Needs

21. For the Nation or State

22. For Those in Public Office

23. For a Governing Assembly

24. For the Head of State or Ruler

34. In Time of Earthquake

35. For Rain

36. For Fine Weather

37. For an End to Storms

---

* MR(2008) just reads *De Communi pastorum*, with no further delineation.

Appendix 4: List of Duplicated Postcommunion Prayers in the 2008 *Missale Romanum*

This appendix lists the 49 postcommunion prayers that are duplicated in the MR(2008), along with the 140 places where a given prayer is duplicated. The prayers are listed in alphabetical order of their Latin incipits.

Note that this list does not include Votive Mass 10.A (Blessed Virgin Mary), which is comprised entirely of a rubric stating that any Mass from the Common of the Blessed Virgin Mary is used in accordance with the various times of the liturgical year.

1. *Cælésti alimónia refécti, súpplices te, Dómine, deprecámur*

   Common of Doctors, II
   1 June (St Justin)

2. *Cæléstibus, Dómine, pasti delíciis, quǽsumus*

   6th Sunday *per annum*
   26 May (St Philip Neri)

3. *Cæléstibus sacraméntis, quǽsumus, Dómine*

   29 June (Ss Peter & Paul, Vigil)
   Votive, 15. Saints Peter and Paul, Apostles

4. *Concéde fámulis tuis, Dómine, cælésti cibo potúque replétis*

   VNO, 8. Ministers of the Church
   Ritual, IV.3.A. Ordination of Several Deacons
   Ritual, IV.3.B. Ordination of One Deacon [*masc. sing.*]
   Ritual, IV.4. Ordination of Deacons and Priests
   Ritual, IX. Institution of Lectors and Acolytes

5. *Consérva in nobis, Dómine, munus tuum*

   Common of Martyrs, I. Outside Easter, A. Several (3)
   26 September (Ss Cosmas & Damian)

6. *Contínua, quǽsumus, Dómine, quos salvásti*

   Friday in Easter Octave
   Friday in Week 2 of Easter
   Friday in Week 4 of Easter
   Friday in Week 6 of Easter
   Saturday in Week 3 of Easter
   Saturday in Week 5 of Easter

7. *Córporis, Dómine, et Sánguinis Fílii tui communióne percépta*

 Masses for the Dead, I.Funeral, E. Baptised Child (1)
 Masses for the Dead, I. Funeral, F. Child Who Died before Baptism

8. *Córporis et Sánguinis Unigéniti tui sacra percéptio*

 Common of Virgins, II. One (2)
 29 July (St Martha)

9. *Da, quǽsumus, omnípotens Deus, ut mysteriórum*

 5th Day in Christmas Octave
 Mondays in Christmastide
 Thursdays in Christmastide

10. *Deus, infirmitátis humánæ singuláre præsídium*

 VNO, 45. For the Sick
 Ritual, II. Conferral of Anointing of the Sick

11. *Deus, qui crucis mystérium in beáto*

 Common of Martyrs, I. Outside Easter, A. Several (1)
 19 October (St Paul of the Cross)
 14 December (St John of the Cross)

12. *Deus, qui nobis supérnam Ierúsalem*

 Common of Ded. of a Church, II. Outside
 9 November (Dedication of the Lateran Basilica)

13. *Deus, qui nos sacraménti tui participatióne contíngis*

 6th Day in Christmas Octave
 Tuesdays in Christmastide
 Fridays in Christmastide

14. *Divérsis plebs tua, Dómine, gubernáta subsídiis*

 7th Day in Christmas Octave
 Wednesdays in Christmastide
 Saturdays in Christmastide

15. *Exáudi, Dómine, preces nostras, ut redemptiónis*

 Thursday in Easter Octave
 Tuesday in Week 2 of Easter
 Tuesday in Week 4 of Easter
 Tuesday in Week 6 of Easter
 Wednesday in Week 3 of Easter
 Wednesday in Week 5 of Easter

16. *Fámiliam tuam, Dómine, réspice propítius*

> Ritual, VI.1. Blessing of Abbot
> Ritual, VI.2. Blessing of an Abbess

17. *Hæc nobis, Dómine, múnera sumpta profíciant*

> Pentecost Vigil
> Votive, 9. The Holy Spirit (C)

18. *Hæc tua, Dómine, sumpta sacra commúnio*

> 11th Sunday *per annum*
> VNO, 17. For the Unity of Christians (A)

19. *Huius, Dómine, virtúte mystérii, in fámulo tuo*

> VNO, 3. For the Bishop
> Ritual, IV.1.A. Ordination of One Bishops (opt. 2)
> Ritual, IV.1.B. Ordination of Several Bishops (opt. 2) [*pl.*]

20. *Maiestátem tuam, Dómine, supplíciter deprecámur*

> Saturday in Week 5 of Lent
> 28th Sunday *per annum*

21. *Mensa cæléstis, omnípotens Deus, in ómnibus festivitátem*

> Common of Pastors, III.B. One Pastor (1)
> 2 January (Ss Basil the Great & Gregory Nazianzen)

22. *Multíplica, Dómine, his sacrifíciis suscéptis*

> 2 November (All Souls, 3rd Mass)
> Masses for the Dead, III.B. Sev. Deceased/All the Dead (1)

23. *Omnípotens sempitérne Deus, qui ad ætérnam vitam*

> 6th Sunday of Easter
> Thursday in Week 2 of Easter
> Thursday in Week 4 of Easter
> Thursday in Week 6 of Easter*
> Monday in Week 3 of Easter
> Monday in Week 5 of Easter

24. *Pane cælésti refécti, súpplices te, Dómine, deprecámur*

> 29 September (Ss Michael, Gabriel & Raphael)
> Votive, 11. The Holy Angels

---

* In regions where Ascension is transferred to the 7th Sunday of Easter.

25. *Plenum, quǽsumus, Dómine, in nobis remédium*

    21st Sunday *per annum*
    Ritual, IV.1.A. Ordination of One Bishop
    Ritual, IV.2.A. Ordination of Several Bishops [*pl.*]

26. *Pópulo tuo, quǽsumus, Dómine, adésto propítius*

    5th Sunday of Easter
    Wednesday in Week 2 of Easter
    Wednesday in Week 4 of Easter
    Wednesday in Week 6 of Easter
    Thursday in Week 3 of Easter
    Thursday in Week 5 of Easter
    Monday in Week 7 of Easter
    16th Sunday *per annum*

27. *Pópulum tuum, quǽsumus, Dómine, intuére benígnus*

    Saturday in Easter Octave
    3rd Sunday of Easter
    Monday in Week 2 of Easter
    Monday in Week 4 of Easter
    Monday in Week 6 of Easter
    Tuesday in Week 3 of Easter
    Tuesday in Week 5 of Easter

28. *Præsta, quǽsumus, Dómine, ut fámuli tui defúncti*

    2 November (All Souls, 1st Mass)
    Masses for the Dead, I. Funeral, C. Easter

29. *Præsta, quǽsumus, omnípotens Deus, ut, quod de sancto altári*

    25 April (St Mark)
    18 Oct (St Luke)

30. *Profíciat nobis ad salútem córporis et ánimæ*

    Most Holy Trinity (Sunday after Pentecost)
    Votive, 1. The Most Holy Trinity

31. *Prosint nobis, quǽsumus, Dómine, frequentáta mystéria*

    1st Sunday of Advent
    Mondays of Advent (before 17 December)
    Thursdays of Advent (before 17 December)

32. *Puríficent nos, quǽsumus, Dómine, sacraménta*

    Thursday in week 4 of Lent
    Ritual, I.1. Election/Enrollment of Names

33. *Quos cæléstibus réficis sacraméntis*

> Holy Family (Sun in Christmas Oct)
> VNO, 12. For the Family

34. *Quos Christo réficis pane vivo*

> Common of Doctors, I
> 3 September (St Gregory the Great)

35. *Redemptiónis ætérnæ partícipes efféci*

> Immac. Heart of the B.V.M. (Sat aft 2nd Sun aft Pentecost)
> Common of the B.V.M., *per annum*, II

36. *Redemptiónis nostræ múnere vegetáti, quǽsumus*

> 4th Sunday *per annum*
> VNO, 18. Evangelization of Peoples (A)

37. *Refectióne sancta enutrítam gubérna, quǽsumus*

> 10 November (St Leo the Great)
> VNO, 1. For the Church (D)

38. *Refectióne tua sancta enutríti, Dómine Iesu Christe*

> 14 September (Exaltation of the Holy Cross)
> Votive, 4. The Mystery of the Holy Cross

39. *Repléti cibo spiritális alimóniæ*

> 2nd Sunday of Advent
> Tuesdays of Advent (before 17 December)
> Fridays of Advent (before 17 December)

40. *Sacerdótes tuos, Dómine, et omnes fámulos tuos*

> VNO, 6. For Priests
> Ritual, IV.2.A. Ordination of Several Priests
> Ritual, IV.2.B. Ordination of One Priest

41. *Sacraménta quæ súmpsimus, Dómine Deus noster*

> Common of Pastors, V. For Missionaries (2)
> 26 January (Ss Timothy & Titus)

42. *Sacramentórum tuórum, Dómine, commúnio sumpta*

> 19th Sunday *per annum*
> Common of Holy Men & Women, I.A. Several Saints (3)

43. *Sacris dápibus satiátos, beáti Ioánnis Baptístæ*

> 24 June (Nativity of St John the Baptist, Vigil)
> Votive, 12. Saint John the Baptist

44. *Sentiámus, Dómine, quǽsumus, tui perceptióne sacraménti*

> Monday in Week 1 of Lent
> VNO, 48. In Any Need (A)

45. *Spíritum nobis, Dómine, tuæ caritátis infúnde*

> 2nd Sunday *per annum*
> Ritual, I.4. Conferral of Confirmation (C)

46. *Suméntes, Dómine, gáudia sempitérna*

> Common of Martyrs, V. Holy Woman Martyr
> 7 March (Ss Perpetua & Felicity)

47. *Súmpsimus, Dómine, sacri dona mystérii, humíliter*

> Saturday in Week 2 of Easter
> Saturday in Week 4 of Easter
> Saturday in Week 6 of Easter
> Friday in Week 3 of Easter
> Friday in Week 5 of Easter
> Tuesday in Week 7 of Easter
> 33rd Sunday *per annum*

48. *Sumpto sacraménto Unigéniti tui*

> 2 November (All Souls, 2nd Mass)
> Masses for the Dead, I. Funeral, D. Other Prayers
> Masses for the Dead, II. Anniversary, C. Easter

49. *Tuam, Dómine, cleméntiam implorámus*

> 3rd Sunday of Advent
> Wednesdays of Advent (before 17th December)
> Saturdays of Advent (before 17th December)

As well as the above, there are some postcommuion prayers (6 groups, 14 prayers in total) with only very slight differences between them:

1. Thursday in week 5 of Lent—Tuesday in Holy Week—8th Sunday *per annum*
2. 2nd Sunday *per annum*—VNO, 17. Unity of Christians (B)
3. Common of Martyrs, I.B.1—4 November (St Charles Borromeo)
4. Common of Pastors, I.1—25 January (Conversion of St Paul)
5. Common of Pastors, IV.A—24 August (St Bartholomew)—Votive, 18. One Holy Apostle
6. Common of Holy Men & Women, I.B.2—10 August (St Lawrence)

APPENDIX 5: ALPHABETICAL INDEX OF FIRST LINES (LATIN)

Cæléstibus sacraméntis, quæsumus, Dómine	29 June (Vigil)
" " " " "	Votive, 15
Cæléstis Agni convívio refécti, quæsumus	24 June (Day)
Cæléstis, Dómine, virtútem sacraménti	8 August
Cæléstis doni benedictióne percépta	Thursday aft Ash Wednesday
Cæléstis participátio sacraménti, quæsumus	Defunct, IV.11
Cæléstis vitæ múnere vegetáti, quæsumus	Saturday aft Ash Wednesday
Caritátis tuæ, Dómine, suméntes sacra subsídia	Defunct, IV.1.B
Cibo refécti, Dómine, potúque salútis,	Votive, 7.1
Cibus, quem súmpsimus, Dómine, in celebratióne	20 August
Concéde, Dómine, Ecclésiæ tuæ, ut, huius sacraménti	Common: BVM, I.5
Concéde fámulis tuis, Dómine, cælésti cibo	VNO, 8
" " " " "	Ritual, IV.3.A
" " " " "	Ritual, IV.3.B [masc. sing.]
" " " " "	Ritual, IV.4
" " " " "	Ritual, IX
Concéde fidélibus tuis, omnípotens Deus, cóngruam	VNO, 27.B
Concéde, miséricors Deus, ut mystéria	13 September
Concéde nobis, Dómine, beáti Ioánnis Baptístæ	29 August
Concéde nobis, Dómine, per hæc sacraménta	Common: Martyrs, I.A.4
Concéde nobis, miséricors Deus, ut Córpore	Votive, 2
Concéde nobis, omnípotens Deus, ut de percéptis	27th Sunday per annum
Concéde nobis, omnípotens Deus, ut, sicut Cena	Maundy Thursday (Eve)
Concéde, quæsumus… ut accépti	Ritual, V.C
Concéde, quæsumus… ut paschális	2nd Sunday of Easter
Concéde, quæsumus… ut, per sacraménta	24 January
Concúrrat, Dómine, quæsumus, pópulus tuus	Ritual, I.2.C
Consérva in nobis, Dómine, munus tuum	Common: Martyrs, I.A.3
" " " " "	26 September
Contínua, quæsumus, Dómine, quos salvásti	Easter Friday
" " " " "	Friday in Week 2 of Easter
" " " " "	Saturday in Week 3 of Easter
" " " " "	Friday in Week 4 of Easter
" " " " "	Saturday in Week 5 of Easter
" " " " "	Friday in Week 6 of Easter
Córporis, Dómine, et Sánguinis Fílii tui communióne	Defunct, I.E.1
" " " " " "	Defunct, I.F
Córporis et Sánguinis Fílii tui, Dómine	Votive, 17
Córporis et Sánguinis Unigéniti tui sacra percéptio	Common: Virgins, II.2
" " " " " "	29 July

Córporis sacri et pretiósi Sánguinis alimónia repléti	Common: Pastors, II.2
Da fidélibus tuis, Dómine, quos et verbi	23rd Sunday *per annum*
Da nobis, Dómine, Fílii tui nativitátem	Christmas Day (Dawn)
Da nobis, Dómine, hoc dono tuo mirábili	24 December
Da nobis, Dómine, hoc sacraménto reféctis	29 June (Day)
Da nobis, Dómine, tuis semper altáribus	Ritual, X.2
Da nobis, Dómine, unitátis sacraménto	11 November
Da nobis, miséricors Deus, ut sancta	VNO, 20
Da nobis, quǽsumus, Dómine Deus noster	Christmas Day (Night)
Da nobis, quǽsumus, Dómine, per hæc sancta	4 October
Da nobis, quǽsumus, Dómine, Unigéniti	Christmas Day (Vigil)
Da nobis, quǽsumus, miséricors Deus, ut sancta	Saturday in Week 3 of Lent
Da nobis, quǽsumus, omnípotens Deus, ut Unigéniti	2 May
Da, quǽsumus, Dómine, ut de percéptis terræ	VNO, 28
Da, quǽsumus, miséricors Deus, ut sancta	VNO, 5
Da, quǽsumus, omnípotens Deus, ut mysteriórum	5th Day in Christmas Octave
" " " " " "	Mondays in Christmastide
" " " " " "	Thursdays in Christmastide
Da, quǽsumus, omnípotens Deus, ut, quæ divína	Tuesday in Week 5 of Lent
De plenitúdine grátiæ tuæ suméntes	VNO, 10
Deus, cuius mystériis mundámur	Friday in Week 7 of Easter
Deus, cuius Unigéniti Corpus	3 July
Deus, cunctárum Pater géntium,	14 February
Deus, infirmitátis humánæ singuláre	VNO, 45
" " " "	Ritual, II
Deus, Pater omnípotens, súpplices te rogámus	VNO, 33.A
Deus, qui ad mensam famíliæ tuæ	VNO, 11.B
Deus, qui beátum Alfónsum Maríam fidélem	1 August
Deus, qui beátam N. pro gémina	Common: Martyrs, IV
Deus, qui crucis mystérium	Common: Martyrs, I.A.1
" " "	19 October
" " "	14 December
Deus, qui Ecclésiæ tuæ cæléstia	Pentecost (Day)
Deus, qui illúminas omnem hóminem	Sun 4 Lent
Deus, qui mirábili sacraménto Ecclésiæ	VNO, 1.C
Deus, qui nobis in cibum spiritálem	VNO, 49.B
Deus, qui nobis supérnam Ierúsalem	Common: Ded Church, II
" " " "	9 November
Deus, qui nos, beáti Petri apóstoli festivitátem	22 February
Deus, qui nos de uno pane et de uno cálice	5th Sunday *per annum*

Deus, qui nos sacraménti tui participatióne	6th Day in Christmas Octave
" " " " "	Tuesdays in Christmastide
" " " " "	Fridays in Christmastide
Deus, qui nos sacraméntis tuis páscere	Wednesday in Week 1 of Lent
Deus, qui nos uno pane réficis	Votive, 19
Deus, qui tuis Ecclésiam iúgiter pascis	VNO, 1.A
Deus, qui Unigénitum tuum ex homínibus	26 July
Divérsis plebs tua, Dómine, gubernáta	7th Day in Christmas Octave
" " " " "	Wednesdays in Christmastide
" " " " "	Saturdays in Christmastide
Divína participántes mystéria, quǽsumus	Defunct, III.B.2
Divínæ tuæ communiónis refécti sacraméntis	Defunct, IV.1.A
Divíni múneris participatióne refécti	Common: Virgins, II.1
Divíni operátio sacraménti, omnípotens Deus	Common: HM&W, V.1
Divínis mystériis veneránter assúmptis	Ritual, VIII.2.A
Divíno múnere satiáti, quǽsumus, omnípotens Deus	17 December
Divíno múnere satiáti, te, Dómine, deprecámur	Defunct, I.E.2
Dómine Deus, cuius Fílius in sacraménto	Defunct, I.A
Dómine Deus noster, qui nos vegetáre	Votive, 9.B
Dómine Deus noster, supplíciter	2nd Sunday of Christmas
Dómine, qui es salus ætérna	Ritual, III
Dómine, qui nos uno pane et uno cálice refecísti	VNO, 32
Exáudi, Deus, tuos sacraménto salútis	Defunct, III.B.5
Exáudi, Dómine, preces nostras	Easter Thursday
" " " "	Tuesday in Week 2 of Easter
" " " "	Wednesday in Week 3 of Easter
" " " "	Tuesday in Week 4 of Easter
" " " "	Wednesday in Week 5 of Easter
" " " "	Tuesday in Week 6 of Easter
Exáudi nos, Deus, salutáris noster	7th Sunday of Easter
Exáudi nos, omnípotens Deus, et famíliæ	Easter Tuesday
Exsúltet Ecclésia tua, Dómine	8 September
Exúberet, quǽsumus, Dómine, méntibus	Easter Monday
Fac nos, Deus, cum exsultatióne	Votive, 14
Fac nos, quǽsumus, Dómine, cæléstium	29th Sunday *per annum*
Fac nos, quǽsumus, Dómine, divinitátis	Corpus Christi
Famíliam tuam, Dómine, divínis ne cesses	14 May
Fámiliam tuam, Dómine, réspice propítius	Ritual, VI.1
" " " " "	Ritual, VI.2
Famíliam tuam, quǽsumus, Dómine, quam de beáti Ioseph	19 March

Fámulos tuos, Dómine, spiritáli cibo	VNO, 14.1
Fórtium esca enutríti in celebratióne	20 September
Grátiam tuam nobis, Dómine, semper accúmulet	Wednesday in Week 7 of Easter
Grátias ágimus, Dómine, multiplicátis	26 December
Grátias de collátis munéribus re,feréntes	19 December
Grátias tibi, Dómine, referímus	32nd Sunday *per annum*
Gregem tuum, Pastor bone, placátus	4th Sunday of Easter
Gubérna, quǽsumus, Dómine, temporálibus	VNO, 26.B
Hæc in nobis sacrifícia, Deus, et actióne	Thursday in Week 2 of Lent
Hæc nobis, Dómine, múnera sumpta	Pentecost (Vigil)
" " " "	Votive, 9.C
Hæc nos commúnio, Dómine, purget	Monday in Week 2 of Lent
Hæc tua, Dómine, sumpta sacra commúnio	11th Sunday *per annum*
" " " " "	VNO, 17.A
His nobis, Dómine, mystériis conferátur	Tuesday in Week 1 of Lent
His recreáti, Dómine, vivíficis sacraméntis	Votive, 13
Hóstia sumpta, Dómine, quam Christi	3 January
Huius mystérii virtúte, confírma, Dómine	Common: Pastors, V.1
Huius quod súmpsimus, Dómine, virtúte	Common: HM&W, II.A
Huius sacraménti, Dómine, virtúte roborátos	7 December
Huius, Dómine, sacrifícii virtúte, institúta	Ritual, V.A
Huius, Dómine, virtúte mystérii, in fámulo	VNO, 3
" " " " "	Ritual, IV.1.A.2
" " " " "	Ritual, IV.1.B.2 [*pl.*]
Huius, Dómine, virtúte sacraménti, da nobis	VNO, 14.2
Immortalitátis alimóniam consecúti	Christ the King
Immortalitátis pígnora, Dómine	VNO, 47
In méntibus nostris, quǽsumus, Dómine	25 March
In natalíciis Sanctórum quǽsumus, Dómine	Common: HM&W, I.A.2
Incarnáti Verbi tui Córpore et Sánguine	Common: BVM, III
Invéniant, quǽsumus, Dómine, fámuli tui	Defunct, III.B.6
Lætíficent nos, Dómine, sumpta	Ritual, VIII.1
Lætíficet nos accéptum de altári	Common: Pastors, IV.B
Lætíficet nos, Dómine, confirmáti	Ritual, VIII.2.B
Largíre nobis, quǽsumus, Dómine	VNO, 30.A
Largíre sénsibus nostris, omnípotens Deus	Wednesday in Holy Week
Laudis hóstia, Dómine, quam pro beáto	31 July
Magníficet te, Deus, Ecclésia tua	31 May
Maiestátem tuam, Dómine, supplíciter	Saturday in Week 5 of Lent
" " " " "	28th Sunday *per annum*
Memóriam beáti Pii papæ celebrántes	21 August

Mensa cæléstis, omnípotens Deus, in ómnibus	Common: Pastors, III.B.1
" " " " "	2 January
Mensæ cæléstis alimónia refécti, te, Dómine	Defunct, IV.3.B
Mensæ cæléstis partícipes effécti, implorámus	15 August (Vigil)
Mensæ cæléstis partícipes effécti, súpplices te	VNO, 2
Mensæ tuæ partícipes effécti, quǽsumus, Dómine	Ritual, V.B
Mensæ tuæ pasti delíciis, te, Dómine	VNO, 11.C
Mentes nostras et córpora, Dómine, quǽsumus	Friday in Week 3 of Lent
Mentes nostras et córpora possídeat	24th Sunday *per annum*
Mirábilem te, Deus, et unum Sanctum	1 November
Multíplica, Dómine, his sacrifíciis	2 November (3rd Mass)
" " " " "	Defunct, III.B.1
Multíplica, Dómine, quǽsumus, per hæc sancta	Ritual, X.1
Munéribus sacris repléti, te, Dómine,	Defunct, IV.4
Mystéria quæ súmpsimus, Dómine Deus noster	Common: BVM, II
Mystéria tua, Deus, eum in nobis	3 December
Mysteriórum tuórum, Dómine, sancta percéptio	22 July
Nostræ libertátis prétium recoléntes	VNO, 43
Omnípotens Deus, qui per hunc panem	VNO, 49.A
Omnípotens sempitérne Deus, orígo cunctárum	VNO, 7.A
Omnípotens sempitérne Deus, Pater totíus	Common: HM&W, I.A.1
Omnípotens sempitérne Deus, qui ad ætérnam	6th Sunday of Easter
" " " " "	Thursday in Week 2 of Easter
" " " " "	Monday in Week 3 of Easter
" " " " "	Thursday in Week 4 of Easter
" " " " "	Monday in Week 5 of Easter
" " " " "	Thursday in Week 6 of Easter*
Omnípotens sempitérne Deus, qui in terra	Ascension (Day)
Omnípotens sempitérne Deus, qui nos Christi	Good Friday
Pane cælésti confirmátum et novi testaménti	VNO, 7.B
Pane cælésti nutrítos et in Christo	Common: Martyrs, I.A.2
Pane cælésti refécti, súpplices te, Dómine	29 September
" " " " "	Votive, 11
Pane mensæ cæléstis… corda nostra confírmet	22nd Sunday *per annum*
Pane mensæ cæléstis… illa sémina maturéscant	VNO, 9
Paschálibus sacraméntis refécti, quǽsumus	Common: BVM, IV
Pasti, Dómine, pretióso Córpore	Common: Martyrs, I.A.5
Per hæc mystéria quæ súmpsimus, Dómine	16 September
Per hæc pacis nostræ mystéria, da nos	VNO, 42

---

* In regions where the Solemnity of the Ascension is transferred to the 7th Sunday of Easter.

Per hæc sacra mystéria, quǽsumus, Dómine	28 June
Per hæc sacraménta, Dómine	20th Sunday *per annum*
Per hæc sancta quæ súmpsimus, Dómine	2 February
Per huius, Dómine, sacraménti virtútem	VNO, 46
Per huius sacraménti virtútem fámulos tuos	VNO, 19
Per huius virtútem sacraménti, quǽsumus	Common: HM&W, II.D.1
Percépta mystéria, quǽsumus, Dómine	Thursday in Week 7 of Easter
Percépta nobis, Dómine, prǽbeant	Ash Wednesday
Percépta nobis sacraménta, quæ súmpsimus	VNO, 39
Percéptis, Dómine, sacraméntis, súpplices	28 October
Percipiéntes, Dómine, gloriósa mystéria	2nd Sunday of Lent
Perfíciant in nobis, Dómine, quǽsumus	30th Sunday *per annum*
Perpétuo, Deus, Ecclésiam tuam	Easter Sunday
Perpétuo, Dómine, favóre proséquere	Saturday in Week 1 of Lent
Plenum, quǽsumus, Dómine, in nobis	21st Sunday *per annum*
" " " " "	Ritual, IV.1.A
" " " " "	Ritual, IV.2.A [*pl.*]
Pópulo tuo, quǽsumus, Dómine, adésto	5th Sunday of Easter
" " " " "	Wednesday in Week 2 of Easter
" " " " "	Thursday in Week 3 of Easter
" " " " "	Wednesday in Week 4 of Easter
" " " " "	Thursday in Week 5 of Easter
" " " " "	Wednesday in Week 6 of Easter
" " " " "	Monday in Week 7 of Easter
" " " " "	16th Sunday *per annum*
Pópulus tuus, quǽsumus, Dómine, cælésti Petri	18 November
Pópulum tuum, quǽsumus, Dómine, intuére	Easter Saturday
" " " " "	Monday in Week 2 of Easter
" " " " "	Tuesday in Week 3 of Easter
" " " " "	Monday in Week 4 of Easter
" " " " "	Tuesday in Week 5 of Easter
" " " " "	Monday in Week 6 of Easter
Præclárum, Dómine, mortis	Ritual, I.3.B
Præsta nobis, miséricors Deus, ut, percipiéntes	VNO, 38.A
Præsta nobis, quǽsumus, omnípotens Deus	3rd Sunday *per annum*
Præsta, miséricors Deus, ut natus hódie	Christmas Day (Day)
Præsta, quǽsumus, Dómine, ut, Carnis	Ritual, I.3.A
Præsta, quǽsumus, Dómine, ut fámuli tui defúncti	2 November (1st Mass)
" " " " " "	Defunct, I.C
Præsta, quǽsumus, Dómine, ut, sicut de prætéritis	Friday in Week 4 of Lent
Præsta, quǽsumus, omnípotens Deus, ut ánima fámuli	Defunct, II.E

Præsta, quǽsumus, omnípotens Deus, ut fámulos tuos,	Defunct, III.B.8
Præsta, quǽsumus, omnípotens Deus, ut fámulus tuus N.	Defunct, I.B
Præsta, quǽsumus, omnípotens Deus, ut illíus salútis	7th Sunday *per annum*
Præsta, quǽsumus, omnípotens Deus, ut, quod de sancto	25 April
" " " " " "	18 October
Præsta, quǽsumus, omnípotens Deus, ut Verbum	27 December
Præsta, quǽsumus, omnípotens et miséricors Deus	Defunct, IV.12
Præstent nobis, quǽsumus, Dómine, sacra mystéria	Common: Martyrs, I.B.1
" " " " " "	4 November*
Précibus nostris et sacrifíciis, Dómine	Defunct, II.B
Profíciat nobis ad salútem córporis	Trinity Sunday
" " " "	Votive, 1
Prosint nobis, quǽsumus, Dómine, frequentáta	1st Sunday of Advent
" " " " " "	Mondays of Adv bef 16 December
" " " " " "	Thursdays of Adv bef 16 December
Prosit, quǽsumus… epíscopi misericórdiæ	Defunct, IV.2.A
Prosit, quǽsumus… sacrifícium Ecclésiæ	Defunct, III.A.2
Purífica, quǽsumus, Dómine, mentes nostras benígnus	Tuesday in Week 4 of Lent
Purífica, quǽsumus, Dómine, mentes nostras per hæc sancta	3 May
Puríficent nos, quǽsumus, Dómine, sacraménta	Thursday in Week 4 of Lent
" " " " " "	Ritual, I.1
Puríficent nos, quǽsumus, omnípotens	Defunct, III.B.9
Quæ ex altári tuo, Domine	Ascension (Vigil)
Quǽsumus, Dómine Deus noster, ut divína mystéria	Common: HM&W, I.A.4
Quǽsumus, Dómine Deus noster, ut, qui in hoc sacraménto	7 October
Quǽsumus, Dómine Deus noster, ut, quod nobis	Wednesday in Week 2 of Lent
Quǽsumus, Dómine Deus noster, ut sacrosáncta mystéria	Thursday in Week 1 of Lent
Quǽsumus, Dómine, ut, huius participatióne	Votive, 3
Quǽsumus, Dómine, ut, refécti Córpore	14 August
Quǽsumus, omnípotens Deus, ut inter eius membra	5th Sunday of Lent
Quǽsumus, omnípotens Deus, ut, huius participatióne	Friday aft Ash Wednesday
Quǽsumus, omnípotens Deus, ut, qui huius sacraménti	Common: HM&W, II.D.2
Quǽsumus, omnípotens Deus, ut, quos divína tríbuis	34th Week *per annum*
Quǽsumus, omnípotens et miséricors Deus	Defunct, IV.2.B
Qui cibum cæléstem, Dómine	VNO, 33.B
Qui tuis nos, Dómine, réficis sacraméntis	VNO, 27.A
Quos cælésti récreas múnere, perpétuo	18th Sunday *per annum*
Quos cæléstibus réficis sacraméntis	Holy Family
" " " "	VNO, 12

---

* With slight changes as noted above, p. 244.

Sacraménta quæ... illíus in nobis vim amóris   1 October
Sacraménta quæ... in commemoratióne   Common: HM&W, I.B.1
Sacraménta quæ... in nobis fóveant   Common: Pastors, I.1
    "   "   "   "   25 January*
Sacraménti salutáris, Dómine, pasti delíciis   Common: HM&W, III.2
Sacraménti tui, Dómine, divína percéptio   Saturday in Week 2 of Lent
Sacraméntis tuis, Dómine, salúbriter enutrítos   17 January
Sacraménto Fílii tui recreáti, te, Dómine   VNO, 1.B
Sacramentórum tuórum benedictióne roboráti   Monday in Week 5 of Lent
Sacramentórum tuórum, Dómine, commúnio   19th Sunday *per annum*
    "   "   "   "   "   Common: HM&W, I.A.3
Sacraméntum caritátis, Dómine, sancta nos fáciat   Sacred Heart of Jesus
Sacraméntum Fílii tui, quod súmpsimus   VNO, 16
Sacri Córporis et Sánguinis pretiósi   12th Sunday *per annum*
Sacris dápibus satiátos, beáti Ioánnis   24 June (Vigil)
    "   "   "   "   Votive, 12
Sacris, Dómine, recreáti mystériis   Common: Martyrs, I.B.2
Sacris mystériis reféctos, da nos   Common: HM&W, III.1
Sacris reparáti mystériis, te, Dómine   Defunct, II.A
Sacro múnere satiáti, cleméntiam tuam   Baptism of the Lord
Sacro múnere satiáti... qui fecísti nos morte   Palm Sunday
Sacro múnere satiáti... quod in festivitáte   Common: HM&W, I.B.2
    "   "   "   "   "   10 August*
Salutáribus refécti sacraméntis, súpplices te   Common: BVM, I.8
Salutáribus, Dómine, fóntibus recreáti   Common: HM&W, II.C
Salutáris gáudii partícipes, Dómine   21 September
Salvatiónis abundántiam tríbue, Dómine   28 December
Sancta tua nos, Dómine, quæsumus, et renovándo   Monday in Week 4 of Lent
Sancta tua nos, Dómine, sumpta vivíficent   Common: Pastors, V.3
Sancta tua quæ súmpsimus, Dómine   30 September
Sancti Spíritus, Dómine, corda nostra   Votive, 9.A
Sanctíficet nos, Dómine, qua pasti sumus   Wednesday in Week 3 of Lent
Sanctíficet nos... mensæ cæléstis participátio   Votive, 5
Sanctíficet nos... mensæ Christi participátio   28 August
Sanctíficet nos... mensæ tuæ participátio   VNO, 18.B
Satiáti múnere salutári, tuam, Dómine   Thursday in Week 5 of Lent
    "   "   "   "   "   Tuesday in Holy Week*
    "   "   "   "   "   8th Sunday *per annum**
Sentiámus, Dómine, quæsumus, tui perceptióne   Mon 1 Lent
    "   "   ",   "   "   "   VNO, 48.A

---

* With slight changes as noted above, p. 244.

Servos tuos, Dómine, in amóre	VNO, 13.A
Sit nobis, Dómine, reparátio mentís	26th Sunday *per annum*
Sit plebi tuæ, Dómine, continuáta defénsio	21 December
Spíritu Sancto, Dómine, perúnctos	Ritual, I.4.A
Spirituális alimóniæ partícipes effécti	Common: BVM, I.7
Spíritum, Dómine, fortitúdinis et pacis	12 November
Spíritum nobis, Dómine… huius sacrifícii virtúte	VNO, 17.B
Spíritum nobis, Dómine… quos sacraméntis	Easter Vigil
Spíritum nobis, Dómine… quos uno cælésti pane	2nd Sunday *per annum*
" " " " " "	Ritual, I.4.C
" " " " " "	VNO, 17.B*
Súbdita tibi família, Dómine Deus noster	15 October
Suméntes, Dómine, cæléstia sacraménta	Common: BVM, I.1
Suméntes, Dómine, gáudia sempitérna	Common: Martyrs, V
" " " " "	7 March
Suméntes dona cæléstia, grátias tibi	Defunct, III.A.3
Suméntes pignus cæléstis arcáni	3rd Sunday of Lent
Súmpsimus, Dómine, Corpus et Sánguinem	VNO, 13.B
Súmpsimus, Dómine, divína sacraménta, sanctórum	3 June
Súmpsimus, Dómine, divínum sacraméntum, passiónis	17th Sunday *per annum*
Súmpsimus, Dómine, læti sacraménta cæléstia	1 January
Súmpsimus, Dómine, pignus redemptiónis	Common: Pastors, IV.A
" " " " "	24 August*
" " " " "	Votive, 18*
Súmpsimus, Dómine, redemptiónis sacraménta	Defunct, III.B.3
Súmpsimus, Dómine, sacraméntum unitátis	VNO, 15
Súmpsimus, Dómine, sacri dona mystérii	Saturday in Week 2 of Easter
" " " " "	Friday in Week 3 of Easter
" " " " "	Saturday in Week 4 of Easter
" " " " "	Friday in Week 5 of Easter
" " " " "	Saturday in Week 6 of Easter
" " " " "	Tuesday in Week 7 of Easter
" " " " "	33rd Sunday *per annum*
Súmpsimus, Dómine, sanctórum tuórum N. et N.	Common: Pastors, III.A
Sumpta mystéria, quǽsumus, Dómine, ætérnis	Common: Pastors, III.B.2.1
Sumpta mystéria, quǽsumus, Dómine, in hac festivitáte	Common: Virgins, I
Sumpti sacrifícii, Dómine, perpétua nos tuítio	Friday in Week 5 of Lent
Sumptis, Dómine, cæléstibus sacraméntis, súpplices	Ritual, VIII.3
Sumptis, Dómine, cæléstibus sacraméntis, tuam cleméntiam	Defunct, III.B.7
Sumptis, Dómine, sacraméntis cæléstibus, te súpplices	22 August

---

* With slight changes as noted above, p. 244.

Sumptis, Dómine, sacraméntis redemptiónis	15 September
Sumptis, Dómine, salutáribus sacraméntis	15 August (Day)
Sumptis, Dómine, salútis et fídei sacraméntis,	Common: BVM, I.4
Súmptis, Domine, salútis nostræ subsídiis	Votive, 10.D
Sumptis munéribus, quæsumus, Dómine	15th Sunday *per annum*
Sumptis salutáribus sacraméntis, implorámus	Defunct, IV.3.A
Sumpto pígnore redemptiónis ætérnæ	4th Sunday of Advent
Sumpto sacraménto Unigéniti tui	2 November (2nd Mass)
" " " " "	Defunct, I.D
" " " " "	Defunct, II.C
Sumpto, Dómine, pígnore redemptiónis et vitæ	Votive, 10.B
Supérno cibo potúque reféctis, Dómine	VNO, 11.A
Súpplices te rogámus... Christi bonus odor	Maundy Thursday (Chrism)
Súpplices te rogámus... tibi étiam plácitis	1st Week *per annum*
Suscipiámus, Dómine, misericórdiam tuam	18 December
Tantis, Dómine, repléti munéribus	14th Sunday *per annum*
Te quæsumus, Dómine, suméntes	VNO, 41
Te súpplices, Dómine, exorámus	VNO, 48.B
Tríbuat nobis, omnípotens Deus, reféctio	Common: HM&W, IV
Tríbue nobis, quæsumus, Dómine, quos ad verbi	Votive, 10.C
Tribulatiónem nostram, quæsumus, Dómine, propítius	VNO, 48.C
Tu semper, quæsumus, Dómine, tuam attólle	Ritual, I.2.B
Tua nobis, quæsumus, Dómine, miseratióne	Votive, 6
Tua, Dómine, súmpsimus dona cæléstia	Common: Martyrs, II.B
Tua nos, Dómine, medicinális operátio	10th Sunday *per annum*
Tua nos, quæsumus, Dómine, sancta puríficent	Saturday in Week 4 of Lent
Tuam, Dómine, cleméntiam implorámus	3rd Sunday of Adv
" " " " "	Wednesdays of Adv bef 16 December
" " " " "	Saturdays of Adv bef 16 December
Tui nobis, quæsumus, Dómine, commúnio sacraménti	Monday in Week 3 of Lent
Tui nos, Dómine, sacraménti reféctio	Friday in Week 1 of Lent
Tui sacraménti caritátis partícipes effécti	Votive, 8
Tui, Dómine, sacraménti veneránda	VNO, 38.B
Unitátis et caritátis mensæ partícipes effécti	VNO, 26.A
Uníus panis alimónia... ut, in tua dilectióne	24 November
Uníus panis alimónia... ut nos in tua iúgiter	Common: Martyrs, II.A.2
Uno pane refécti, quo humánam famíliam	VNO, 29
Uno pane, qui cor hóminis confírmat	VNO, 31
Vígeat in hac Ecclésia tua, Dómine	VNO, 1.E
Vísita, quæsumus, Dómine	Monday in Holy Week
Vitálibus refécti sacraméntis	Defunct, III.A.1
Vivíficet nos, quæsumus, Dómine, divína quam obtúlimus	13th Sunday *per annum*
Vivíficet nos, quæsumus, Dómine, huius participátio	Tuesday in Week 3 of Lent